COMPUTER
DICTIONARY

COMPUTER DICTIONARY

Pamco Publishing Company, Inc.

Copyright © 1992 by
Pamco Publishing Co., Inc.
118 East 28 Street
New York, New York 10016

Compiled and edited by J. Radcliffe

ISBN: 1-881275-18-3

Contents

A

abend, (*abnormal ending*) the termination of a program because of a program error or system fault

abend dump, a data dump at an abend to allow the programmer to determine the cause of error

abend exit, a means of regaining control of a program after an abend

abend, unrecoverable, an abend with no provision in the program to restart or to determine the cause

abort, to stop a procedure or program which is in progress

absolute address, direct address; a group of characters which indicate the location of specific data stored in memory which can be accessed directly by the computer

absolute coding, program coding accessed directly by the computer

absolute instruction, a command in absolute coding which specifies the execution of a computer operation

absolute language, machine language

absolute value, the magnitude of a number without regard to its sign

abstract, to make a brief summary of a document; the document thus created

A-bus, the main communication circuit in the ALU of certain microcomputers

ACC, (*accumulator*) the CPU register which stores the results of arithmetic operations

acceptance test, a test to demonstrate the capabilities of a new computer system

access, to retrieve data from storage, or place it into storage; the

ability to retrieve and store data

access arm, the arm that moves the head in a disk drive

access code, an identification number or a password which allows access to a computer system

access, instantaneous, the ability to quickly obtain data or place data in memory

access method, any software procedure that enters and retrieves data from memory

access, parallel, simultaneous access to more than one element at a time

access, random, a system which allows data to be addressed independent of the last access; compare sequential or serial access

access, sequential or serial, a system that retrieves data by reading through all of the records until it finds the search object; compare random access

access time, the lapsed time between the moment when the computer asks for data from a storage unit and the moment when the data becomes available

accounting checks, techniques to insure accuracy such as control totals or cross totals

accounting machine, a device which prepares accounting reports from punched cards

accumulator, a CPU register which stores the results of an arithmetic operation

accumulator register, same as **accumulator**

accumulator shift instruction, instruction that directs the right or left shift of the contents of the accumulator register

accuracy control characters, specific character or characters that indicate when data is faulty, to be abandoned, or unsuitable for a particular device

accuracy control system, a system which detects errors and signals their presence

ac dump, to remove power from a system or component by design, accident, or program conditions

ACIA, (asynchronous communications interface adapter) a device that provides data formatting and control in order to transfer data between asynchronous communications systems and bus oriented systems

ACK, (acknowledge) a control signal which confirms that transmitted data has been accepted by the receiving unit

ACK/NAK transmission, an error-correcting scheme in which the receiver sends a negative acknowledgment (NAK) requesting repeat transmittal whenever there is a transmission error or excessive dead time

acknowledge (ACK) a control signal which confirms that transmitted data has been accepted by the receiving unit

acknowledge, negative, (NAK) a control signal which indicates that a transmission error occurred in the last data block sent

ACM, Association for Computing Machinery

acoustic coupler, a unit which connects a modem to a telephone line through the telephone hand set

acoustic modem, a modem which accesses a telephone line through an acoustic coupler, converts digi-

tal computer signals to sound for sending and encodes sound which it receives back to digital

ACPA, Association of Computer Programmers and Analysts

acronym, the first letter or letters of a compound name formed to make a word; for example, COBOL is derived from COmmon Business Oriented Language.

action, performance in response to a command; the results of the completed response

active file, a file which is in use and which may be referenced or modified

active master file, an active permanent file, as opposed to a **static file**

active memory card, a card, similar to a credit card, with a magnetic surface onto which data can be recorded

activity, the access, use of or changes to, a record in a master file

activity ratio, the ratio of the records which have been accessed, used or changed compared to the total records in the file

actual decimal point, a decimal point which requires a space in storage as opposed to an **assumed decimal point** which does not

ACU, (automatic calling unit) a device which automatically dials telephone numbers in a predetermined sequence

ada, a structured, modular computer language developed for the U.S. Department of Defense

ADAPSO, Association of Data Processing Service Organizations

adapter, a device which connects parts of one or more systems, enabling them to interact

adapter, channel, a device which allows connection between data channels of different equipment

adapter, data, a processor which translates input and output signals to and from computer codes

adapter, on-line, a high speed computer memory to memory link

adapter plug, a coupler which modifies a jack, socket, or receptacle to accommodate an otherwise incompatible connector

adaptive system, a computer or program which learns from past activity; for example, a scanner or hyphenation system which, when corrected, retains a record for future use.

ADC, analog to digital converter

A/D converter, a device that changes analog signals into digital signals

adder, a device which outputs the sum of two or more inputs

addition, combining quantities

addition, destructive, deletion of the augend each time a new augend is created when an add instruction is executed.

addition record, a new record filed during the processing of a file

add-on, a component added to an existing system to increase its memory, improve performance, or enable a new capability

address, the location in memory, identified by name or number, where data is stored; to call up data or write it to memory

addressable register, a device in storage which has a specific location number

address, arithmetic, locations used to hold computation results

address, base, the location which is combined with a relative address to derive a final address; the address of the beginning of a program or data file; any address which is a reference point for other addresses

address bus, a circuit which carries information identifying memory locations or input/output devices

address computation, the processing which produces or alters the address in a computer instruction

address conversion, converting a relative or symbolic address into an absolute address

address counter, the register which contains the address of the next command to be processed

address, direct, (first level address) an address in a computer instruction which is explicit; the precise storage location of an operand

addressed memory, a memory area that contains a specific register

address, effective, address actually used to execute a computer instruction; the address which results from converting a relative or symbolic address

address, extended, an op code followed by two bytes which specify an absolute address

address, external device, an address which specifies which external device is being referenced

address, first level, a direct address

address format, the specific arrangement of the parts of an address in a computer instruction

address, immediate, an address of data which is included in the instruction which operates on that data

address, implied, an address derived from other data or reference to specific registers

address, indirect, an address in computer instruction which references another address

addressing, assigning memory locations to instructions or data

addressing capacity, the amount of memory available for programs, data and other functions

addressing, direct, a procedure in which memory locations are identified by explicit addresses; a method of identifying the operand in a program by its address

addressing, fixed position, a system which sets aside a specific address location for data of a predetermined size (such as fields in a data base) storage of which does not alter the position of adjacent data

addressing, immediate, the inclusion of the address of data in the instruction which operates on that data

addressing, implied, a system whereby an address is derived from other data or reference

addressing, indexed, data addressed through an index

addressing, indirect, an instruction wherein the address cited references another address

addressing level, the relative directness of addressing; direct addressing is first-level

addressing mode, the specific method of addressing data or instructions in the computer, such as absolute address, direct address, indexed address, indirect address or relative address

addressing, multilevel, using an instruction that references the ad-

dress which contains the data address

addressing, relative, a method of providing absolute addresses by modifying a given address when a program is run

addressing, second-level, an instruction which contains the address of the memory which contains the address of the data

addressing, symbolic, identifying a location in memory by assigning a name representative of the data contained therein

address, instruction, the location of an instruction in computer storage

address mode, the specific method of addressing data or instructions in the computer, such as absolute address, direct address, indexed address, indirect address or relative address

address modification, the process of altering or changing the address of a machine instruction during the running of a program

address register, the register in a CPU where an address is stored

address, relative, an address which is to be altered to a direct address when a program is run

address, specific, in absolute code, an exact storage location

address, symbolic, a location in memory identified by a name or other symbol instead of by its absolute address

address, zero level, immediate address; an address of data included in the instruction which operates on that data

add time, the time taken by the computer to perform one addition operation, excluding time to access data or store the result

add to storage, the process of transferring a sum to memory from the accumulator

adjacent channel, the channel with a frequency band next to the band of the reference channel

adjacent channel interference, interference generated when two communications channels are too near in frequency

adjacent channel selectivity, the ability focus on the selected channel and reject nearby signals

administrative data processing, data processing associated primarily with management and administrative functions

ADP, automatic data processing

AEDS, Association for Educational Data Systems

AFIPS, American Federation of Information Processing Societies

agc, automatic gain control

agenda, an ordered list of the major operations in a procedure for a program

AI, (artificial intelligence) a reference to the characteristics which make a computer more self-sufficient in terms of problem-solving, learning, adapting, etc.; the amplification of human intelligence through the use of the computer's ability to organize and assemble a mass of data in a short period of time

alarm, a tone which sounds to indicate that an error has occurred

algebra, Boolean, developed by George Boole in the 1850's, a system based on binary logic in which there are only two variables, 1 (true) and 0 (false)

alias, an assumed name, usually symbolic; a name given to a procedure, a file, an instruction, an ar-

ray, a peripheral, etc. to more easily reference it in a program

algebraic expression, a statement containing mathematical symbols and signs, which observes mathematical syntax

ALGOL, (algorithmic language) a computer language designed to handle arithmetic and logical problems

algorithm, an ordered sequence of a finite number of very precise instructions with a definite stopping place, designed to solve a specific problem

algorithmic routine, a computer routine which directs the solution of a problem directly without using trial and error

alignment, synchronizing the components of a system to interact properly

alignment pin, a pin or guide that facilitates the correct physical alignment of connecting components

allocate, to assign the resources of the computer to specific tasks

allocation, to reserve specific computer storage and memory locations for particular instructions or blocks of data

allocation, dynamic storage, the system of assigning storage to the first space available in order to make the best use of disk space

alphabet, a set of letter characters which excludes numerals and punctuation

alphabetic, containing only the letters of the alphabet and punctuation marks

alphabetic coding, abbreviation codes using letters only for input into a microcomputer

alphabetic-numeric, containing the letters of the alphabet, numbers, punctuation marks and special characters

alphabetic string, a series, or string, of letters

alphameric, short for alphanumeric

alphanumeric, short for alphabetic-numeric

alphanumeric character set, a character set which includes letters, numbers, punctuation marks and, usually, special characters

alphanumeric instruction, computer instructions in which either alphabetic or numeric data can be manipulated

alter, to change, delete, or insert data

alteration switch, a switch, either physical or contained in program instructions, which can be set to alter coded machine instructions

alter mode, a program mode which allows changes and updates to data in memory

alternate routing, a secondary path for communication when the primary path is unavailable

ALU, (arithmetic and logic unit) the chip in a the microprocessor which performs arithmetic and logic operations

ambient conditions, conditions in the area where a computer is located such as temperature, humidity, air pressure, or noise

ambient temperature, temperature of surrounding air as opposed to internal temperature of a computer

ambiguity, having more than one meaning, as in a program instruction

ambiguity error, an error, often fatal to a program run, which may cause the formation of incorrect data or an abend

American National Standards Institute, (ANSI) an organization which develops and publishes industry standards; the coordinating body for the voluntary standards in the computer and information processing industry in the U.S.

American Standard Code for Information Interchange, (ASCII) a standard code for representing printable and control characters in binary numbers

amplification, augmentation of a signal to make it stronger

amplifier, a device which boosts the input signal to create a stronger output

amplitude, magnitude of a signal; one of the two parameters of a signal, the other of which is time or duration

analog, representation of data as a continuous variable, such as a slide rule or mercury thermometer; contrasted to **digital**

analog adder, an amplifier which outputs a variable signal equal to the sum of two or more variable input signals

analog channel, a channel which defines signal limits and can transmit at any value between those limits

analog computer, a computer that accepts and stores data in analog form (voltage, resistance, etc.) rather than in discrete values

analog data, digital or discrete data representation of analog values, such as the representation on a monitor of a circular form in a graphics program

analog device, a device which represents numbers in linear form such as a slide rule or thermometer; an analog computer

analog gate, a logic gate which controls output as a linear function of input

analog input scanner, a programmable device that connects any of several sensors to measuring equipment

analog multiplier, a device which calculates a variable equal to the product of two or more variable input signals

analog network, circuits which represent physical variables in such a way that mathematical relationship between the variables can be examined by checking the relationship of the electronic signals in the circuit

analog signal, an electric signal which varies in amplitude or frequency to transmit information

analog to digital converter, a device that changes data from analog into digital form for use by a computer

analysis, a method to determine the nature of a thing by breaking it down and scrutinizing its parts, in computer science, the methodical investigation of a problem or condition

analysis area, the storage area which holds data required to monitor or debug programs

analysis mode, a computer operation in which statistical and analytical data is stored for later retrieval by the analyst

analysis, numerical, the analysis of a problem which has been reduced to or expressed in mathematical terms; the methods of computing

answers to numerical problems

analysis, operations, the use of data, manipulated and redefined by the computer to scrutinize operational problems; **numerical analysis**

analyst, a person skilled in the analysis of problems and the design of solutions

analyzer, differential, an analog computer that uses several integrators to solve differential equations

AND, a logical operator that gives a value of true only when both variables associated with the *AND* are true

AND gate, a logic device of two inputs and one output which delivers a value of true when both inputs are true and a value of false for any other condition

AND operator, a Boolean operator that gives a value of true only if the value of the two statements on which it operates are true; any logic operation that uses the AND operator

AND NOT gate, a logic device of two inputs and one output which delivers a value of true when the first input is true and the second input is false

angstrom, a unit for measuring wavelength; a hundred millionth of a centimeter, or 0.003937 millionth of an inch

annotate, to include non-essential notes or descriptions in a program for reference

annotation, a supplemental description or comment

annotation symbol, a flow chart symbol which denotes an annotation as apart from a step or process in a program

ANSI, American National Standards Institute

ANSI compatible, a product which complies with ANSI standards; usually refers to standard versions of programming languages or escape code sequences

ANSI keyboard, a standard typewriter keyboard featuring a choice of upper-case letters only, or of upper-case and lower case

anti-coincidence gate, a gate which performs the *exclusive OR* operation wherein output is true if the inputs are different, and false if the inputs coincide

anti-virus program, a program designed to offer protection against other programs which might compromise the integrity of a disk or its files

aperture card, a punched card with an opening for mounting a frame of microfilm

APL, (A Programming Language) an interactive programming language especially well suited to complicated operations involving arrays

append, to add something to; a DOS command which enables programs to open data files in specified directories as if those files were a part of or appended to the current directory

application, a program which uses the computer for a specific task such as inventory control, word processing, spread sheet calculation, etc.

application, business, a business-oriented computer program such as payroll, accounting, etc.

application development language, a programming language used to develop a particular computer application

application development system, a series of programs used for the development of custom designed applications

application generator, a system which allows the user to create custom designed applications

application, inquiry, a computer instruction that enables scanning and selecting records from stored data such as a data base

application-oriented language, a language used for creating a specific type of application

application package, a set of programs and routines which perform the tasks associated with a particular application

application program, a program or software package which uses the computer for a set of related tasks such as inventory control, word processing, spread sheet calculation, etc.

application program library, a collection of application programs; usually refers to programs in memory at a work station or accessible from a host

application software, the program which is loaded into a computer to perform the required task

applications program, an interactive program which allows the user to select from a number of tasks related to a specific application, and to control data input and output

applications programmer, a programmer who writes application programs; in contrast to a **systems programmer**

applications programming, writing an interactive program which offers the user access to a number of tasks related to a specific application, such as inventory control, word processing, spread sheet calculation, etc.

applied mathematics, mathematics put to practical use, in contrast to theoretical mathematics

approximation, a value which is inexact because the number has been rounded or truncated

arbitrary access, allowing equal access time to all memory locations

architecture, the internal design of a microprocessor or of a computer system which defines its word size, registers, input/output operations, data paths, etc.

architecture, network, the configuration of a communications system

archive attribute, a file characteristic which indicates that the file has been changed since last backed up

area, in computers, a part of storage set aside for a specific purpose

area, analysis, the storage area which holds data required to monitor or debug programs

area, constant, a storage area set aside for a constant value

area, fixed, a storage area set aside for specific files or data and which may not be changed or used by any other files or data

area, input/output, a storage area set aside for holding input (data coming into the computer) and output (data going out of the computer)

area, instruction, that area of storage set aside to hold program instructions

area search, examination of a large quantity of data to find and select

those specified in the search instruction

area, temporary storage, the memory area set aside for temporary files and work in process

area, user, the storage area available for user programs and data in contrast with areas reserved for system functions

argument, in a computer program, refers to variable or variables assigned to a function to create the value of the function: for example, if *SQR* is a function which finds square root, the expression *SQR(16)* has *16* as its argument and the value of the expression is 4

arithmetic address, a location where mathematical computation results are held

arithmetical instruction, an instruction to perform an arithmetic operation

arithmetic and logic unit, (ALU) the chip in a the microprocessor which performs arithmetic and logic operations

arithmetic check, verification of the results of a mathematical operation

arithmetic expression, any program statement which employs a mathematical operator and can be reduced to a numeric value

arithmetic instruction, an instruction which employs a mathematical operator, as contrasted to a logical operation

arithmetic operation, a procedure performed on a number which employs any of the mathematical operators: addition, subtraction, multiplication, division, square root, etc.

arithmetic overflow, a condition

which occurs when the result of an arithmetic operation is larger than the space allocated to hold it; a condition often caused by an incorrect allocation of a fixed position address in the program; the bits or numerals which exceed the space allocated for them

arithmetic, parallel, a method of operating on more than one digit at a time, in contrast to **arithmetic, serial**

arithmetic processor, a math coprocessor; a special device which operates in conjunction with a CPU and which performs high-speed arithmetic operations

arithmetic register, a register in the ALU on which arithmetic and logical operations can be performed

arithmetic relation, an expression which consists of two values separated by a relational operator such as a comma

arithmetic, serial, mathematical operation on one digit at a time, in contrast to **arithmetic, parallel**

arithmetic shift, moving binary digits in a register one place to the left or right which is the means of multiplying or dividing the number by 2

arithmetic statement, a mathematical expression separated by an equals sign from a variable to which a value has been assigned based on the expression

armed interrupt, an interrupt that accepts and remembers an interrupt signal

armed state, the state of an interrupt level at which it can accept and remember the interrupt signal

ARQ, automatic request for repeat; an error detection system which requests that transmission be repeated when an error in transmission is detected

arrangement, the order in which items are located in a set

array, a collection of data (data set) identified by a single name, organized so that each item can be identified by its position within the set

array, data, the arrangement of a set of data on tape, disk, etc.

array, gate, the pattern of gates on a chip which can be interconnected to perform specific functions

array, indexed, an array in which individual items can be accessed through the use of a subscript

array, one-dimensional, an arrangement of data consisting of a single row or line of elements

array processor, (also, **vector processor**) a microprocessor which can perform an operation on an entire array in a single step

array, virtual, an array in linear form which simulates a two or more dimensional array

arrows, cursor, the keyboard keys which move the cursor without altering data

artificial cognition, a procedure whereby scanned characters are identified by comparison to parameters contained in memory

artificial intelligence, a reference to the characteristics which make a computer more self-sufficient in terms of problem-solving, learning, adapting, etc.; the amplification of human intelligence through the use of the computer's ability to organize and assemble a mass of data in a short period of time

artificial language, a programming

language created for a specific purpose and conforming to a previously established set of rules.

ARU, audio-response unit, a device that connects a computer to a telephone in order to provide a recorded voice response to incoming human queries

ASA, American Standards Association, the predecessor to American National Standards Institute

ascending sort, arranging data records in order from low number or letter to high

ASCII, American Standard Code for Information Interchange

ASCII keyboard, a keyboard with keys representing the printable ASCII character set, and a control key for accessing the extended character set and non-printing control characters

ASCII terminal, a keyboard terminal capable of sending and receiving the full set of ASCII codes

ASM, Association for Systems Management

ASP, Attached Support Processor

aspect ratio, the ratio of horizontal to vertical dimensions in a computer graphics display

assemble, to translate instructions into machine language

assembler, a program that translates assembly language into a machine language which can be understood by the computer

assembler directive commands, commands which enable the programmer to produce data and values based on conditions at the time of assembly

assembler error message, a message displayed when the assembler detects an error in the source code

assembling, the process of converting a symbolic source language program into machine instructions

assembly, the translation of a program written in assembly language into a program in machine language

assembly, conditional, an assembly which is programmed so that sections of code may be added or deleted based on system variations

assembly language, a low-level computer language in which each statement corresponds to one machine language statement

assembly language listing, a printout showing the binary equivalents of the symbolic instructions as an aid to debugging a program

assembly language processor, an advanced assembler with compiler capabilities and the ability to handle words, statements, and phrases

assembly language program, a program written in assembly

assembly listing, a printout showing both the symbolic and the machine form for elements of an assembly program's instructions

assembly mnemonics, the instructions for an assembly language which are abbreviated words designed to be easily remembered

assembly program, same as **assembler**

assembly routine, same as **assembler**

assembly system, an assembly language with its assembler

assignment statement, a computer program statement that calculates the value of an expression and assigns that value to a specific variable name; $A=A+1$ is an assignment statement which increases the value of *A* by one each time the statement is executed

associative memory, a high speed search based on memory content rather than memory address

associative processor, a processor which accesses data according to memory contents

associative storage, a system in which storage locations are distinguished by content rather than by address or name

associative storage registers, registers which are identified by their content rather than by their address or name

assumed decimal point, the position in a computer stored number where the decimal point is assumed to be located; the assumed decimal does not occupy space in storage contrasted with **actual decimal point**

asynchronous, not synchronized; the transmission of data as it becomes available as contrasted with transmission in specified blocks or at timed intervals

asynchronous circuit, a circuit which is triggered by signals rather that timing synchronization

asynchronous communication, the transmission and recognition of data or instructions one character at a time characterized by the use of stop bits between characters as contrasted to a timing signal to distinguish characters

asynchronous communications interface adapter, a device that provides data formatting and control in order to transfer data between asynchronous communications systems and bus oriented systems

asynchronous computer, a computer in which an operation is started as soon as a previous operation is completed or a part of the computer is available, as contrasted to synchronous computer which relies on a timing signal

asynchronous data transmission, a procedure for transmitting data dependent only on line capacity without timer restraints

asynchronous device, a unit whose operating speed does not rely on anything to which it's connected

asynchronous operation, a system of computer processing in which each operation is completed before the next is started

asynchronous transmission, a method of sending data wherein characters are separated by stop bits rather than timer breaks

ATE, (automatic test equipment) a device which tests circuit boards containing large scale integrated chips and microprocessor devices and displays any faults

attached processor, a CPU connected to the main CPU, acting as an extension of it, sharing software, memory and peripheral devices

attached support processor, a CPU connected to the main CPU, operating in conjunction with it to increase the efficiency of running a series of short-duration jobs

attenuation, reduction in signal strength as it passes through a system

attribute, one of the properties which describe a thing; in computer data, refers to such things as type, location, length, etc.

audible alarm, a tone which sounds

to indicate that an error has occurred

audio, sound frequencies within the range of human hearing

audio cassette recording, a form of mass storage using a standard cassette tape player or a similar device

audio cassette record interface, a device that converts digital signals to audio frequencies and back

audio response, the use of recorded or synthesized voices to answer queries or to reiterate keyboard entries and command responses

audio response device, an audible output device

audio response unit, a device that interfaces a computer and a telephone to provide audible response to incoming voice queries

audio system, computer equipment which can process and store data from voice input

audio tape storage unit, a unit which stores computer data on audio cassette tapes

audio-visual, material which incorporates and integrates sight and sound in the final presentation

audit, a process for verifying the validity of data

audit, in-depth, a detailed audit of a single transaction; usually a subroutine in a program to verify data identified as questionable in a cursory audit or to isolate the defective portion of invalid data

auditing, the job of executing an audit

audit program, a program designed to validate data

audit software, programs designed to detect possible errors by tracing data flow and sampling files

audit trail, a method of confirming the validity of transactions, locating lost data, verifying programming steps, etc. which requires tracing an element through every stage of its activity

augend, a value to which an addend is added to produce a sum

augment, to increase in value

author, an originator; the designer or writer of a computer program; the writer of instructional material

auto-answer, a function which allows the automatic answering of incoming phone calls

auto-answer modem, a modem with auto-answer capability

auto bypass, the ability of the computer to circumvent terminals and peripherals which are turned off, and allow those which are on-line to continue functioning

autochart, an application program or application within a larger program that automates the production of charts, updating them whenever the source information is updated

auto dial, the ability of a modem to generate phone calls automatically in a pre-determined sequence or on command as from a personal phone directory in the computer

auto-index, a computer program which generates an index of text or a program; the index generated by a special computer program

auto-indexed addressing, altering an address by a specific factor each time a particular instruction is executed

auto loader, a program stored in ROM which directs program loading to be triggered by a timer (for example, records processing or a backup program started at the same time each day, or during the night), by an eventuality (such as a printer malfunction which starts a program to switch printers or save to disk), from a remote location via telephone or teletype, or from a tape, cassette or disk

automata theory, a study of the relationship of the operation of automated devices with various theories of behavior in man

automated data processing, the use of computers and other electronic devices to process data

automated management, management tasks accomplished with the aid of data processing equipment, such as, production planning, financial planning, scheduling, design, etc.

automatic, refers to processes and devices designed to operate without human involvement

automatic backup, a backup program linked to the computer clock which performs a complete system backup at regular intervals, such as daily or weekly, without operator intervention; a program feature which saves the old version of a file whenever the file is altered: DOS's edlin incorporates this feature, saving the old version with the extension .BAK, whereas some of the more sophisticated application programs allow the user to select this option; a program feature which saves at regular intervals, a copy of changes whenever a file is active

automatic calling unit, a device which automatically dials telephone numbers in a predetermined sequence

automatic carriage, the device that moves paper through a printer

automatic check, the testing devices built into the computer to examine its operation

automatic checking, a continuous process within a computer to verify that all systems are functioning properly

automatic coding, the process of converting symbolic source language into machine instructions

automatic computer, a computer which is programmed to perform its tasks without further human involvement

automatic controller, an electronic device which regulates the operation of equipment and processes

automatic data processing, the use of computers and other electronic devices to process data

automatic dialing unit, a modem or other device which automatically generates pulses for dialing

automatic error correction, techniques employed to detect and correct errors which occur during the routine operation of a system without involving the user or interfering with that operation

automatic error detection, techniques which discover errors in the operation of a program or system, display the source of the error and, sometimes, correct them

automatic exchange, communication between terminals without human involvement

automatic gain control, a device which maintains an incoming signal at a predetermined level

automatic interrupt, a program-controlled, temporary or permanent, switch to a new location for the purpose of performing a different function

automatic link, automatically updating text and graphics held in common by linked documents or files whenever the data is changed in any one

automatic loader, the ROM program which initializes the operating system when the computer is first turned on

automatic message switching, the automatic rerouting of messages to another destination after receipt and analysis of the contents by the processing unit

automatic message-switching center, a center which routes messages according to the information they contain

automatic program interrupt, a feature which causes the computer to stop (or interrupt) a task in order to perform one of higher priority after which control returns to the original task

automatic program interrupt and time sharing, an interrupt feature which allows control to alternate between two tasks (shared time) for more efficient operation

automatic programming, the ability of a computer to write some of its own code from minimal input by the user

automatic programming language, a programming language which enables the computer to generate parts of a program

automatic queue, registers which automatically sort a LIFO or a FIFO stack

automatic recovery program, a procedure which detects system faults and automatically switches to backup equipment when a fault occurs

automatic request for repeat, an error detection system which requests that transmission be repeated when an error in transmission is detected

automatic routine, a routine which is programmed to execute when certain conditions occur

automatic segmentation and control, a technique for conserving memory which involves segmenting a program, its data and its overlays so that it can be instructed to load in only those portions of the program needed at any given time

automatic sequencing, the ability of a computer to put material in proper order without human involvement

automatic stop, the suspension or cessation of a process when an error is detected which it cannot correct internally

automatic switchover, a procedure that allows switching to a second piece of equipment when a fault is detected in the first

automatic teaching machine, computerized instruction which features interaction between the user and the computer program

automatic test, the running of a test procedure and comparing the results with expected levels

automatic test equipment, a device which tests circuit boards containing large scale integrated chips and microprocessor devices and displays any faults

automatic transaction recorder, a routine which records data relating to transactions

automatic voltage regulator, a

device which maintains a constant voltage output regardless of fluctuation in input

automation, the replacement of tedious manual operations with machine operations, especially by computer-controlled systems; the application of fully automatic procedures in performance and control of operations involving a large scale sequence of complex, standardized, repetitive processes

automonitor, a program instruction which directs a computer to keep a record of its information handling

autonomous devices, those units making up a computer system in which none of the units is dependent on another unit for its timing

auto plotter, a program applied to plotting graphs

auto restart, the feature of a power fail interrupt program which restarts the computer after the interrupt at the point of interruption without loss of data or instruction

auxiliary console, any console other than the main

auxiliary data, data such as comment, backup, etc. which is related to data being processed, but not a part of it

auxiliary equipment, equipment which is not controlled by the CPU

auxiliary memory, memory in addition to that available to the user which may include RAM or ROM, and which is dedicated to transparent machine operations and functions

auxiliary operation, a task performed by equipment which is not under the constant control of the CPU; also **peripheral operation**

auxiliary processor, a processor which is a server to the primary processor, designed to handle a specific task

auxiliary routine, a program routine which assists the computer in its operation or in debugging other routines

auxiliary storage, any external storage available to the computer in addition to, but not including, its internal storage, such as magnetic tape, floppy disk, external hard drive, compact disk, etc.

availability, represents the percentage of available time during which data processing or other equipment is operating correctly

available time, represents the total amount of time equipment is accessible for use

available machine time, represents the total time equipment is accessible and operating correctly

available resources, that portion of a computer's capability free to perform an additional task after discounting commitment to tasks of higher priority

average, moving, represents a statistical average based on a string of data which is updated by adding new data to the end of the string and deleting corresponding data from the beginning of the string; for example, a six month average which is recalculated by adding a seventh month and deleting the first month

average transfer rate, the average time required to move data through a channel or line based on a relatively large sample

average, weighted, a statistical device for calculating an average which places added emphasis on values that are considered more important than others

awareness, network, a system in which the CPU is always informed of the state of the elements in a network

axes, (plural of **axis**) reference lines used in a Cartesian coordinate system; the horizontal is the x-axis, the vertical the y-axis, and the line parallel to the line of view the z-axis

B

Babbage, Charles, inventor of the analytical engine, forerunner of the computer, in 1833

back coupling, a device which allows the energy output from an amplifier to be reversed back to its source

back-end processor, a computer devoted to data processing, as contrasted to computation or other routines

background, refers to operations which are performed out of the user's control and sight; the computer resources engaged in such processing

background noise, extraneous data which must be removed in the course of processing; extraneous material picked up by an optical scanner, especially troublesome in OCR processing; errors introduced into the system by electrical or other fluctuation; in general, any disturbance which interferes with operations

background processing, refers to automatic processing not under user control which occurs using available resources while foreground or user-controlled tasks are being performed

background program, a program of lower priority than that which is running and which will be executed only as computer resources become available

background reflectance, relates to the reflective qualities of the surface which contains material for optical scanning

backing memory, memory in auxiliary or backup storage characterized by unlimited capacity and long access time

backing storage, any external storage available to the computer in addition to, but not including, its internal storage, such as magnetic tape, floppy disk, external hard drive, compact disk, etc.

backlit supertwist LCD, a computer display screen, used mainly for portable microcomputers, which uses LCD technology coupled with the addition of a backlight panel for a brighter screen and improved contrast

backup, to make an additional copy of program or data

backup and recovery, the procedure which facilitates the backup of programs and data from a fixed disk, and recovery (or reloading) of the backup material in the event of a hardware or software failure

backup, automatic, a backup program linked to the computer clock which performs a complete system backup at regular intervals, such as daily or weekly, without operator intervention; a program feature which saves the old version of a file whenever the file is altered; DOS's edlin incorporates this feature, saving the old version with the extension .BAK; some of the more sophisticated application programs allow the user to select this option; a program feature which saves at regular intervals, a copy of changes whenever a file is active

backup copy, a duplicate of computer data kept as protection against loss of the original; duplicate of a file saved with a different name on the same device as the original; a set of program or data files saved on a different medium such as magnetic tape, floppy disk, external drive, compact disk, etc.

backup, manual, making duplicate copies of program or data files on demand as contrasted with an **automatic backup**

backup system, a standby system available for use when the primary system is down and which takes control either automatically or at the user's command; a system combining several sophisticated techniques for the detection and correction of errors

Backus-Naur Form, (also *Backus Normal Form*) a formal notation for describing the syntax of a computer language

backward compatibility, the ability of a program or peripheral to work with programs and data files created from an earlier version

backward read, the transfer of data from one tape to another or to computer memory by running the source tape backward

badge reader, a device designed to read the magnetic code implanted on a small card such as a credit card or employee badge

band, a range of frequencies between two specific limits; a group of recording tracks on a hard disk or magnetic drum

band, clear, in optical character recognition, a border which must be free of extraneous material

band, narrow, referring to a communication line similar to a voice grade line but operating at a lower frequency

bandwidth, in communications, the range of frequencies in a band

bank, a unit of main memory in a computer; a group of fixed contacts for electrical connections

bank, data, a collection of information which is available to the computer

banner word, the first word in a data file

bar chart, a graphic representation of relative values expressed as bars of varying lengths

bar code, a pattern of lines representing characters and numbers which can be read by an optical device; see also, **Universal Product Code**

bar code reader, any device used to read bar codes and translate them for the computer

bar, fixed type, a long, narrow bar holding the font used by a printer which cannot be changed by the user

bar, interchangeable type, a type bar which can be replaced by a different font

bar printer, a printer which uses a series of long, narrow bars each of which contains a font of type and supports one print position

base, the number on which a mathematical system is founded, for example, the binary system is base 2, the decimal system is base 10, etc.

base address, the location which is combined with a relative address to derive a final address; the address of the beginning of a program or data file; any address which is a reference point for other addresses

base, data, a file containing specific data which is accessible to the computer; the aggregate of all data accessible to the computer; usually a file of like data for a number of subjects, for example, a name and address file

base displacement method, a means by which a program can be stored and run from anywhere in memory through the technique of notating the base address

base number, the number of characters available for use in a numbering system; the base of a numbering system

base register, a computer register which modifies an instruction prior to its execution

base time, a precise time function by which a process is controlled or measured

BASIC, (beginner's all purpose symbolic instruction code) a high-level interactive language which is one of the easiest to learn, it has derived considerable power with the introduction of several sophisticated interpreters and compilers

basic code, computer code which uses absolute addresses and operation codes

basic coding, instructions written in machine language

BASIC graphic extensions, special functions and commands in BASIC which permit it to perform graphics

operations

BASIC immediate (or **execution**) **mode,** the BASIC mode in which each statement is interpreted and executed as soon as it is entered

basic input/output system, (BIOS) the part of the CP/M or MS-DOS operating system which controls the screen, the keyboard, printers and other peripheral devices

basic linkage, an interconnection of routines or programs which uses the same calling sequence in a routine, program, or system each time it is used

basic operating system, (BOS) a program which controls the essential functions of computer operation, such as reading the keyboard, accessing disk drives, monitor display, communicating with the printer, etc.

basic programming support, a minimal operating system

basic sequential access method, a data-base system wherein all records are read in turn until the search record is found

basic telecommunications access method, a system to control the transmission of data between main storage and local or remote terminals

batch, a group of records to be processed at one time without further user input

batch command, the name of a batch file; the instructions executed when the name of a batch file is typed

batch entry, remote, the facility for assigning a task from a remote location for processing by a main computer which is linked to the remote location by communication channels

batch file, a file used to execute a series of commands or short program which is activated by typing the file name without the extension

batch processing, a technique whereby a quantity of records is processed at one time without user involvement

batch processing interrupt, the suspension of batch processing to allow execution of a real-time transaction

batch processing, remote, batch processing from a remote location

batch total, the sum of selected data in a batch of data records often to validate the run

batch transfer program, a program which controls and allows execution of data transfer from local to remote terminals

battery backup board, a device which provides temporary power for dynamic memory in the event of an external power failure

baud, a unit measuring the rate of data transmission, equivalent to one carrier pulse per second

baud rate, the speed at which information is exchanged between computers or peripherals

BBS, bulletin board service

BCD, binary coded decimal

BCD coding, the use of binary coded decimal notation in order to conserve memory

BDOS, (basic disk operating system) the part of CP/M which handles files on diskettes

BDOS error, an error in reading from or writing to a diskette

beat, (also, **word time**) the time required for a computer word to pass a given point

beginning of file label, data at the beginning of a file which describes its contents

beginning-of-information marker, an indicator on magnetic tape which indicates where recording may begin

bell character, an ASCII control character that activates a tone: used in programs to alert the user to an error condition, an end of processing, etc.

BEMA, Business Equipment Manufacturers Association

benchmark program, a routine used to determine the relative speed and efficiency of a computer or peripheral

benchmarking, rating different computers by comparing the speed with which they complete a task or routine

benchmark problem, a routine used to determine the relative speed and efficiency of a computer or peripheral; same as a **benchmark program**

bias, the degree to which the average of a group of values differs from a reference value; an unbalanced range of error

bias checking, a technique for varying equipment operating conditions (voltage, etc.) to isolate defective parts; **marginal testing**

bi-directional bus, a bus with the ability to carry signals in either direction

bi-directional flow, the capability of flowing in either direction

bi-directional lines, bi-directional and asynchronous bus lines

bi-directional operation, an operation such as reading, writing, or searching which may be executed in either direction

bi-directional printer, a printer in which the print head makes impressions while moving in both directions

bifurcation, a logic condition that branches to one of two possible selections

BIM, beginning-of-information marker

binary, using only two digits; a term used to represent anything in the binary system

binary addition, addition in the binary system, where $1 + 1 = 10$ ($1 + 1 = 0$ plus 1 to carry $= 10$)

binary arithmetic, any mathematical operation using the binary system

binary cell, the basic unit of memory which can assume either of two stable states: 0 or 1, *true* or *false*, *yes* or *no*

binary chain, a series of binary circuits arranged so that each affects the condition of the circuit which follows

binary chop, a system for searching a list of sequenced data by repeatedly seeking the search object halfway through the list and discarding the half that does not contain the symbol

binary code, the depicting of letters, numbers, and other symbols with groups of binary digits

binary coded character, a character represented by a binary coding system, such as ASCII or EBCDIC

binary coded decimal, (BCD) a technique in which a decimal is represented by four binary digits, allowing the packing of a digit in the same byte

binary coded decimal number, a number consisting of successive groups of four binary digits in the BCD system

binary coded digit, one decimal digit as depicted in the BCD system

binary counter, a counter which can be set for 0 or 1; a device which counts in the binary system

binary digit, a bit; either of the two numerals in the binary system, 0 or 1

binary division, division performed on binary numbers, executed by repeated subtraction in the binary system

binary dump, the contents of all or part of memory displayed or printed out in binary form

binary element, a data component which is expressed as 0 or 1

binary logic, logic elements which are limited to one of two possible choices

binary look-up, a technique for finding an item in an ordered list by dividing the list in half and discarding the half that does not contain the search item

binary multiplication, multiplication using addition and **shift registers**

binary notation, a system of notation that expresses numbers in base 2

binary number, a number represented in base 2

binary operation, a procedure requiring strict adherence to the rules of Boolean algebra

binary point, the separation between the whole and fractional part of a binary number, equal to the decimal point in a decimal number

binary search, a system for searching a list of sequenced data by repeatedly seeking the search object halfway through the list and discarding the half that does not contain the symbol

binary signaling, communication by means of binary codes transmitted by signal variations

binary subtraction, the technique of subtracting binary numbers which is accomplished by the addition of the negative of the subtrahend to the minuend

binary system, the number system in base 2

binary-to-decimal conversion, the task of calculating the base 10 equivalent of a binary number

binary-to-hexadecimal conversion, the task of calculating the base 16 equivalent of a binary number

binary-to-octal conversion, the task of calculating the base 8 equivalent of a binary number

binary variable, a variable which can have one of two values

bind, to assign an absolute address to a symbolic name in a program

binding time, the point at which the compiler replaces a symbolic name or address with an absolute address

bionic, descriptive of a device that resembles or simulates a living organism in the way it functions

bionics, the study of living organisms with the intention of developing mechanical systems that simulate them

BIOS, basic input/output system

bipolar, having two poles; containing both positive and negative charges

bipolar CPU slice, a CPU chip which can be coupled with other similar chips to form a more complex device

bipolar transistor, a transistor formed by sandwiching a layer of P- or N-type semiconductor between two layers of the opposite type, as contrasted to a **field-effect transistor**

biquinary code, a seven-bit decimal code in which the first two bits represent 5 or 0 and the other five bits represent the numbers 0 through 4

bi-stable, capable of assuming either of two stable states, thereby storing one bit of information

bi-stable circuit, a circuit capable of assuming either of two stable states which is changed by an energy pulse; a flip flop

bi-stable device, any device which can assume either of two stable states such as yes or no, true or false, on or off

bi-stable multivibrator, a circuit which requires two energy pulses to complete a cycle from one stable state to another

bi-stable relay, a relay which requires two energy pulses to cycle through two states

bi-stable trigger circuit, a circuit which can be changed into either of two stable states; a flip-flop

bit, (binary digit) the smallest unit of information in the binary system, represented by 0 or 1

bit, check, a binary check digit

bit density, the volume of bits contained in a unit of length or area on the storage media

bit, guard, a file protection device; a bit contained in a computer word to denote that the contents of memory cannot be altered

bit, information, a bit which is part of the data, in contrast to a check bit, guard bit, etc.

bit, link, a special bit flag in a register which allows its contents to be combined with another register to form a double-length computer word

bit map, the memory area which holds binary coded graphic images

bit-mapped graphics, computer graphic images on screen or printed in which each pixel is represented by a bit in memory and can thus be manipulated; a system which creates high resolution graphics

bit-oriented protocol, a data transmission technique which handles data bit by bit

bit parity, a simple error detection and correction system which adds an extra bit to each word in order to make the sum of all bits either even (even parity) or odd (odd parity) depending on the system used

bit position, the location of a bit in memory or in time

bit rate, the number of bits which are transmitted over a specific length of time

bit set/clear mode addressing, an addressing mode which can set or clear any specific bit on page zero of memory

bit, sign, a bit set to represent plus or minus

bit-slice architecture, a design in which a CPU is constructed from several chips which allows the designer to set word length to suit a specific purpose

bit-slice microprocessor, a microprocessor containing several modular chips which have been joined to produce a CPU with a specified word size

bit-slice micro program, the instructions which make up the machine code for a bit-slice microprocessor

bits per inch, a measure of data density on disk or tape

bits per second, a measure of the speed at which information is transmitted

bit, start, in asynchronous transmission, the bit which signals the start of transmission of data

bit, status, a bit stored in a register which indicates the status of a computer or the information it is processing

bit, stop, in asynchronous transmission, the bit which signals the end of transmission of a group of data bits

bit stream, the sequence of bits in a binary signal with no regard to stop bits, parity bits, etc.; a reference to a string of bits transmitted with no separation between groups of characters

bit stream transmission, a technique for transmitting a bit stream using timed intervals

bit string, an array of binary digits in which the position of each is set as a separate unit

bit stuffing, a communication technique which adds a zero bit after each sequence of five one-bit sets to insure that a flag character does not appear in a data field

black box, generally any control device built for a special purpose; one that predictably but inexplicably causes a system to function in a non-standard manner

blank, a signal characterized by a

lack of information or content; a control character (not the same as space or zero)

blank character, the printed character which, based on program instructions, represents a blank such as *B* or a blank space

blank instruction, an instruction which tells the computer to advance to the next instruction and which functions only to hold a place for another instruction which is to be added later

blank transmission test, a test to detect the existence of blank positions in a data field

blast, to clear areas of memory no longer required by a program

blind, the transmission of data in which certain portions are not displayed at the receiving end

B-line counter, a programmable index register

blinking characters, elements displayed on a CRT which flash on and off, as the cursor in a word processing application

block, a sequence of characters, words, records, etc., treated as a unit; a contiguous data string of fixed size for transmission; in word processing, contiguous data selected by the user for manipulation such as formatting, moving, copying, etc.

block access, access to data base records that are physically grouped together in storage

block check characters, check bits which comprise the final portion of a block transmission used to confirm validity of the data in the block

block command, in word processing, an instruction which manipu-

lates a block of selected data, such as copy, delete, formatting, etc.

block diagram, a schematic; a graphic representation of hardware or software elements which shows interrelationships

blocked list, a index of operations waiting for CPU time or the completion of an I/O process

block gap, the space on magnetic tape which separates blocks of data

blocking, the combining of records into blocks

blocking factor, the number of records per fixed block; the ratio of logical records to physical records on tape or disk

block-input processing, handling a unit of data as a block instead of character by character, as in formatting, moving, etc.

block length, block size expressed in bytes, characters, words, records, etc.

block loading, a technique for loading sections of a program into contiguous sections of the computer's main memory

block mark, the indicator in storage which signals the end of a data block

block move, the command to move a selected block of text in word processing

block parity system, a system which uses parity bits to detect errors in block data transfers

block register, a register which contains the address of storage blocks available for incoming data

blocks, physical records (as contrasted to logical records) which are transferred to and from magnetic tape as a unit; units of storage for data records on magnetic tape

block sequencing, a procedure to insure that data is received in proper sequence and that no blocks are lost or duplicated

block sort, a method of sorting data which involves dividing first into major categories, then into subsequently smaller groups which can be more easily sorted

block storage, a section of main memory treated as a single element

block structure, a technique for blocking program segments

block synchronization, verification of the beginning and ending of blocks as they are transmitted

block transfer, the moving of a block of data as a unit to memory between memory locations, or from memory to another device

block transfer function, the instruction which eases the transfer of blocks

BNF, Backus Naur Form, or Backus Normal Form

board, an electrical panel which is wired by the user to change its function

board, plotting, the surface of a plotter on which the graphics are displayed

board, plug, the wiring panel which is inserted into a data processing machine to govern its functions

bomb, a situation in which the computer becomes inoperable as the result of a hardware failure or a program error and from which there is no recovery except to shut down and restart; a **crash**

bookmark, a device used in some application programs to mark data in a file which can be referenced by the user at a later data for the purpose of updating linked objects, compiling an index, etc.

Boolean algebra, developed by George Boole in the 1850's, a system based on binary logic in which there are only two variables, 1 (true) and 0 (false); an algebraic system using logical functions instead of arithmetic relationships

Boolean calculus, Boolean algebra modified to include time

Boolean equation, an expression which sets up a relationship between logic functions

Boolean logic, problem solving with variables which may represent either of only two possible values; problem solving using the logical operators AND, OR and NOT

Boolean operation, a logic operation using Boolean algebra

Boolean operator, a logic operator such as AND, OR or NOT whose operands and whose result may have either of two values

Boolean search, information retrieval in which the Boolean operators AND, OR, and NOT are a part of the search criteria

Boolean variable, a logic variable with one of two values: 1 (true) or 0 (false)

boot, to initialize a computer; to load an operating system into a computer; to power up a computer which automatically loads an operating system available to it from a disk drive

booting, using a bootstrap loader to initialize a computer immediately after turning it on; loading the operating system

bootleg program, a program created outside the purview of athorized operation; proprietary software illegally received or transferred; **pirated software**

bootstrap, a program which contains instructions to enable it to run the computer; a program designed specifically to initialize the computer

bootstrap loader, a program which loads the operating system when the computer is turned on

bootstrap loading, loading a program or routine from a program built into the computer

bootstrap memory, a protected section of memory in which loading instructions are stored

bootstrap, ROM, a bootstrap loader in read only memory

BOP messages, bit-oriented protocol messages

bore, the inside diameter of the hub on a magnetic tape reel

borrow, a negative carry operation in subtraction

BOS, basic operating system

bound, the allowable upper or lower limit of a value or range of values

boundary register, in a multi-user system, a register which stores the upper and lower addresses of each user's block of memory

box, a logical unit of computer programming, represented by a rectangular symbol in a flowchart

box, black, generally any control device built for a special purpose; one that predictably but inexplicably causes a system to function in a non-standard manner

bpi, bits per inch

bps, bits per second

BPS, basic programming support

branch, a program instruction to move to a new section of the program; a GOTO statement

branch, conditional, an instruction to move control to a new section of the program if a certain condition is met

branching, switching between alternate sets of instructions in response to program commands

branch instruction, a conditional instruction which directs a computer to choose one of two sets of subsequent routines

branch point, the point in a routine where branch instructions are contained

branch, regular or unconditional, an unconditional instruction to move control to a new section of the program

breadboard, an experimental hardware model constructed for testing, etc.

breadboard construction, the construction of electronic circuits and elements during the design or experimental phase of development; a temporary device

breadboard, intelligent, a breadboard which can be connected to a console for development and testing

break, an interruption in transmission or operation

break key, a key which temporarily interrupts the transmission of data or execution of a program

breakpoint, a place in a program where execution is interrupted, often as an aid in debugging

breakpoint, conditional, a place in a program where execution is interrupted if certain conditions exist

breakpoint instruction, a command which causes the computer to interrupt execution unconditionally, based on conditions or as a result of conditional branching

breakpoint, program, a breakpoint set by a programmer as an aid to debugging

breakpoint symbol, an optional symbol in a program to indicate a breakpoint

B register, an extension of the accumulator used for multiply and divide processes; a register containing a computer word which can modify an instruction; a register containing a value used to modify an address

briefcase computer, forerunner of the laptop

brightness, the reflective quality of an optical medium such as paper, critical to optical character recognition techniques

broad band system, in data transmission, the ability to handle a greater frequency range than voice grade

broad band transmission, the transmission of signals using a band width of a greater frequency range than voice grade

broadcast, to transmit the same message simultaneously to several terminals

brute force approach, using existing equipment or routines to solve a problem that does not require precise computation and for which the equipment or routines are not designed

BSAM, (basic sequential access method) a database system procedure

BTAM, basic telecommunications access method

BTP, batch transfer program

bubble memory, a type of random access memory which uses movable magnetic fields in a solid state device

bubble memory chip, a semiconductor chip using bubble memory

bubble sort, an algorithm for sorting a list in which the first two items are sorted, then the second and third, third and fourth, etc. forcing the highest item to the end of the list and the process is repeated until the entire list is in order

bucket, a casual term for space reserved for temporary storage; a buffer, counter or queue

buffer, a device reserved for temporary storage of data

buffer, data, a temporary storage for data flowing from a faster device to feed to a slower device, such as, from the computer to the printer

buffered computer, a computer which uses buffers to permit it to perform more than one operation concurrently, such as input and output, and to compensate for variations in speed among peripherals

buffered I/O, input-output which is buffered to permit concurrent operations at optimum speed

buffer, input/output, the temporary storage area for computer input and output

buffer, refresh, temporary storage for screen display information as screen image is refreshed

buffer register, a temporary register able to receive or send data at different I/O rates

buffer, sender/receiver, temporary storage which allows input to be collected before being transmitted

buffer storage, a device which temporarily stores information during transfer; a secondary storage for data to be transferred between internal and external storage; a synchronizing element between internal and external storage, devices of differing speeds, etc.

bug, an error in a computer program; a defect in a computer, printer or other peripheral; generally, anything wrong with a system, hardware or software

bug, logic, a computer program error caused by faulty logic in a program statement or statements

bug monitor, any program which is designed to seek out problems with hardware or software

bug patch, an added instruction or routine in a program to circumvent a bug

bug, syntax, a computer program error caused by failure to follow the rules of the programming language

building block principle, the concept of developing a computer system or program from modules; **modular construction**

built-in check, a provision built into computer hardware to verify that it is functioning correctly

bulk eraser, a device which deletes the data on an entire reel of tape without scanning the tape

bulk storage, large capacity external storage which supplements internal storage

bulletin board service, a computer message center, accessed by modem, which can be called up from a remote terminal to get information and exchange messages or programs

bundled, descriptive of hardware, software, and/or services priced and sold as a unit

burn-in, a testing method for new devices which involves operating for a specified period of time to check for component failures

burst, to separate the sheets of continuous or fan-fold paper

burst mode, a mode of communication which involves reading or writing data without an interrupt

bus, a collection of wires or paths for data, address, commands, control codes, etc. on which information is moved between the CPU, memory and I/O devices

bus arbitration, a technique that permits only one device to control the bus at a time

bus available signal, the signal which indicates that one transaction is complete and the bus is available for the next

bus circuit, a group of wires which provide communication between two or more devices

bus driver, a circuit added to a data bus to guide the transfer of data from several memories in line

bus hub, the place on a control panel where pulse signals enter and exit

business application, a computer program which handle ordinary business routines such as payroll, accounting, etc.

business compiler, a language compiler for business oriented tasks such as COBOL

business data processing, data processing dedicated to business oriented applications

business graphics, representation of business data as graphs, charts, etc.; software used to enable such representation; audio-visual presentation and the enabling software; desktop publishing and the enabling software; CAD, CAD/CAM, engineering drawings, schematics etc., and the enabling software

business programming, creation of applications specifically for business needs, with emphasis on data manipulation such as accounting and planning functions, mailing lists, etc.

busing, daisy chain, the process of sending signals along a bus to a series of devices wherein those devices which do not require the signals pass them through to the next device

bus, input/output, a set of lines for sending and receiving data, commands, device addresses, status, and control information

bus master, any device, CPU or peripheral, which has control of a bus transaction

bus, multiplexed, a bus wherein is combined address and data signals supported by independent control lines

bus multiplexing, transporting data and address over the same bus

bus, network, a communication line which connects the stations of a local area network

bus, peripheral, a bus which interfaces with a peripheral device

bus slave, any device, CPU or peripheral, which is receiving or transmitting data on instructions from a bus master

button, emergency, a button or switch which stops a computer operation in the event of a malfunction

button, panic, an emergency button; a fictional alarm button which is pressed in emergency

button, reset, the button on a microcomputer which reboots after a crash without the necessity of shutting off the system

bypass procedure, a procedure to get the most critical data into the main computer when the line control computer fails

by product, peripheral data developed by a procedure designed to perform some other function

byte, a computer word; the memory space required to store one printed character, usually eight bits; the smallest group of bits which can be addressed individually

byte, hexadecimal, an eight bit byte referenced as a two-digit hexadecimal number

byte location, effective, the actual location of a byte in storage

byte mode, transmission of data one byte at a time

byte multiplexer channel, a channel which interleaves bytes from different sources

byte multiplexing, delegating time slots on a channel to different sources so that bytes can be interlaced in sequence

C

C, a high-level, structured programming language, which is similar to PASCAL

cable, a wrapping of conductors which may be used separately or in groups

cable, coaxial, a transmission line comprised of an inner conductor and an outer conductor layer

cable, connecting, a cable which transfers electricity between two pieces of equipment

cable connectors, the cable terminals or plugs which are necessary for connecting the cables to each other or to equipment

cable, optic, a set of optic fibers

cable, ribbon, a wide, thin transmission line in which the wires are aligned side by side

cable, tape, a cable comprised of flat metallic ribbon conductors

cache memory, extremely fast buffer memory in a CPU which loads frequently used files from main memory in anticipation of need

cache memory hit ratio, a measure of the effectiveness of the cache; the number calls for files which are found in the cache (hits) compared to the total number of calls

cache register, high-speed memory for storing frequently used data

CAD, (computer aided design) a graphics program which uses a computer to assist in the design of products or components

CAD/CAM, (computer aided design /computer aided manufacturing) a graphics program which uses a computer to assist in the design of products and manufacturing systems

CADD, computer aided design and drafting, a CAD system which assists in the creation of engineering drawings

CAE, computer aided engineering; use of the computer to analyze the design of structures, electrical components, etc.

CAI, computer aided instruction; use of a computer in the teaching of a student; use of a computer by a teacher for preparing lessons, record keeping, etc.

CAL, computer-augmented learning; conversational algebraic language

calculator, any device which performs numeric calculations

calculator chip, a chip with a built-in processor programmed to perform numeric calculations

calendar date, a date expressed as day, month and year in any order as contrasted to **Julian date**

call, the transfer of control to a program subroutine

calling sequence, the set of instructions which directs program control between the main program and a subroutine

call instruction, a command which calls a subroutine and directs resumption of the program when the subroutine is completed

call word, the word used to identify a computer program subroutine

CAM, (computer aided manufacturing) the use of a computer program to control an automated manufacturing system; (content-addressable memory) a memory location which is identified by the data or type of data which it contains rather than by its address

CAM devices, content. addressable memory devices

cancel, stop or abort a program or procedure

cancel character, a control character indicating that data is to be disregarded

CANCL, a status word which indicates that a remote computing system has deleted something

canned routines, routines provided by the manufacturer in machine-readable form

canned software, software designed for a specific application, but not a specific user, often available on the open market

capability, stand-alone, the ability of a device to function independently

capacitance, a measure of how much electric charge can be stored in a capacitor

capacitor, a device which stores an electrical charge

capacity, the ability to accept, store or process; the amount of information a memory device can hold

capstan, the rotating shaft that moves magnetic tape past the recording heads

CAR, computer-assisted retrieval; cataloguing of documents by a computer to facilitate retrieval and examination

card, a printed circuit board; a punched card used in data processing

card cage, a frame inside a microcomputer which can hold a number of printed circuit boards

card deck, a set of punched cards containing related data; a file of data base records on punched cards

card edge connectors, the electronic connectors which connect a card to the computer

card encoder, a device which places information on the magnetic strip of a credit card, security card, or key card

card, fax, a device, mounted in a computer, which allows the transmission and receipt of facsimile copies

card frame, the card connectors and guides in a card cage

card guide, the part of a card frame which holds the card

card, logic, one of several cards in a computer containing electrical components and wiring circuits

card, magnetic, a card containing a magnetic strip on which data can be stored

card, master, a punched card which contains pertinent data about a card deck

card, memory, a card, similar to a credit card, containing one or more imbedded magnetic chips to which data can be recorded

card, punched, a card on which data is stored in the form of holes punched in columns

card reader, a device which reads the holes in punched cards; a device which reads information from the magnetic strip of a credit card, security card, etc.

card sorter, a device which sorts punched cards

card sorting, the process of arranging cards in a stack based on the information punched in them

caret, a symbol (^) to indicate the radix point or exponential

carriage, the part of a printer which holds the paper

carriage return, (CR) a keyboard function key, also called *enter* or *enter key* which is used to move the cursor to the beginning of the next line or, in some programs, to direct execution of a selected command; in some word processing application programs, inserts an end-of-line or paragraph marker

carrier, a transmission signal of constant frequency which can be modulated to carry data to a receiver such as a telephone or computer

carrier, data, the medium on which data is conveyed, such as punched cards, magnetic disk, etc.

carrier noise, undesirable variations in the frequency of a signal caused by the physical medium which is carrying the signal

carry, the transfer of a digit in arithmetic operations when the sum of a column exceeds the base

carry flag, an indicator that signals an overflow or under flow condition created by a mathematical operation in the accumulator

carry time, the time required to process a carry

Cartesian coordinate system, a system for indicating the shape of a solid by means of three planes intersecting at right angles to each other at a point called the origin from which any point in space with coordinates x, y, and z can be located; the means used in a CAD system to represent a three dimensional object on screen

cartridge, a container, usually for a magnetic recording device

cartridge, ribbon, a printer ribbon housed in a plastic container for ease of replacement in the printer

cartridge, tape, magnetic tape which is enclosed in a protective container

cascade carry, a carry process in parallel addition

cascade connection, two or more components arranged so that the output of one is connected to the input of the next

cascade control, a control system in which each unit regulates the next unit in line

cascade merging, a system of com-

bining used in a sort program

case, referring to a property of text, whether upper case or lower case

case conversion, a technique in some word processing programs for changing the case of characters without retyping which involves selecting the character or text block, then entering, or selecting from a menu, a command which converts the text to all caps, caps and lower case or all lower case

case shift, in word processing, the transfer of keyboard function from lower to upper case

cassette, a self-contained package of reel-to-reel magnetic tape, such as that used in stereo systems and video recorders which can be used to store computer data

cassette interface, the circuits which control transfer of data between a computer and a cassette tape recorder

cassette recorder, in computers, a device designed to interface with a computer and record digital data

cassette-user tape system, a system which includes hardware and software necessary to store data and programs on a cassette tape

catalog, an inventory of programs files, etc. in an ordered fashion for easy reference; to make such an inventory

catastrophic error, a series of errors or a single error with such far reaching effects that the job must be terminated

catastrophic failure, a total failure in which the computer shuts down and any data not in storage is lost

catena, a closely connected series; a series of components

catenate, to connect in series

cathode ray tube, (CRT) a display device attached to a computer or used as a remote terminal; a vacuum tube which sprays a stream of electrons onto a fluorescent screen such as a television set or computer display

CBBS, computerized bulletin board service

CBEMA, Computer and Business Equipment Manufacturing Association

CBL, computer-based learning

CCD, charge-coupled device

CCD memory, charge-coupled device memory; a form of volatile random access memory

CCIA, Computer and Communications Industry Association

CD ROM, compact disk read-only memory; unalterable data stored on a compact disk

CD ROM drive, the device which holds and reads a compact disk

cell, a memory location that holds a single unit of information; a data element in a spreadsheet

cell, binary, the basic unit of memory which can assume either of two stable states: *0* or *1*, *true* or *false*, *yes* or *no*; an elementary unit of storage

cell, data, the smallest unit of data equal to one bit

cell, magnetic, a basic unit of memory in which a bit is characterized by a magnetic flux in one of two directions

centisecond, one hundredth of a second

central processing element, (CPE) a two- or four-bit section of a processor which is arrayed in parallel with other, like sections to form a processor of the desired word length

central processing unit, (CPU) the part of a computer where operations are performed and instructions are executed; the unit which controls operation of the computer; in a microprocessor, an integrated circuit contained on a single chip

central processor, (CP), the main processor, which contains arithmetic, logic and control capabilities

CGA, color graphics adapter; the original standard for color monitors on IBM® and compatibles which provides a resolution of 320 pixels across the screen by 200 pixels down

chain, to link records with pointers which indicate the location of the next element; elements so linked

chained files, data files containing pointers which indicate the location of previous and subsequent blocks

chained list, a list in which each element contains a reference to the location of the next, without regard to storage order

chained sectors, disk sectors that contain a sequential units of data but are not necessarily contiguous on the disk

chain field, the field in a record which indicates the location of the next record

chaining, connecting parts, sections, or blocks by the use of pointers which indicate the location of previous and subsequent elements

chaining, program, a program written in modules which are automatically called in order when the preceding module is completed

chaining search, a technique for

searching data in which each data element points to the next element, until the search element or the end of the chain is reached

chain printer, a line printer whose characters are mounted on a moving chain

change dump, a printout of all the memory locations in which contents have changed

change file, a computer document which contains a collection of transactions which are to be merged with the master file to update it

change record, a record used to update information in a master file

channel, a communications link between two devices; an electrical link between two points; the link which carries data signals

channel adapter, a device which allows connection between data channels of different equipment

channel, analog, a channel that can accommodate a signal at any value within its defined limits

channel bandwidth, the number of line-signal elements per second (baud rate)

channel capacity, the maximum number of bits per second that a channel is able to carry

channel command, an instruction which directs that an operation be performed

channel, dedicated, a communications channel reserved for a specific use

channel, DMA, a channel for direct memory access

channel, duplex, a channel capable of transmitting in both directions simultaneously

channel, input, a channel which accepts signals to the computer

channel, input/output, a channel which links a peripheral device and a computer

channelizing, to divide wide band transmission facilities into several narrower channels

channel, read/write, a bi-directional data path linking main memory and a peripheral device

channel, simplex, a channel able to communicate in only one direction

channel switching, connection of an I/O device to more than one channel to optimize processing

channel synchronizer, a device which controls the transfer of data at proper times and sequence

channel, voice grade, a channel capable of voice transmission

character, any one of a set of symbols, as letters, numbers or punctuation marks; a symbol which can be processed and stored by a computer

character, alphanumeric, the letters of the alphabet, numbers, punctuation marks and special characters

character, bell, an ASCII control character that activates a tone: used in programs to alert the user to an error condition, an end of processing, etc.

character/block transmission, the ability to act on characters one at a time or in blocks, which expands editing capabilities

character code, the group of binary digits which represents a character

character, command, a character, which represents a control function

character crowding, a technique which reduces the space or time interval between characters in order to maximize storage or reduce transmission time

character density, the number of characters which can be stored per unit of disk area or tape length

character fill, to replace unwanted data with a character such as 0 or X; in programming, to indicate space for an, as yet, unknown character

character generator, the chip which stores the pixel patterns for characters displayed on a screen

character graphics, a form of low-resolution graphics using an extended character set of predefined lines, bars, corners, etc.

character highlighting, any method for distinguishing a character or characters from surrounding text, such as blinking, reverse video, higher intensity, or underlining

character, illegal, a character transmission rejected as invalid by a computer or other device; a character in a data base rejected as invalid based on parameters laid down in the program

character, magnetic, a character printed with magnetic ink

character, new-line, a control character that moves the print head to a new line; a line feed

character, non-printing, a control character

character, numeric, a digit, integer or numeral

character pitch, the number of characters per inch of printed text

character, print-control, any of a number of characters which control the operation of a printer

character printer, a printer which contains a fixed font similar to a

typewriter, such as a daisy-wheel printer; a printer which, although not limited to a fixed font, cannot print graphics other than those in an extended character set

character reader, a magnetic or optical device used to scan printed or written characters which it converts into digital data

character recognition, the ability of a scanning device to recognize a printed or written character; reading characters with a scanner

character set, the aggregate of all the characters associated with a given device or system; a font of type

characters, machine-readable, stylized characters which can be interpreted by humans or by scanners such as OCR or MICR

characters per second, a common measure of the speed of a printer

character shift, a program code or printer switch which toggles control between outputting standard characters and graphics symbols

character, special, a character other than a letter or number

character string, a series of characters processed as a unit

charge-coupled device, a semiconductor characterized by high density storage and low power consumption

chart, detail, a flowchart which shows the step by step execution of a series of operations

chart, logic, a program flow chart which shows the logical steps applied to solve a problem

chart, run, a flow chart of a computer run which shows input and output

chart, system, a schematic of a

system which shows the information flow

chassis, the base on which the electronic components of a computer are mounted; the framework of a computer

check, a test of condition; the means by which data is verified; tests of machine operations; the performance of such tests

check, arithmetic, verification of the results of a mathematical operation

check bit, a binary check digit

check character, a parity character added to a group for the purpose of error detection

check, cyclic, a system of error detection that checks every nth bit

check digit, a calculated digit used to verify the accuracy of a transmission

checker, grammar, a program, either stand alone or part of a word processing application, which reviews a document for grammatical errors

checker, spell, a program, either stand alone or part of a word processing application, which proofreads for errors in spelling

check indicator, a device which indicates that an error has occurred

check indicator, overflow, a device which indicates that an operation has produced a number too large for the system to handle

checking, automatic, a continuous process within a computer to verify that all systems are functioning properly

checking, bias, a technique for varying equipment operating conditions (voltage, etc.) to isolate defective parts; **marginal testing**

checking loop, a procedure for checking data transmission by sending it back to the source to match it with the original data

checking, odd-even, a system for confirming the accuracy of an operation through an extra bit in a computer word which indicates whether the word had an odd or even number of 1's

checking program, a diagnostic program which analyzes other programs or data for errors

check light, an indicator light which goes on when there is an error condition

check number, a number which is transmitted to test data transmission equipment

checkout, a set of routines inserted by a programmer to assess the performance of a program under operating conditions

check, parity, a test for transmission accuracy which compares the sum of the bits in a computer word with a previously calculated sum bit which indicates an even or odd number of 1's in the original word

checkpoint, a place in a program where the value of variables is checked and recorded; a point at which records are saved in case a restart is necessary

checkpoint and restart procedure, a procedure in data base management which enables a restart from the last checkpoint, in contrast to starting from the beginning

checkpoint/restart, a system that designates checkpoints in the run of a database program when records are saved so that processing can be continued from that point in the event of a crash

check problem, a problem which tests the operation of a program

check program, a short program which tests the validity of a part of a larger program; a hardware testing program run on a computer which does not have automatic or self-checking

check register, a register which holds information to be checked against the next transfer of the same information

check, selection, a verification that the correct input/output device was selected for a routine

check, sign, a test for change in the sign of a data field

check sum, a number used to verify the accuracy of a transmission; the sum of a group of digits, such as the total of the ASCII codes for a block of data, used to verify accuracy by comparison with a previously calculated sum of the same digits

check, system, a test of system performance

chip, an integrated circuit; a small piece of silicon to which impurities have been added in a pattern to form transistors and other circuit elements

chip architecture, the arrangement and interconnections of the ALU, registers, and control bus structures on a chip

chip, bubble memory, a semiconductor chip using movable magnetic fields in a solid state device

chip card, a smart card

chip, CPU, a large-scale integrated circuit; a microprocessor which contains all the elements of a central processor on a single chip, including accumulator, registers, ALU, I/O ports, and some memory

chip, logic, a circuit chip which performs logic functions and, in conjunction with other chips, is used to create more complex circuits

chip, memory, a semi-conductor used to store data

chip, microprocessor, a CPU chip; a large-scale integrated circuit which contains all the elements of a central processor on a single chip, including accumulator, registers, ALU, I/O ports, and some memory

chip-select input, a gating input that calls a specific chip or couples it with another circuit

CIM, (computer input microfilm) a system which utilizes a scanner to recognize and translate images from microfilm to computer language for input

circuit, a complete path for an electric current; a system of electrical conductors with a power source, a switch to open and close the conductor path and a device which has resistance

circuit, anti coincidence, a gate which performs the *exclusive OR* operation wherein output is true if the inputs are different, and false if the inputs coincide

circuit, asynchronous, a circuit which is triggered by signals rather that timing synchronization

circuit, bi-stable, a circuit capable of assuming either of two stable states which is changed by an energy pulse; a flip flop

circuit, bi-stable trigger, a circuit which can be reset to either of two stable states

circuit board, a printed circuit card to which other devices may be affixed

circuit, bus, a group of wires which provide communication between two or more devices

circuit, bus driver, a circuit added to a data bus to guide the transfer of data from several memories in line

circuit capacity, the number of channels in a circuit which can be accessed concurrently; the amount of information a circuit can process, in bits per second

circuit card, a printed circuit board which contains electronic components

circuit chip, a device containing complex, microscopic circuitry

circuit, computer, any of the circuits used in a digital computer

circuit, dedicated, a circuit reserved for a specific use

circuit diagram, schematic drawing of an electronic circuit

circuit, integrated, a mass-produced solid state circuit containing a number of elements designed to work together

circuit, inverting, a circuit which functions as a NOT gate

circuit, logic, a circuit which performs logic functions, such as AND, OR, etc.

circuit noise, electrical or other interference which distorts a signal interference

circuit, printed, a circuit whose elements are linked by printed or etched conducting paths

circuits, control, the circuits which interpret program instructions and cause their execution

circuits, discrete, electronic circuits constructed of individual components, as opposed to integrated circuits

circuit, sequential, an electronic circuit that incorporates a logic element with storage element that provide data on the previous state of the inputs

circuit, single-shot, a circuit which standardizes imprecise input to produce output which meets the criteria of the target device

circuit, storage, a circuit which stores the value of the last signal received until changed by a subsequent signal

circuit tester, a device with a processor and memory which runs programs to test individual circuits

circular shift, a shift in which bits shifted off one end of a register fill in from the other end

circulating register, a register which performs shift operations

circulating storage, a device that stores information in a train of pulses which, when they reach the end of the device, are reinserted at the beginning

CIU, (computer interface unit) a device which matches and connects a computer to its peripheral devices

cladding, material which protects optic fiber from external light

class, a group whose members share similar characteristics

classify, to arrange or catalogue a collection by class

clear, to set all values to zero; to erase the contents of a memory device by resetting all values to zero

clear band, in optical character recognition, a border which must be free of extraneous material

cleared condition, the condition of memory after a destructive read

clearing, replacing the contents of a register or memory location with zeros

clear to send, (CTS) control signal which indicates that a data link is available

click, to press a mouse button and release it quickly, usually to reposition the cursor or highlight a menu item in an applications program

clip art, ready made art which is available for use in documents, flyers, etc.

clip art file, a computer file of artwork which can be accessed, altered and inserted into other documents

clipping, the truncation of the image near the edge of a CRT

clock, a time keeping or synchronizing device in the computer; an electronic circuit which generates regular pulses for timing signals within the computer; **master clock**

clock, day, an electronic device in the computer used for real-time processing

clock, digital, a timer whose output is expressed in discrete numbers

clocked signals, signals controlled by clock pulses

clock frequency, the cycle of pulses generated by a clock to regulate signals; **master clock frequency**

clock generator, the device that produces clock signals and synchronizes messages sent to peripherals

clocking, internal, bit-timing in communications provided by the computer rather than by a modem

clock pulse, the pulse used for timing operations

clock rate, the pulses per second produced by a clock

clock, real-time, time maintained in conventional manner in order to execute program instructions which contain real-time commands

clone, a computer which is compatible with IBM microcomputer technology

closed, the state of a circuit that is turned on enabling a flow of current; the state of a data file which is not available for editing

closed loop, a set of instructions with no provision for escape without programmer intervention; a programming error in which the output modifies the input so that an ending value is never attained; a technique involving data feedback for verification

closed loop system, a technique in which a program controls an external program or process without human involvement

closed routine, a remote routine which is called up by the main program

closed subroutine, an external routine which can be called from a specific location

clustering, grouping items which have similar characteristics

CMI, (computer-managed instruction) the use of a computer to assist in the administrative tasks associated with classroom teaching

CML, (current-mode logic) a type of transistor which responds to slight changes in input current which results in very fast switching speeds

CMOS, complementary metal oxide semiconductor; a type of integrated circuit that requires low power and is relatively immune to outside noise and changes in temperature

coalesce, to combine two or more files into one

coaxial cable, a transmission line comprised of an inner conductor and an outer conductor layer

COBOL, common business oriented language; a high level structured language designed for business applications

CODASYL, Conference On Data Systems Languages

code, data represented by symbols, characters, or words; a series of machine or assembly-language instructions; text or data which has been encrypted; to translate an algorithm to computer language

code, absolute or **basic,** program code accessed directly by the computer

code, binary, the depicting of letters, numbers, and other symbols with binary digits

code, biquinary, a seven-bit decimal code in which the first two bits represent 5 or 0 and the other five bits represent the numbers 0 through 4

code, command, operation code; that part of a computer instruction which identifies the operation to be performed

code conversion, translating from one code structure to another, as from source code to machine code; changing the bit patterns from one data code into those of another

code converter, a device which automatically changes the code of input data to output in a different code such as a compiler

coded data, data depicted by symbols; sets of characters assigned to represent items of data

coded decimal number, a number in which each digit is coded individually

code dictionary, an alphabetical listing of computer codes in the order of their definitions and in the order of the codes themselves

code, direct, code which specifies a computer command and address in machine language

coded program, a program written in the syntax of a programming language (source code) or in machine language

code, error detecting, a system whereby errors produce a forbidden code combination

code, false, a character which is not accepted as valid by the computer

code, function, a code which directs the operation of a peripheral device

code, gray, in graphics, a numeric code in which each number inside a finite range differs from the previous number by one digit

code, instruction, a set of all instructions, symbols, names, etc. understood by a particular computer or system

code, internal, the structure of data representation in a computer, such as 8 bits per computer word, byte or character

code interpreter, a device which translates interim or program code to machine code

code line, a line of code within a program; one computer instruction on one line

code, line-feed, a command which causes the paper in a printer to be moved up one line

code, MICR, magnetic ink character recognition; a code developed to machine-read documents to control banking transactions

code, minimum access, a code designed to reduce delays in the transfer of data or instructions between storage and other components

code, mnemonic, code devised with a built in memory aid; a code whose name is a reminder of what it represents, such as ACC for accumulator

code, mnemonic operation, operation codes written in assembly-language mnemonics

code, numeric, a code system which uses only numbers

code, object, the code produced by a compiler or assembler translation from source code

code, one-out-of-ten, a ten-bit binary word in which a decimal digit value is represented by a 1 in the position which corresponds to that numeral, 0 through 9

code, operation, a symbol which directs the computer to execute an operation; a single instruction in assembly language

code, optimized, the most direct solution to a problem; a program which contains no unnecessary instructions

code, pseudo, a simplified form of program code which details the program structure and on which the final program is based

coder, a program which translates input in one code into output in another code, such as source code to machine code; a compiler or assembler; a person who writes program code

code, reentrant, programming that can be shared by several users at the same time

codes, any symbolic representation of something else; rules and conventions which outline the processing of commands, communications, etc.

code, self-checking, a system for detection of errors by adding an extra bit to computer words

code, self-complementing, a machine language in which the code of the complement of a digit is the complement of the code of the digit

code, self-correcting, a system of coding numbers in which detection and correction of transmission errors is automatic

code set, a code structure; the group of symbols, letters, and numbers which comprise a particular code

code, skip, a code which directs the computer to skip specified memory fields

code, symbolic, source code

coding, the act of writing code; converting an algorithm into programming language or source code

coding form, a printed sheet with positions blocked so that code can be written in the same form in which it will appear on a screen or punched card

coding, numeric, coding which uses only numerals to depict instructions and data

coding, skeletal, pseudo code; preliminary coding of a program in which some information is completed later

cognition, artificial, a routine in which scanned characters are compared to stored matrixes in or-

der to select the most likely representation

cognition, machine, a type of artificial intelligence; the recognition
by a computer of patterns which
are then stored for use in future
decision making

COGO, (coordinate geometry) a high-
level language used to solve geometric problems

coincidence AND signal, a circuit
which produces an output only if
all input signals are the same

coincidence circuit, an AND gate

coincidence gate, a logic circuit
which produces output that relies
on specific input

cold boot, the start-up procedure
performed when power is first
turned on; restarting a computer

cold start, starting a computer after
it has crashed or been turned off

collate, to merge two or more ordered sets of data to create a new
set ordered in the same fashion as
the original sets

collating sequence, the order in
which various items are merged

collating sorting, sorting data to
produce an ordered sequence

collator, a program which merges
data from two or more sources; a
machine which merges two sets of
punched cards

collection, data, the process of
bringing data to a central point for
processing

collection station, data, a remote
terminal such as on a factory floor
which is used to collect employee
time and production information

collection system, data, a system
which collects, sorts and stores
data from remote collection stations

colon, a delimiter in programming
code, indicating a pause, break, or
stop depending on the syntax of
the particular code

column, the vertical characters in a
two-dimensional array; the position
of a bit in a computer word; a vertical arrangement of elements; vertical positions in a punched card

COM, (computer output microfilm)
microfilm or microfiche generated
from computer output; communications, as in **COM port**

combinational logic, an arrangement of circuits to determine output by subjecting input to a number of logic tests

combination operation, the performance of two or more operations
simultaneously

combined read/write head, a tape
head that can read and write

combined symbol matching (CSM),
a system of optical character recognition based on detecting recurring
patterns

command, a computer instruction
which specifies that an operation
be performed; a code or signal to
start or stop and operation

command chained memory, dynamic memory in which storage locations are designated by a sequence of commands

command, channel, an instruction
which directs that an operation be
performed

command character, a character,
which represents a control function

command code, operation code;
that part of a computer instruction
which identifies the operation to be
performed

command control program, the
program which processes the

commands originating from the user console

command decoder, the device which interprets commands from the user console

command driven program, an interactive program that requires the operator to employ a set of commands which drive the program directly

command file processor, a system which allows a series of commands to be entered as a file and processed as a type of higher level operating system

command functions, codes which direct the CPU to perform various tasks

command language, a procedural syntax for directing performance of basic functions

command line, the line, at the system prompt, on which instructions for the system are typed; the instruction, with any parameters, typed to start an application or issue any other system command

command list, a sequence of CPU generated routines for the performance of an I/O operation

command processing, the processing of computer commands as distinguished from the processing of data

comment, a programmer's notation which describes a task or routine without affecting operation of the computer

comment line, a line in a program containing a notation by the programmer which does not affect processing by the computer; in some applications, comments by the user which are not printed in the final document, often used in

text or spreadsheet files to relay messages between users who share responsibility for input the file

commercial FORTRAN, a programming language combination of FORTRAN with elements of BASIC and/or COBOL, designed for business use

common block storage, a section of main memory used by both the main program and a subprogram

common business-oriented language, (COBOL) a high level structured language designed for business applications

common carrier, any of the organizations, regulated by the government, which provide telecommunication services for the general public

common field, a data field which is designated as available to more than one program routines

common language, a computer language which is recognized by a number of different computers; a single code recognized by devices from more than one manufacturer

common software, programs and routines in a language common to a number of different computers

common storage, a part of memory accessible to all programs

communicating word processors, desktop computers which are connected to other devices such as phone and fax modems; word processors programmed for direct communication with other units in the system

communication, the transfer of information from one place to another; transmission of data or control signals between a computer and peripherals or between two computers; transmission of data over telephone lines; transmission of messages between terminals

communication channel, the physical path which carries the signals to transfer information

communication control character, a character that regulates operations performed by a peripheral device, such as a printer

communication data system, a real-time system that connects a remote data collection terminal and a computer

communication input/output control system, the routines for handling I/O operations

communication link, the physical connection between devices which allows them to communicate with each other; the hardware and software which furnish the means for two devices to interact

communication network, the complex of channels, transmitters, and receivers required to carry data from one installation to another

communication protocol, standards by which hardware and software operate in order to ensure successful transfer of information

communication, real-time processing, the receipt of data from remote locations while the transactions producing it are taking place, such as shop floor data collection, automated bank teller transactions, etc.

Communication Satellite Corporation, (COMSAT) the US member of a commercial corporation which provides worldwide satellite communications

communications buffer, a device in a communications network which provides temporary storage of data to compensate for different rates of data flow between components in the network

communications code, the representation of characters, numbers, symbols, and control functions in binary form

communications, computer, passing information between two computers, or between a computer and a remote terminal

communications device, input/output, a device which sends or receives information from a data communications system

communication settings, settings which specify the parameters for the transfer of information between the computer and other devices

communications executive, a control routine which sets protocol for various communication line disciplines and terminal types

communications monitor, an operating system designed specifically to control communications

communication software, software which deals with interrupts, message queuing, and error control in communication systems

communication statements, statements which call subroutines and return them to memory

communications processing, the management of information transmitted from a remote terminal which is not connected directly to the computer

communications system, a computer which manages real-time, on-line applications

communications system, data, data processing which involves the use of terminal devices, communications software, and the transmission and receiving of data over common and private lines

communications transparency, the ability of a computer to communicate in the background with no apparent interrupt or delay in foreground operations

communication theory, a branch of mathematics which deals with the properties of message transmittal

compaction, compressing; rearranging scattered or fragmented files on a disk in order to make the best use of storage space; any technique which refines processing to make the best use of space, bandwidth, transmission time, generation time, or storage space

compandor, compressing and expanding converter, a D/A and A/D converter which compresses an analog signal for voice communication and expands it at the receiving end

companion keyboard, an auxiliary keyboard located in an area away from the main unit

comparator, a device which confirms the accuracy of data by comparing two transmissions of the same data

compare, an instruction which subtracts one word from another to determine which, if either, is larger; to determine the size of one data element in relation to another

comparing control, the checking of data fields against each other to confirm the accuracy of any form of transmission

compatibility, the characteristic of various software and hardware devices to work together

compatibility, equipment, the capability of two computers or devices to share data

compatibility, program, the ability of programs to interact or to be integrated with each other

compatibility, systems, the compatibility of components in a computer system

compatible, describing devices and programs which may be used together

compatible hardware, a computer and peripheral devices which may be used together

compatible software, software which can be run on a particular computer without modification; software programs which be used in conjunction with each other

compilation, the process of converting a source code program to an object code program; translating source code to machine language

compilation time, the time required to translate a source program into an object program

compile, to translate a program written in a source code into machine language

compile and go, loading, compiling, and executing a program all in one step

compiler, a program which translates a high level program language or source code into machine language

compiler diagnostics, a list of program errors detected during compiling

compiler, incremental, a compiler which compiles a program one line at a time allowing on-line editing

compiler, interactive, a program which compiles another program one statement at a time as it is received; a compiler which allows on line editing while producing a compiled program

compiler language, a language used to write compilers

compiler, on-line, a program which compiles a source code program one line at a time, allowing on-line editing while producing a fully compiled object program; an interactive, incremental compiler

compiler, resident, a compiler program which resides within the computer for which it is compiling programs

compiling program, same as **compiler**

complementary bipolar integrated circuit, an integrated circuit that employs both *npn* and *pnp* transistors in the same substrate

complementary metal oxide semiconductor (CMOS), a type of integrated circuit that requires low power and is relatively immune to outside noise and changes in temperature

complementary operation, any Boolean operation that is the negation of the original operation

complementary operator, the NOT of a given operator

complete carry, a carry which results when the addition of carries is allowed to propagate

complete operation, an operation that obtains an instruction, retrieves operands from memory, processes the data and returns the results to memory

component, a single part or element of a whole system

component, computer, any of the elements which make up a computer

component, integrated, a group of electrical elements which cannot be disassociated without disabling the component's function

COM port, communications port; a serial or parallel port of a computer

composite cable, a cable which is made up of wires of different gauges or types

composite card, a data processing punched card which contains information used in more than one process or application

composite video, the standard system for producing a TV image and for communicating between a computer and a TV or monitor

composite video signal, a single signal using one channel or wire which consists of the display signal combined with a timing or synchronization signal and the blanking pulses between images

composition error, an error which is detected as soon as it is entered and can be immediately corrected

compound logical element, circuitry which provides a single output from multiple inputs

compress, to compact data so as to take less storage or transmission space

compressed video, a system of transmitting video signals over telephone lines

compression, data, reduction of the space required for data storage and transmission through elimination of blanks, redundancies, etc.

computer, a general purpose programmable device which is capable of accepting data and manipulating it, as well as reporting and storing the results

computer aided design, (CAD) a graphics program which uses a computer to assist in the design of products or components

computer aided design and drafting (CADD) a CAD system which assists in the creation of engineering drawings

computer aided engineering, (CAE) use of the computer to analyze the design of structures, electrical components, etc.

computer-aided instruction, (CAI) use of a computer to assist in the teaching of a student; use of a computer by a teacher to assist in lesson preparation, record keeping, etc.

computer aided manufacturing, (CAM) the use of a computer program to control an automated manufacturing system

computer, analog, a computer which interprets data in analog form and operates by directly measuring and manipulating the electric current which represents the data

computer analyst, a person skilled in the analysis of problems and the design of solutions for the computer; one who certifies the capability of a computer system and designates the tasks for which the system will be used

computer animation, animated cartoons, motion pictures, television commercials, etc. produced with the assistance of computer technology; animated figures controlled by computer

computer application, a task to which the computer is suited; a function for which the computer is to be used

computer architecture, the internal design of a computer; the components which make up a computer, particularly its electronics

computer art, artwork produced by or with the assistance of a computer or computer technology

computer-assisted instruction, (CAI), the use of computers to assist in teaching or to assist in planning and administrative functions related to education

computer-assisted retrieval, (CAR) cataloguing of documents by a computer to facilitate retrieval and examination

computer, asynchronous, a computer in which an operation is started as soon as a previous operation is completed or a part of the computer is available, as contrasted to synchronous computer which relies on a timing signal

computer-augmented learning, (CAL), a form of instruction in which traditional teaching methods are supplemented by computer programs

computer-based learning (CBL), instruction in which a computer using special programs is the primary teaching device

computer bomb, a situation in which the computer becomes inoperable as the result of a hardware failure or a program error and from which there is no recovery except to shut down and restart; a **crash**

computer, buffered, a computer which uses buffers to permit it to perform more than one operation concurrently, such as input and output, and to compensate for variations in speed among peripherals

computer center, a data processing center; an area which houses computer equipment and peripherals as well as the personnel responsible for computer operations and their office space

computer circuit, any of the circuits used in a digital computer

computer code, the system of machine code used for a particular computer; the set of instruction codes for a computer

computer communication, interaction between the units in a computer system; transmission between two computers or between a computer and remote terminal

computer communications system, a microcomputer system which handles real-time applications; the hardware which makes up a communication system which is controlled by computer such as telephone and fax modems, etc.

computer component, any of the elements which make up a computer

computer designer, an individual who designs the electronic circuitry of a computer

computer, desktop, a computer designed to fit on a desk, as contrasted to being built into the desk or requiring floor space; a **personal computer** (PC)

computer, digital, a computer which uses digital (as contrasted to analog) signals and data

computer engineering, the study, analysis and development of computer hardware

computer family, a group of CPUs which all have essentially the same architecture but vary in such things as efficiency, size and speed; a group of computers which use the same operating system and software

computer field, a data field; the columns of a punched card used for a standard item of data; the elements of an assembly source statement

computer game, a computer program written for recreational use

computer graphics, graphs, charts, pictures and animation created on the computer, contrasted with word processing characters; the generation and processing of visual images by the computer with peripherals such as scanners, paint and draw programs, type generation programs, etc.

computer image processing, the use of computer programs to change or enhance an image, especially for reproduction as audio-visual presentation material ' or desk top publishing

computer-independent language, a programming language which is not restricted to any particular computer, but which requires a machine-dependent compiler or interpreter

computer input microfilm, a system which utilizes a scanner to recognize and translate images from microfilm to computer language for input

computer interface unit, a device which matches and connects a computer to its peripheral devices

computerized bulletin board service, (CBBS) a computer message center, accessed by modem, which can be called up from a remote terminal to share information, exchange messages and trade programs

computer instruction set, the set of instructions indigenous to a particular computer; the instructions recognized by a particular computer and which it is capable of performing

computer kit, a computer package which requires assembly by the purchaser

computer language, machine language; a language understood directly by the computer

computer, laptop, a computer which is small enough to be held in the lap, often as powerful as a desktop and which can usually be connected to other computers and peripherals such as printers, etc.

computer, large scale, a computer with complex and powerful programmable logic designed for the performance of extremely complex tasks

computer learning, a self-adjusting routine in which the parameters of a function are modified to suit conditions such as the density of a scan for OCR recognition; the modification of program or data by a computer based on its experience while executing the program

computer literacy, knowledge (by an individual) of basic computer operation and computer terms

computer-managed instruction, (CMI) the use of a computer to assist in the administrative tasks associated with classroom teaching

computer network, a system composed of two or more independent computers which are connected in order to share software, data and peripherals, or to allow users to communicate with each other

computer, object, the computer which executes an object program, which may be different from the **source computer** which assembles the program or stores input

computer on a chip, an integrated circuit; a computer in which all main components (CPU, RAM, ROM, clock, etc.) are contained on a single chip

computer operator, the person responsible for operating a mainframe computer as contrasted to a programmer or user

computer oriented language, a low-level language which translates quickly into machine language

computer output microfilm, (COM) microfilm or microfiche generated from computer output

computer, personal, (PC) a computer system of relatively small physical size designed for use by an individual

computer, portable, a computer in its own carrying case and rechargeable battery pack which can carried about with relative ease; **notebook computer; laptop computer**

computer power, the speed of a computer, generally expressed in millions of cycles per second, as 12 MHz (megahertz), 20 MHz, etc.; the word size of a computer's CPU, such as 8-bit, 16-bit, etc.; the ability of a computer to handle background processing or multitasking

computer programmer, one who designs, writes, codes, tests, debugs, and documents programs for a computer

computer run, the processing of a set of instructions under control of one or more programs; the performance of a routine or several linked routines without human involvement

computer, satellite, a secondary computer which supports a larger system; a **satellite processor**

computer science, the study, analysis and development of computer software

computer security, protecting computer equipment and data from unauthorized access

computer, self-learning, a computer which has been programmed to modify future action based on experience

computer, sequential, a computer in which instructions are followed one after the other, in sequence

computer, serial, a computer which processes each bit, word or command one at a time, in order

computer services organization, a company which provides computer access to individual customers through time sharing or batch processing; a company which designs and develops customized software programs; a consulting firm which specializes in computer related projects

computer, single-board, a computer which is designed with all of the vital components wired to a single printed circuit board

computer, slave, a computer which is under the control of another computer as a backup against failure of the main computer, as a repository and controller of file storage, as a device for background processing, etc.

computer, source, a computer which prepares or stores input for another computer

computer storage, the memory in a computer system, managed by the computer, where data, instructions, programs, etc. are stored

computer, synchronous, a computer in which operation is controlled by the pulses of a timing signal

computer system, a computer or computers and all of the associated peripherals and software

computer, target, a computer specifically designated to run a program which is being written or translated; a computer designated as the receiver of data or instructions from another computer

computer virus, any undesirable instruction which adversely affects the performance of a computer or program; a program or instruction maliciously hidden in another program which replicates itself and destroys files, changes files, clogs the system or performs any other action which is detrimental to the computer and its programs

computer, wired program, a computer in which the program instructions are characterized by wired connections on a board

computer word, a fixed-length sequence of bits manipulated as a unit in processing and memory storage; a unit of data in a computer

computing, calculating using arithmetic functions; using a computer for any purpose

COMSAT, Communication Satellite Corporation; the U.S. member of the international corporation which provides worldwide satellite communications

concatenate, to link together; to join together two or more character strings

concatenated data set, a data set which is formed by joining data from two or more files

concatenation, the linking of two or more character strings, such as *micro* concatenated with *computer* equals *microcomputer*

conceptual modeling, creating a model which characterizes a result and experimenting to confirm the validity of the model

concurrent operations, several instructions or operations running at the same time

concurrent processing, performing two or more tasks at the same time

condition, the status of a computer in terms of programs running, peripherals committed or operations being performed at a given time; parameters within a program which dictate a course of action

conditional assembly, an assembly which is programmed so that sections of code may be added or deleted according to the system on which it is run

conditional branch, an instruction to move control to a new section of the program if a certain condition is met

conditional breakpoint, a place in a program where execution is interrupted if certain conditions exist

conditional code, code which describes program conditions which affect the execution of instructions

conditional jump, a conditional branch

conditional statement, a statement which describes a condition and contains instructions to follow if

that condition is met

conditional stop instruction, an instruction to stop processing if certain conditions are met

conditional transfer, a **conditional branch**

condition codes, codes which describe the result of the last CPU action

conductor, a material through which electrical current can flow

configuration, the way in which a specified assemblage of computers and components are connected and programmed to work as a unit; the settings and operating mode of a device

configure, to specify settings on a computer or peripheral which make it compatible with connecting devices, such as setting communication ports and speeds

confirmation message, a message from the computer requesting verification that a command or instruction is to be executed, usually reserved for destructive commands, such as deleting a file

conjunction, the logical AND operation

connecting cable, a cable which transfers electricity between two pieces of equipment

connector, a logical operator which indicates the relationship between two parts of a logic statement; in a flowchart, a representation of the convergence of flow lines; the flowchart connector symbol

connectors, cable, cable terminators to which the cable wires are attached, necessary for connecting to each other or to hardware devices

connector symbol, a flowchart

symbol indicating the convergence of flow lines

connector, variable, a flowchart symbol representing a conditional connection; a routine that may introduce other routines depending on the operation of the program; a multiple branch point

connect time, the period of time a remote user is on-line in a time-sharing computer system

consecutive, relating to items in space or events in time that are sequential with nothing intervening

consistency check, a test to determine that data is within a specified range or of a specified type

console, the device which an operator uses to communicate with a computer, consisting of a control panel and usually a keyboard; a computer user's station consisting of a terminal or screen and a keyboard

console, remote, a terminal which is located away from the computer and which is connected to it enabling normal communication

console, visual display, an operator's console which allows a visual display of computer contents

constant, information which has a fixed value; a symbol or name which represents a fixed value; data which is not subject to change

constant area, a storage area set aside for a constant value

constant, numeric, a value which does not change; a self-defining numeric

consultant, a technical advisor

content, data held in a memory location or main storage

content-addressable memory, (CAM) a memory location which is

identified by the data or type of data which it contains rather than by its address

contention, conflict; a condition in which two CPUs attempt to control the same device at the same time; in communications, two locations attempt to transmit to the same receiver at the same time

contention system, a system of transmitting data in which the sender tests for conflict, i.e., a busy line, and does not attempt to transmit until the channel is free

contents, data held in a memory location or main storage

contents directory, a listing of the material in a specific memory area

context sensitive help, a program feature wherein the response to a request for help is directly related to a highlighted menu item, dialog box or error message

contiguous, elements that are next to each other with nothing between

contingency interrupt, a program suspension caused by any action or condition which has priority over the program routine or which prevents completion of the routine in the normal manner, such as a keyboard interrupt, an arithmetic overflow, an invalid operation code, address of a device which is off-line or not functioning properly

continuity check, an audit to verify an open channel for the transfer of information

continuous-data-stream mode, serial data transmission without timed periods between words

continuous processing, on-line or real-time processing as contrasted to batch processing

continuous simulation, simulation

using continuous variables sampled at regular intervals to create discrete data

continuous-tone image, an image, such as a photograph, in which areas of color gradually blend into each other as contrasted with a screened image in which the impression of blending is created by varying density of the screen

contour analysis, a system of character recognition in which the outline of characters is analyzed for comparison

contrast, the relative reflective characteristics of a medium in optical character recognition

control, to command, direct, or manipulate, as in *control* of a program or peripheral; a mechanism which permits manual operation; a fixed or relative standard by which deviation is measured; instructions which induce conditional jumps in a program

control block, a storage area consisting of information to control processing tasks, functions, etc.

control bus, a set of 10 to 100 lines which carry synchronization and control information necessary for computer operation

control cards, punched cards which carry computer control information

control character, a non-printing character used to control the action of a peripheral device such as a printer; a character which, in a particular context modifies a control operation or function

control circuits, the circuits which interpret program instructions and effect their execution

control clock, the electronic device which times the progress of instructions and data through the computer system

control, comparing, the checking of data fields against each other to confirm the accuracy of any form of transmission

control console, the console used by a computer operator to control and monitor processing

control counter, the register which holds the address of the next instruction

control data, information used in control functions such as identifying a routine or set of data

control, dynamic, an interactive program which can alter its instructions while computing or executing commands

control field, a memory location in the computer which contains control information

control flag, a flag, or code, which indicates whether a transmission is data or control information

control function, an operation which directs the function of a device such as to advance the printer paper feed, execute a carriage return, stop transmission, etc. while processing information

control information, information which is transmitted from one device to another to direct the functions of the second device

control instruction, an instruction which manages data, memory and other instructions in a program

control key, a shift key on the keyboard, labeled CTRL, which when pressed in conjunction with another key, modifies its signal to one recognized by the computer as a control code

controller, an electronic circuit which enables a CPU to communicate with peripheral devices

controller, hard disk, the electronic component which controls the computer's disk drive

controller, intelligent, a control device which interprets feedback from the controlled device

controller, program, that part of a processor which controls the order and execution of instructions

control messages, handshaking; data which is passed between devices communicating with each other to confirm compatibility and regulate the transfer of data

control-oriented micro-computer, a microcomputer which can access and drive a number of command-and-status or data paths of varying bit widths

control panel, the part of a console which contains manual controls and switches; a removable board which can be wired to control equipment operation

control print character, print-control character, any of number of characters which control the operation of a printer

control program, a process control system; operating system, the program which handles the routine functions of computer operation such as reading the keyboard, accessing memory, managing input and output, etc.

control program for microcomputers, (CP/M) the trademark for a family of operating systems used in microcomputers

control punch, an instruction code on a punched card which directs the computer to perform a particular function

control read only memory, (CROM) an area in a CPU which contains instructions for basic CPU operations

control, real-time, control functions which manage real-time operations such as entries from a keyboard

control register, a register which contains the address of the next program instruction; sometimes, the storage unit which contains the current instruction

control routine, a routine which performs control functions

control section, the electronic components in a computer or peripheral which control the processing of instructions

control sequence, determination of the order in which program instructions are to executed; the processing of program instructions in order sequentially unless a branch is encountered

control sequencer, a device which denotes the next instruction to be executed

control signals, signals which insure the proper flow of information in a computer system

control statement, a program statement which controls the flow of a program

control, supervisory, a system which permits the computer operator to oversee control of a process or operation

control system, open loop, a routine for checking transmission without feedback, in which the check data is contained in the transmission data, such as a parity check

control system, output module, a device which stores program commands and converts them into control signals

control unit, (CU) the part of the CPU which receives program instructions, decodes them and transmits control signals for execution; the hardware component in a computer or peripheral which controls its functions

control word, a computer word which is the first or last word of a record or a block which contains information pertinent to that record or block; a word which transmits processing information

conventional equipment, peripheral equipment which, although not part of the computer itself, is usually part of a computer system, such as a printer or monitor

conventional programming, programming in a procedural language such as BASIC or COBOL

conventions, standard and generally accepted procedures, symbols, etc. in programming

conversational algebraic language a language created for solving relatively simple problems in an interactive environment

conversational compiler, a compiler which translates a program one line at a time which allows online editing while producing a fully compiled object program

conversational guidance, the use of on-screen prompts or menus to elicit user input

conversational language, a programming language such as COBOL, which uses command statements which approximate their spoken language equivalents

conversational mode, a procedural mode in which the computer and user interact, usually an applications program

conversational system, a system in which the user or a device employed by the user can communicate directly with the computer

conversion, converting the file format of data in memory; changing data code, as from ASCII to EBCDIC or changing the numeric base; moving data from one recording medium or memory device to another; restructuring a program to run on a system other than the one for which it was written; converting data from analog to digital or digital to analog

conversion, binary to decimal, the task of calculating the base 10 equivalent of a binary number

conversion error, an error created in transmitting or translating data; an error in the value of a decimal number which is the result of truncating intermediate values during a series of calculations

conversion table, a representation of equivalent values in different systems, such as metric to English, EBCDIC to ASCII, etc.

convert, to change the file format of data in memory; to change data code, as from ASCII to EBCDIC; to change the base of numeric data; to move data from one recording medium or memory device to another; to restructure a program to run on a system other than the one for which it was written; to change data from analog to digital or digital to analog

converter, a device which facilitates the conversion of data or commands from one format to another

converter, code, a device which automatically changes the code of input data to output in a different code such as a compiler

converter, data, a device which changes data from one format to another

coordinate geometry, (COGO) a high-level language used to solve geometric problems

coordinate indexing, the use of two elements, such as row and column number, to locate data, as on a graph or monitor screen

coordinate paper, graph paper; continuous feed paper designed for use on a plotter

coordinate storage, coordinate indexing

coordinate system, two lines, intersecting at right angles used as axes to create a graph

co-processor, a secondary CPU which manages time-consuming tasks, freeing the main processor to handle program control

co-processor, math, a special device which operates in conjunction with a CPU and which performs high-speed arithmetic operations

copy, to make a duplicate; to transfer information without change in content; material for input such as hard copy to be scanned or records for a data base

copy and correct, a procedure for copying data from a source file, making specified corrections and saving to a target file; also, **correct and copy**

copy, hard, information or data on a permanent, portable, physical medium such as paper

cordless plug, a connector which

has no flexible portion

corner cut, the diagonal cut at the corner of a punch card which insures that the card is in the correct position in a deck

corona wire, the wire on a laser printer which generates a strong electrical charge to attract toner from a drum to the surface of the page

correction, anything done to emend an error condition; the quantity by which an erroneous value must be changed to arrive at the accurate value

correction program, a routine used after a malfunction or error which restarts the program from the checkpoint immediately prior to the malfunction

correction routine, a routine used after a malfunction to reconstruct the program that was being run

corrective maintenance, maintenance performed after a malfunction is detected as contrasted to preventive maintenance

cost benefits analysis, a comparison of the cost to develop, install, and operate a new system with the cost to operate an existing system

cost effectiveness, the savings or additional cost based on a cost benefits analysis; the cost of a measurable unit of output based on the price of a new system compared to the value or market price of the same unit of output

count, a record of the number of times an event occurs

counter, a program variable which records the number of times a routine or procedure has occurred; a **cycle index counter**

counter, B-line, a programmable

index register

counter, control, the register which contains the address of the next instruction

counter, cycle index, a program variable which records the number of iterations of a program loop

counter, location, a register which holds the address of a particular element of a program or data

counter, program, a register which contains the address of the next instruction

counter, repeat a software routine which records the number of iterations of an event or other routine; also **cycle index counter**

couple, to connect two computers, computer systems or peripherals so that they can communicate with each other

coupler, acoustic, a unit which connects a modem to a telephone line through the telephone hand set

courseware, computer software programs designed for use with a specific course of instruction

CP, central processor; CPU or CPE

CPE, central processing element

cpi, characters per inch

CP/M, Control Program for Microcomputers

CPM, critical path method; cards per minute

CPP, card punching printer; a machine which punches cards as they are being printed

cps, characters per second; a measure of the speed of a printer

CPU, central processing unit

CPU card, a circuit card which contains a CPU and all necessary support chips

CPU chip, a large-scale integrated circuit; a microprocessor which contains all the elements of a central processor on a single chip, including accumulator, registers, ALU, I/O ports, and some memory

CPU handshaking, interaction between a CPU and peripheral devices to confirm recognition, compatibility and regulate the transfer of data

CR, carriage return

crash, a situation in which the computer becomes inoperable as the result of a hardware failure or a program error and from which there is no recovery except to shut down and restart; a **bomb**

CRC, cyclic redundancy check; a bit check which is performed at both ends of a transmission to detect incorrect data

credit card reader, an optical device with a microprocessor which can read and save data from the magnetically encoded strip on a credit card, security card, etc.

criterion, a comparison value used in testing; a rule, value or test which is basis for decision making

critical path, the longest path through a timed network of operations or procedures which indicates the shortest possible time required for completion

critical path method, (CFM) a technique which orders the operations in a project showing their lapsed time requirement and interdependency, thus allowing the identification of those events which are most critical to timely completion of the project

CROM, control read only memory

crop, to trim or put a frame around a graphic element, as from a **clip**

art file

cross assemble, to write and translate programs designed to run on a different computer

cross assembler, a program with the capability of generating an executable program to run on another machine

cross-check, the use of two different checking methods to test the results of an operation

cross compile, to use one computer to write and compile programs which are designed to run on a different computer

cross compiler, a program which translates or compiles another program which is to run on a different computer

cross hair cursor digitizer, a type of cursor (+) used for inputting individual points of data onto a graph; in desk-top publishing, the cursor used to draw lines, circles, etc.

cross-reference dictionary, a listing of the labels in the order they appear in an assembly program with the element that the labels identify

crosstalk, an interference signal from an adjacent channel

crowding, character, a technique used to reduce the time or space intervals between characters in order to optimize storage space and performance

CRT, cathode ray tube

CRT highlighting, the capability of a CRT to highlight text by displaying a different level of intensity from surrounding text, by underlining or by blinking

CRT, monochrome, a console which displays in one color only,

most often white, green, or amber

CRT terminal, a console which displays information on a CRT

cryptographic, a reference to methods of encoding data to prevent unauthorized access

CSM, combined symbol matching; a system of optical character recognition based on detecting recurring patterns

CTC, conditional transfer of control; a conditional branch

CTRL, control; a shift key on the keyboard, which, when pressed in conjunction with another key, modifies its signal to one recognized by the computer as a control code

CTS, clear to send; a control signal which indicates that a data link is available

CU, control unit; the part of the CPU which receives program instructions, decodes them and transmits control signals for execution; the hardware component in a computer or peripheral which controls its functions

current, a flow of electrons through a conductor

current instruction register, the register which contains the instruction being executed

current-mode logic, (CML) a type of transistor which responds to slight changes in input current which results in very fast switching speeds

cursor, the marker on a display screen which shows the insertion point of the next command; a position shown by a block, an underline or a dash

cursor arrows, the keyboard keys which move the cursor without altering data

cursor control keys, keys which change the position of the cursor on a display screen without altering data on the screen; cursor arrows, home, end, page up, and page down

cursor positioning, moving the cursor to a specific location on the screen in anticipation of the next command

cursor tracking, controlling the cursor movement in a graphics display with a stylus or mouse

curve, a graphic illustration of the relationship between variable coordinates on an x and y axis

curve fitting, illustration of a curve on a display terminal using mathematical expression

curve follower, a peripheral device which reads data depicted on a graph

custom IC, an integrated circuit which is manufactured to meet a customer's requirements

custom microprocessor, a computer chip designed to meet a customer's requirements

custom software, any program designed and written to meet the special requirements of a customer

cut and paste, text editing which involves highlighting or selecting text in a document and moving to another location in the document or to another document with the choice of deleting the original text or leaving it intact

CUTS, cassette-user tape system; a system which includes hardware and software necessary to store data and programs on a cassette tape

cycle, frequency, the time needed for an electromagnetic wave to complete a cycle from zero through its positive and negative maxima and back to zero; one iteration of a repetitive operation; the interval during which one set of events is completed

cycle counter, a circuit which keeps track of a cycle index

cycle criterion, the number of times a cycle is to be repeated

cycled interrupt, the programmed transfer of control to the next instruction

cycle index, the number of times a routine has been or is to be executed

cycle index counter, a program variable which records the number of iterations of a program loop; a reverse counter set to a value and reduced by one each time a cycle is completed

cycle stealing, periodically taking a machine cycle from the execution of the program which is running to perform a peripheral operation

cycle time, the time required for the completion of a particular function

cyclic check, a system of error detection that checks every nth bit

cyclic feeding, automatically feeding documents at a constant rate through a document reader

cyclic memory, memory which allows access at multiples of a fixed time interval

cycle, operation, the time lapse from the retrieval of an instruction to the completion and storage of the results of executing that instruction

cyclic redundancy check, a bit check which is performed at both ends of a transmission to detect incorrect data

cyclic shift, a shift in which digits dropped at one end of a computer word are set in at the other end

cyclic storage access, cyclic memory; memory which allows access at multiples of a fixed time interval

cylinder, the parallel tracks in the same vertical position in a stack of magnetic disks

D

D/A, digital to analog

DAC, digital and analog converter; data acquisition and control system

D/A converter, digital/analog converter; a device which converts digital information to analog form

DAD, data base action diagram; a diagram which details the way in which data is processed in a data base

daisy chain, a system of transmitting signals along a bus to several peripherals in a series so that it affects only the peripheral for which it is intended; peripherals connected in a series

daisy-chain bus, a bus in which connections are made in series instead of in parallel

daisy chain busing, the process of sending signals along a bus to a series of devices wherein those which do not require the signals pass them through to the next device

daisy wheel, a printing device in the form of a rotating wheel which produces a quality comparable to that of a good typewriter

daisy wheel printer, an impact printer in which the printing device

is a set of wheels with formed characters around the edge

DAR, data access register

DAS, digital analog simulator; a digital device which emulates the action of an analog device

DASD, direct-access storage device; disks or drums, as contrasted to tape

data, (plural of datum) a general term used to describe material which can be processed by a computer; material contained in computer files; information which has yet to be entered into the computer or processed

data access register, (DAR) a register which computes memory addresses and has sub-registers for the program counter, stack pointer, and operand address

data acquisition and control system, (DAC) a modular system of real-time processing units used to control data acquisition and processing

data adapter, a processor which translates input and output signals to and from computer codes

data administration, management and control of data processing; the group in an organization responsible for the data processing needs of that organization

data, analog, digital or discrete data representation of analog values, such as the representation on a monitor of a circular form in a graphics program

data array, the arrangement of a set of data on tape, disk, etc.

data bank, a collection of information which is available to the computer

data base, a file containing specific

data which is accessible to the computer; the aggregate of all data accessible to the computer; usually a file of like data for a number of subjects, for example, a name and address file

DAD, data base action diagram; a diagram which details the way in which data is processed in a data base

data base administrator, (DBA) a person responsible for the management and control of an organization's data processing

data base/data communications, (DB/DC) software which controls the functions of maintaining a data base and data transmission

data base designer, a data base administrator

data base file, a collection of related information, an accumulation of individual records, each made up of data fields which hold a single element of information such as name, address, etc.

database layering, data arranged in a three-dimensional matrix such as in a CAD database

data base machine, a computer which is designed specifically for data processing

date base management, supervision of the orderly storing, updating, and retrieval of information in a data base

date base management system (DBMS), an interactive software package created to control access and security for a collection of data files

data base manager, a data base management system; an individual responsible for controlling access and security for data files

data base mapping, outlining the interrelationship of data base files such as fields in common and interdependent fields

data base, on-line, a data base which can be continuously updated and is readily accessible, such as the reservations and seating database used by airlines or a fully automated inventory program

data base protocol, a convention in which instructions to alter or manipulate the data base are limited to those which come from the host processor and certain specified data fields

data base, relational, a data base organized associatively by rows of related records, such as an employee list, and columns of fields containing like data elements, such as employee name or number

data base server, a software engine which runs on a LAN server to provide data processing services for the network, in contrast to downloading files to work stations

data block, all of the data affected by one set of operations which is input at the same time; the results of that set of operations as output

data buffer, a temporary storage for data flowing from a faster device to feed to a slower device, such as, from the computer to the printer

date buffer register, a data buffer

data bus, a set of bus lines dedicated to the movement of information

data capturing, data collection

data carrier, the medium on which data is conveyed, such as punched cards, magnetic disk, etc.

data cartridge, a magnetic tape cartridge

data cell, the smallest unit of data, equal to one bit

data center, the department of an organization responsible for control and maintenance of data base and information services

data channel, a bi-directional data path connecting I/O devices and main memory which permits simultaneous I/O operations and other processing

data code conversion, the translation of alphanumeric data into a form which can be read and manipulated by the computer

data collection, accumulation of data by means of hard copy, automatic recording of transactions such as shop floor collection or at a cash register, etc.; the process of bringing data to a central point for processing

data collection station, a remote terminal such as on a factory floor which is used to collect employee time and production information

data collection system, a system which collects, sorts and stores data from remote collection stations

data communications, transmission of information via phone lines or other forms of external communication

data communications buffer, a buffer which temporarily stores information to adjust for variation in the speeds of communicating devices

data communications equipment, the hardware components necessary for transferring data; equipment which uses RS-232 serial communications

data communications network, the hardware components and the connections between them necessary for transferring data between one or more remote stations and the data base

data communications systems, data processing which involves the use of terminal devices, communications software, and the transmission and receiving of data over common and private lines

data compacting, elimination of extraneous material through the use of special coding techniques

data compression, reduction of the space required for data storage and transmission through elimination of blanks, redundancies, etc.; the display of binary data in hexadecimal form to conserve display time and space; **data compacting**

data concentration formatting, the binary formatting of data which makes the most efficient use of memory or of transmission signals

data control block, a storage area comprising control information which is used with access routines to supply information required to receive and store data

data conversion, changing the way in which data is presented such as sorting on different fields or limiting the fields which display in a printout; changing the data medium as from punched cards to disk or hard copy to magnetic tape; changing the way in which data is stored such as altering field specifications or creating additional files with linking fields; changing the way in which data is accessed such as recoding for use in a different system

data converter, a program which

changes the format, coding, media, etc. of a given body of data

data delimiter, a flag character which marks the beginning or end of a string of bits or characters

data, digital, material which is fixed in discrete form as contrasted to analog form

data editing, reviewing data to confirm formatting and probable accuracy prior to or immediately after inputting; correcting and updating data in the system

data element, data field; a specific item of information in a data record

data element dictionary, (DED) a directory of data elements or fields with a description of the information contained therein

data encryption standard, (DES) a technique employed to scramble binary code before transmission over public lines to insure its security

data entry, recording information in a data file by typing from a terminal, by reading from an input source such as punched cards or microfilm, or by direct access such as shop floor collection

data entry, OCR, data entry by means of optical character recognition, either through a device which reads and directly translates special characters from a source document or through a program which identifies and translates characters which have been scanned and imported as graphics

data entry program, a program which controls the recording of data for entry into a computer; a program of routines for testing the legality and probable accuracy of

data entered in a file, document or data field such as the presence of numbers in a name field or letters in a quantity field

data error, inaccurate input information discovered at the time data is entered or in subsequent testing prior to processing; indication of the discovery of data which has been incorrectly altered during processing

data evaluation, to examine and analyze data; a program procedure which examines data for validity before processing

data field, the basic unit of a data record; the part of a data record which contains a single item of information; an area in main memory which contains a data record

data file, an accumulation of data records all of which contain the same data fields usually pertaining to the same informational objective

data flow diagram, a type of flowchart which shows the movement of data in an organization, including communications and storage by personnel as well as by machine operations

data format, a description of the proscribed form for data in a file or record, such as the legality of leading, following or imbedded spaces, restriction of numbers in a name field or letters in an amount field, etc.

data hierarchy, data organized into sets and subsets so that data in a subset is of a lower order than the data of the set to which it belongs

data independence, refers to a system in which the data base is separate from the software which operates on it, so that changes to the logical or physical structure of the data base do not require change in the application software

data library, the collection of database files stored in main memory

data link, a connection between terminals which allows them to exchange and share information

data link protocol, the standards which govern the interchange of data through a communication link

data management, the access and control methods used in a data base system; the individual responsible for management and control of the system

data management system, the collection of hardware and software available to perform all data processing functions within a particular organization

data manipulation language, (DML), a language which allows communication between an application program and a data base

datamation, data animation; automatic data processing

data medium, the medium on which data or information is stored, such as punched card, magnetic tape or floppy disk

data name, one or more words used to identify a record in a data base

data, numeric, data which consists only of numerals

data origination, data entry; creating a record in a database file from any one of several sources

data parse, converting data from one file format to another, such as from a spreadsheet to a database, by breaking down the data strings which comprise the records from the source file to logical fields or columns to be entered into the target file format

data path, the bus for transmitting data and data control signals

data preparation, organizing data into a form suitable for computer input and processing

data processing, (DP) generally, used to describe any type of computer processing; specific manipulation of data such as selecting, sorting, etc.; the production of information and reports from stored data

data processing center, the location within an organization where the bulk of the data processing equipment, operating personnel and administrators are located; an organization which provides data processing services to other organizations

data processing manager, the person responsible for the data processing and information services within an organization

data processing, on-line, data processing which is performed by computer, without user interaction

data processing system, the aggregation of hardware and software components in a specific situation devoted to data processing functions; the procedures for handling data processing in a particular situation or organization

data processor, a device which manipulates data according to specific instructions; a person engaged in activities which involve the manipulation of data

date purification, testing and removing errors from new data prior to inputting to an automated data processing system

data, raw, data which has not been

processed in any way

data record, the basic element of a data file; a set of data elements or fields that contains information on one of the items in a file

data reduction, using statistical analysis to produce intelligible information from raw data

data registers, CPU registers which store data temporarily while data processing operations are in progress

data reliability, a ratio which expresses the degree to which data is expected to be error free

data security, any method, employed to protect data from unauthorized access, such as encryption or password protection

data set, a data file; a collection of related data records

data set, concatenated, a data set which is formed by joining data from two or more files

data sheet, a printed form with positions blocked so that data can be written in the same form in which it will appear on a screen or punched card

data source, a device which originates data signals for transmission such as a keyboard or remote collection device

data station, a remote terminal with a viewing monitor and keyboard input used for communications or off-line jobs; a terminal; a work station

data storage device, any device which stores data, such as a magnetic disk, tape drive or floppy disk

data stream, a method of transmission in which data flows in a continuous stream as a single read or write operation with no breaks

data structure, the system by which an assortment of data or information is organized

data tablet, an electromagnetically sensitive board which enables a user with a stylus to input graphic images

data terminal, a modem; a work station composed of a viewing monitor and a keyboard; any device for inputting information

data terminal equipment, (DTE) any device where a transmission path begins or ends

data transfer register, a temporary storage device which facilitates the flow of information

data transmission, the sending of data from one location to another

data validation, a program procedure which tests data for improper elements such as imbedded spaces, numbers in an alpha field, etc.; **data purification**; **data entry program**

datum, singular of *data*; a single piece of information

date, calendar, a date expressed as day, month and year in any order

date, Julian, a date expressed as a five digit number of which the first two digits are the year and the last three the days since the beginning of the year, for example, January 5, 1993 is 93005

day clock, an electronic device in the computer used for real-time processing

DBA, data base administrator; a person responsible for the management and control of an organization's data processing

DB/DC, data base/data communications; software which controls the functions of maintaining a data base and data transmission

DBMS, Data Base Management System, an interactive software package created to control access and security for a collection of data files

DCA, document content architecture; a common text file format which many application programs will accept for importing text from another application

DC dump, the removal of direct current power from a computer system or a component

DCE, data communications equipment; the hardware components necessary for transferring data; equipment which uses RS-232 serial communications

DC flip-flop, a flip-flop which passes on the steady state quality of a signal and eliminates its oscillating attributes

DC signaling, a transmission method which uses direct current

DCTL, direct-coupled transistor logic; logic devices using only transistors

DD, digital display; a display of data in digital format

dead band, a range of values within which an incoming signal can be altered without affecting its output

dead file, a data file which is no longer used, but has not been deleted

dead halt, a cessation in processing from which the system cannot recover to continue

deadlock, a cessation in processing which occurs when two devices try to access the same device at the same time

dead time, a programmed delay between two related actions; lost

time due to malfunction of computer hardware or software; time during which a system is not in use

deblocking, reversing a blocking command; returning a block of copy to its unblocked state; breaking up a data block into individual records

debug, to find and correct errors in a program; to find and correct malfunctions in a computer; to confirm that a routine functions correctly; to examine and work out problems in a new program, computer or peripheral

debugged program, a program free from detectable errors

debugger, software designed to assist in identifying and correcting errors in other software

debugging aid, a routine which assists in checking a program by allowing the programmer to access certain portions of memory

debugging, interactive, debugging a program while it is in progress by analyzing a memory dump

debugging program, a special program which allows the programmer to observe how a program being tested is affecting registers and memory and to change their contents, if necessary

debugging statement, a special statement placed in a program temporarily to assist in detecting and correcting errors in that program

debugging suppression, the means of preventing the repeated printing of the same errors

debug macros, macros built into a program to assist in debugging

decay time, the time it takes for

voltage to drop to 10% of its maximum value

decentralized processing, the performance of some operations at remote stations or terminals rather than at the data processing center

decimal, numeric representation in base ten

decimal code, a style in which each decimal digit, rather than the whole number, is expressed in binary code

decimal digit, the characters 0 through 9

decimal, packed, storing two digits or a digit and code in one byte

decimal number, a number represented in base 10

decimal point, actual, the decimal point printed as a character; a system wherein the decimal point uses a position of storage

decimal point, assumed, a position in fixed length record storage where the decimal point is supposed to be

decimal-to-binary conversion, changing a number in base ten into its equivalent in base two

decimal-to-hexadecimal conversion, changing a number in base ten into its equivalent in base sixteen

decimal-to-octal conversion, changing a number in base ten into its equivalent in base eight

decision, the choice made between alternatives

decision box, the flowchart symbol which signifies a conditional branch

decision circuit, a circuit which performs a logical operation on one or more bits of data and outputs the results

decision element, a circuit which performs a logical operation

decision gate, a logic circuit whose output depends on the combination of two or more inputs

decision making, the process of selecting a suitable alternative from a set of options

decision support system, (DSS) the computerized analysis of information to assist in the decision making process

decision table, a graphic aid which displays possible courses of action for a given situation

decision tree, a graphic representation of all possible options in a series of program branches

deck, a set of related punched cards such as those of a program or data set

declaration statement, a instruction which defines variables or labels

declarative operation, a procedure which provides symbolic labels and operation codes for data and constants

declare, to state; in some programming languages, a reserved word which precedes a statement of the attributes of a variable

decode, to translate coded data into a understandable form; to ascertain the meaning of instructions written in machine language

decoder, a device which translates a set of signals; a circuit which translates data from one code to another; a circuit which converts binary numbers into decimal numbers

decoder, command, the part of a CPU which processes program or keyboard commands

decoder, instruction, the part of the CPU which converts program instructions into control signals

decollate, the process of separating the parts of a multi-part printed form

decollator, a machine which separates multi-part printed forms

decrement, to decrease a variable by a fixed amount; the amount by which a variable is decreased

decrement field, part of a computer instruction used to modify a register or storage location

DED, data element dictionary

dedicated, a machine, program, etc. which is designed for or used for one specific purpose or function

dedicated array processor, a computer built to do repetitive arithmetical operations on large arrays of data

dedicated channel, a circuit which is reserved for a single function or set of functions

dedicated circuit, a circuit reserved for a specific use

dedicated computer, a computer designed for a specific task or a set of related tasks

dedicated line, a communication line set aside for a specific purpose and no other

dedicated machine control, the management of production machinery by microcomputer

dedicated storage, a portion of memory set aside for a specific purpose

dedicated system, a computer system built for one specific application such as desk top publishing or data processing

default, an instruction built into a computer or program which is executed if no other instructions are given; an assumption made by the computer or program

default directory, the directory in a microcomputer designated as the location of the files associated with a particular program; within an applications program, the directory designated as the location for data files

default drive, the disk drive which a microcomputer selects in the absence of other instructions when looking for program or data files

default option, the default; the choice elected when no other option is selected

default value, the value assigned to a variable if no other value is given

deferred addressing, a type of indirect addressing; a routine in which an addressed location contains the address of the target data rather than the data itself

define, to fix a value for a variable or symbol

definition, the number of addressable picture elements on a view screen, a determinant of the quality of the image; **resolution**

degauss, to demagnetize or to remove all data from a magnetic tape

degausser, a device which produces a magnetic field to erase the data on a magnetic tape

degradation, a reduction in the performance or quality level in a system while it continues to operate

degradation testing, measuring the performance of a system at the extreme limits

delay circuit, a circuit which delays a pulse or signal in order to synchronize with other signals

delay line, a line designed to delay

the transmission of a signal

delete, to remove, as a file, a record, a command, etc.

deletion record, a record which serves as a model for the deletion from a master file of records which contain matching data

delimit, to fix the limits or bounds

delimiter, a computer character which marks the limits of a string of characters

delimiter, data, a character which marks the beginning or end of a string of bits or characters

DEMA, Data Entry Management Association

demand fetching, introducing program elements into memory only when they are called for

demand processing, real-time processing; manipulating data as soon as it becomes available

demodulate, to retrieve discrete data from an analog signal; to convert an analog signal to a digital signal

demodulation, the recovery of the signal from a modulated carrier wave

demodulator, a device which translates the analog signal of a telephone into digital signals

demultiplexer, a circuit which can route a single line of digital information to several lines

density, the compactness of data on a storage medium

density, recording, the number of bits or bytes per unit of length or area on magnetic tape or disk

dependent variable, a variable whose value is contingent on the value of another variable

DES, data encryption standard; a technique employed to scramble

binary code before transmission over public lines to insure its security

descending sort, a sort in which the output is in descending, or reverse, order as an alpha sort from Z to A or a numeric sort from 100 to 1

description, problem, a programmer's assignment; a statement of the problem to be solved or task to be performed by a proposed program

descriptor, a word used to define the characteristics of a data element

design, the specifications for a computer system including the CPU and all peripherals as well as their relationship to each other

design automation, refers to the use of computers to aid in the designing of computers

designer's console, a control panel which allows a programmer to monitor and control the operation of a system

design objective, the planned performance goal for a system

desk check, the debugging of a written program or routine without the aid of a computer

desktop, referring to items which might be found on a desk: appointment book, address book, calculator, note pad, etc.; computer emulation of items which might be found on a desk

desktop computer, a computer designed to fit on a desk, as contrasted to being built into the desk or requiring floor space; a **personal computer** (PC)

desktop publishing, refers to the generation of print quality type and graphics on a microcomputer

desktop publishing software, one of a family of application programs used for desktop publishing

desktop utility, referring to a software package in which several items associated with the desktop are bundled in a single program and designed to be used interactively, as an alarm clock which signals the time for an appointment or a calculator which shows the results of computations recorded in a note pad

despike, to remove voltage surges

destination address, the address to which data is being transmitted

destination file, the file to which data is being transmitted after processing

destination warning marker, (DWM), a reflective spot on magnetic tape which is sensed photo electrically to indicate proximity to the end of the tape

destructive read, a situation in which data read from a storage device causes the data to be erased from the device at the same time

destructive readout, (DRO) a destructive read; a reading of data which erases the source data

detachable keyboard, a keyboard which is connected by a cable to a computer or terminal, contrasted to being built into the same housing

detail chart, a detail flowchart

detail file, an update file containing data which is to be added to a master file

detail flowchart, a flowchart which shows the step by step execution of a series of operations

deterministic model, a prototype in

which there is a fixed relationship between elements; a mathematical study of direct cause-and-effect relationships

development time, the time required to test and debug new hardware or routines

device, a mechanical or electronic component; sometimes, a special routine or method

device control character, a character used to control a device

device driver, an operating system program which controls a peripheral devices

device independence, a situation in which a computer requests input and output operations without regard for which device will actually be used

device independent, refers to an operation which can take place without regard to the peripheral called

device, logic, any circuit in the computer which performs a logical operation such as a gate

device priority, the sequence in which a computer acknowledges I/O requests from peripheral devices

device selection check, an audit to verify that the program instructions were transmitted to the correct device

device status word, (DSW) a computer word in which the bits indicate the status of a device

DFT, diagnostic function test; a program which tests overall system reliability

diagnosis, the process of determining the cause of error or malfunction in a program or device

diagnosis, single-step mode, detailed examination of a program, one step at a time, by stopping after each instruction is executed; examining a program's effect on memory, registers and flags after each instruction has been executed

diagnostic, referring to the detection, description, and isolation of a malfunction or error

diagnostic function test, (DFT) a program which tests overall system reliability

diagnostic message, the error message displayed when an interpreter or compiler encounters errors in a program; an error message which usually includes the location and type of error such as incorrect syntax, data exception, etc.

diagnostic program, a testing program which is run on a computer to identify and locate hardware malfunctions

diagnostic routine, a special routine, sometimes inserted in an existing program, to locate and identify a malfunction in a device or a program

diagnostics, a system of integrated routines to assist in debugging programs; a system of tests to measure relative performance of hardware

diagnostics, on-line, running diagnostic routines which monitor the computer while it is performing other tasks

diagnostic test, a special routine, sometimes inserted in an existing program, to locate and identify a malfunction in a device or a program

diagram, a schematic drawing of data flow, computer circuitry or wiring, logic paths, etc.

diagram, flow, a flowchart

diagram, logic, a graphic representation of the interconnection of logic elements in the computer

dialog box, a window which appears in response to a command or menu selection, requesting confirmation, additional information, querying the selection, conveying information, etc.

dichotomizing search, a search through sequenced data using binary look-up

dictionary, a directory of code names used in a program or routine with a description of meanings or functions; a directory of code names used in a system; a directory of reserved words used by a compiler or assembler

differential amplifier, a circuit whose output is the difference between two inputs

digit, a symbol representing a numeral smaller than the base of the system used; an integer

digital, discrete, expressing distinct values; using the numbers of a given base to represent values

digital/analog converter, a device which converts digital information to analog form

digital camera, a pocket-sized camera which takes photographs, displays them on a small screen and stores them in digital form for uploading to the computer

digital clock, a timer whose output is expressed in discrete numbers

digital computer, a computer which uses digital signals and data to perform arithmetic and logical operations

digital data, material which is fixed in discrete form as contrasted to analog form

digital data processor, a computer which processes digital data; a digital computer

digital display, (DD) a display of data in digital format; a display of alphanumeric data

digital imaging, creating graphics from information which is stored in digital form

digital multiplier, a device which multiplies the representation of two digital numbers by shift and addition

digital recording, transcribing information in digital form as discrete fields of magnetic polarity on disk or tape

digital signal, a signal whose various states are separated by discrete intervals

digital sorting, a sorting technique in which sorting time is proportional to the number of characters in the key and the total volume of data

digit, binary, either of the two numerals used in the binary numbering system; 0 or 1

digit, high order, a most significant digit

digitization, the converting of an analog signal to a digital signal

digitize, to convert the analog value of a physical variable into a discrete digit

digitizer, a device which converts analog values to digital form

digitizer, crossed-hair cursor, a type of cursor (+) used for inputting individual points of data onto a graph; in desk-top publishing, the cursor used to draw lines, circles, etc.

digitizer, graphics, a device which converts line drawings and other forms of pictorial representation into digital data

digitizer tablet, an electromagnetically sensitive drawing surface which converts the location of an attached stylus into digital data

digitizer, three dimensional, a device which inputs three dimensional coordinates by moving a stylus over a three dimensional object

digit, least significant, the rightmost digit in a number, therefore, the digit of least consequence in determining the value of the whole number

digit, low order, a least significant digit

digit, most significant, the leftmost digit in a number, therefore the digit of most consequence in determining the value of the whole number

digit place, the position of a numeral in a number

digits, significant, the left-most digits of a computer word; the digit place of important value to the accuracy of a number

diode, a device which allows electric current to pass in one direction only

DIP, dual in-line package; a package of integrated circuits with two parallel rows of leads which plug into the circuit board

dipole modulation, binary digits described on a magnetic medium

DIP switch, one of a series of toggle switches built into a DIP which allows certain of the connections to be switched on or off

direct access, refers to storage in which each site has a unique address so that the medium or the accessing device is able to move directly to any site specified; the ability to read and write data to any location in memory in a constant amount of time; **random access**

direct-access storage, storage in which access is independent of the last location accessed

direct-access storage devices, devices which allow fast access to storage locations such as disks or drums

direct address, (first level address) an address in a computer instruction which is explicit; the precise storage location of an operand

direct addressing, a procedure in which memory locations are identified by explicit addresses; a method of identifying the operand in a program by its address

direct code, code which specifies a computer command and address in machine language

direct connect modem, a modem which is linked directly to a telephone line from the computer

direct control, command of one device by another without user involvement

direct-coupled flip-flop, a flip-flop in which the active elements are coupled with resistors

direct current, (DC), a current which flows in only one direction through a circuit

direct data capture, the recording of data from actual transaction input such as at a cash register

direct insert routine, a subroutine which is written into the main program in contrast to being called up as a subroutine

directing character code, code at the beginning of a message which indicates destination

directive, a pseudo-instruction in a program, used to control translation

directive commands, assembler, commands which enable the programmer to produce data and values based on conditions at the time of assembly

directive statement, a statement which defines program structure

direct memory access, (DMA) the direct transfer of data between memory and a peripheral

directory, a file which contains information about the content of other files on a mass storage device; in microcomputers, a storage section which holds a group of related program or data files

directory, default, the directory in a microcomputer designated as the location of the files associated with a particular program; within an applications program, the directory designated as the location for data files

direct reference address, an absolute address; refers to an instruction which contains the actual address where data is stored

direct view display storage, storage of images or data on a direct view storage tube

direct view storage tube, (DVST) a high resolution screen which maintains a constant image, used with CAD, DTP or other graphics programs

disabled, refers to the state of an interrupt feature which has been repressed or **masked**

disarmed state, an interrupt level

state which cannot accept an interrupt input signal

disassembler, a program which converts machine language into assembly language, usually used to decipher an existing program

disassembly, the conversion of machine language into assembly language

disaster dump, a dump to the printer triggered by a non-recoverable program error

disconnect, fail-safe, the provision for an automatic disconnect from transmission lines in the event of an abnormal condition

discrete, separate and distinct, as contrasted to continuous

discrete circuits, electronic circuits constructed of individual components, as contrasted to integrated circuits

discrete component, an electronic component which is not part of an integrated circuit

discrete data, a coded symbol for a variable which represents one of several distinct conditions, such as marital status, sex, etc.

discrete semiconductor, a semiconductor which serves a single function

discrimination, passing over certain program instructions as a result of a conditional branch

discrimination instruction, a conditional branch

disjunction, same as OR

disjunctive search, a search defined by a logical sum which uses the inclusive OR operator

disk, a magnetic storage medium; in large computers, a disk pack, which consists of a number of disks joined together on a spindle;

in microcomputers, a hard disk (also called a fixed disk or a hard drive) or a floppy disk (also called a diskette)

disk accessing, reading data from or adding data to a disk

disk crash, the result of the read/write head of a disk drive coming into contact with the surface of the disk causing fatal damage and, usually, complete loss of data; commonly, a term to describe any disk failure whether or not data is lost

disk, double-sided, a diskette which can store data on both sides, thus doubling disk capacity, contrasted to a single-sided disk which is, for the most part, obsolete

disk drive, the part of the computer which holds, drives, and reads a magnetic disk or diskette

diskette, in a microcomputer, a small external disk which can be read to and from the computer; a floppy disk

diskette initialization, the process of initializing a disk to prepare it for use by recording a pattern of reference marks on it; also called *formatting*

disk file, a set of records retained as a unit on a disk and identified by a unique name

disk, floppy, an external device which can be read to and from the computer; also, a diskette; a form of magnetic storage

disk formatting, the process of initializing a disk to prepare it for use by recording a pattern of reference marks on it

disk fragmentation, a condition which occurs when files are updated frequently and various parts of the file are scattered in pieces throughout the disk

disk full error, a message from an application program which does not detect sufficient space in memory for it to work

disk, hard, a form of magnetic storage medium which in a large disk system is contained in a removable cartridge or pack and in a microcomputer is permanently fixed in the computer housing

diskless work station, an interactive terminal which has no provision for accessing floppy disks

disk library, a collection of disks containing programs and data available to the system

disk memory, disk file storage as contrasted to internal computer memory

disk operating system (DOS), an operating system for microcomputers; the program which controls all of the computer functions and from which other programs are run

disk pack, a number of magnetic disks connected by a spindle and packaged for insertion in a hard disk drive

disk reader, a device which converts information on a disk to signals which are sent to the computer

disk sector, a portion of a disk track; the amount of data which a computer can read into memory in one step

disk sector formatting, part of the initialization of a disk; marking a disk to indicate the sectors and tracks

disk storage, computer memory using hard or floppy disks; the area in which are saved copies of

data and program files

disk system, the components required for disk management including drives, heads, support chips, and software

disk system, peripheral, file storage on a disk system outside the computer

disk tracks, the concentric circles of a disk on which data is stored

dismount, to remove a disk from its read/write device

disorderly close-down, a stopping of a system such as by a power failure in which data and program files are not properly saved and closed

dispatcher, a routine which controls communication within the computer system

dispatching priority, the order of activities as determined by the dispatcher; in a real-time system, the assignment of resources to meet demand

dispersed data processing, data processing tasks which are shared with remote terminals

displacement, an index; the number a computer must add to a base address to get the effective address

display, visual representation of information or graphics on a monitor screen

display capacity, the total number of character positions on a monitor screen, expressed as the number of characters per line (horizontal) times the number of lines (vertical)

display console, a monitor which displays on a screen the contents of a program, a file, entries from a keyboard, computer messages regarding status, etc.

display console keyboard, a keyboard attached to the computer or workstation whose entries are displayed on a monitor

display cursor, a marker which displays position on the monitor screen

display, digital, a display of alphanumeric characters on the monitor screen

display editing functions, word processing or similar commands which permit the editing of text displayed on the monitor

display highlighting, a display editing function to indicate blocks of text selected for editing; any of the techniques to set off selected text such as reverse video, underlining, blinking, etc.

display RAM, the area of RAM memory which contains the necessary information to produce a video display

display resolution, the fineness of detail in the image on a display monitor

display scrolling, moving the screen image horizontally or vertically without changing its contents

display unit, any device which displays information on a screen

display window manager, software which allows a CRT to be partitioned into sections or windows which can each display different information and each of which can be edited without affecting the content of the other windows

distortion, undesirable change in a signal

distributed date processing data processing tasks which are shared with other computers

distributed processing network, data processing shared by two or more host computers in a network of computers and terminals

distributed processor, a computer containing several processors which share the task of running a program

distributive sort, a sorting procedure which divides the data to be sorted into two or more sets

dithering, dispersing colored dots on a screen to create the illusion of blended colors or black and white dots to simulate gray tones

DMA, direct memory access; the direct transfer of data between memory and a peripheral

DMA channel, a channel for direct memory access

DMA interleaved processing sharing a memory bus to alternately process DMA and CPU operations

DML, Data Manipulation Language

document, a word processor file; a physical copy of information stored in the computer; to provide information on the nature and operation of software or hardware

documentation, a printed text or manual which provides information needed to load and run packaged software; printed information necessary to set up and operate a hardware device; comments within a program which describe the flow of data, mission of subroutines, etc.

documentation, on-line, information which is displayed as a program is being run or which can be called up by the user as needed

document content architecture, (DCA) a common text file format which many application programs will accept for importing text from another application

documentor, a program that produces and maintains program documentation in the form of flowcharts, text, tables, and graphs, using data processing methods

document reader, any device which can scan hard copy and translate the characters into digital data; a device which scan special codes for translation into digital data

document retrieval, locating and accessing documents stored by the computer

document, source, the origin or hard copy from which data or information is obtained for entering into the computer; when transferring data between computer files, the file from which transfer data is obtained

do-loop, in high-level languages, a routine which is to be repeated until a specified condition is met

domain, refers to the information in a single field for all records in a database file

do-nothing instruction, a dummy instruction; a line in a program whose only purpose is to mark a space as to fulfill a program structure requirement or to hold it for future use

dopant, an impurity such as phosphorous added to a silicon semiconductor to increase its conductivity

doping, the process of adding minute quantities of impurities to a semiconductor to make it more conductive

DOS, disk operating system; an operating system for microcomputers; the program which controls all of the computer functions and from which other programs are run

DOS booting, loading the disk operating system at the time the computer is turned on

dot matrix, a rectangular array of dots from which characters and graphic symbols are formed on a CRT or on a printer

dot matrix printer, a printer which forms characters and graphics from a rectangular array of dots

dots per inch, (dpi) an expression of the fineness of input, as from a scanner, or output, as from a printer; the number of data dots in a linear inch, which determines how the eye perceives the quality of an image, normally 300 dpi, with extremely fine resolution at 1800 dpi or higher

double buffering, the use of one buffer to manipulate data while another performs input-output operations

double click, to press and quickly release a mouse button twice in succession, usually to reposition the cursor and cause the next logical action to the element at the cursor position

double density disk, a type of floppy disk or diskette which can store twice the binary data per unit area as a single density disk

double length number, a number requiring great accuracy which is represented by a binary number of double the binary digits that the computer's word length allows and uses two registers or storage locations; a double precision number

double precision, descriptive of data which requires two computer words for storage and computation

double precision arithmetic, arithmetic which requires greater accuracy than that provided by the computer's single word length

double precision number, a double length number

double-sided disk, a diskette which can store data on both sides, thus doubling disk capacity, contrasted to a single-sided disk which is, for the most part, obsolete

double-sided printed circuit, a device with circuits printed on both **sides** and connectors between the sides

double word length, see double length number

double word register, two computer registers which can be used together to accommodate a double length word

down, said of a computer which is not running for any reason

download, to transfer data or a program to a remote system or terminal from the main system; to transfer special font or graphics data to a printer which has been programmed to use them

downloadable font, a font which is stored in the computer and sent to the printer as needed; also called a soft font

down time, the time during which a computer is not operating regardless of the reason

downward compatible, a program which can run on an earlier, smaller or less sophisticate model of computer than the one for which it is designed; a program designed to run with another program which can also be run with earlier versions of the program; a new version of a program which can use data files created by an earlier version without translation

DP, data processing

dpi, dots per inch; an expression of the fineness of input, as from a scanner, or output, as from a printer; the number of data dots in a linear inch, which determines how the eye perceives the quality of an image, normally 300 dpi, with extremely fine resolution at 1800 dpi or higher

DPMA, Data Processing Management Association

drag, to reposition a selected item on screen by positioning the mouse pointer over the item, then pressing a mouse button and holding it down while dragging the item to a new location

DRAM, dynamic RAM; random access memory using capacitors which must be refreshed to retain data

drift, an undesirable change in the output of a circuit caused by voltage fluctuation

drift error, in an analog computer, an error caused by a change in temperature or power supply

drive, a device which moves magnetic tape or disk past the read/write head

drive, default, the disk drive which a microcomputer selects in the absence of other instructions when looking for program or data files

drive designation, the letter, number or code which the computer recognizes as a valid memory device driver

drive, disk, the part of the computer which holds, drives, and reads a magnetic disk or diskette

drive letter, the letter assigned to a particular memory device driver, as A for a 5-¼" floppy drive, B for a 3-½" floppy drive and C for a hard disk drive

drive, network, a disk drive which is the main storage of data for users of a network; also called a file server

driver, a control or system program which manages external or peripheral devices

driver, device, an operating system program which controls a peripheral devices

driver, line, an amplifier which receives a signal, augments and retransmits it

driver, party line, a driver which controls terminals, workstations, etc. along the same line

driver, peripheral, an interface module between a digital device and a non-digital peripheral device

DRO, destructive readout; a reading of data which erases the source data

drop-dead halt, a cessation in processing from which the system cannot recover to continue; dead halt

drop down menu, in some interactive programs, options menus which appear when subject headings are selected by the user

drop-in, the reading of a false signal which overrides the correct signal

dropout, a temporary loss of signal; failing to identify a bit during the transfer of data

dropout count, the number or dropouts detected in a specific number of reads

drum, a magnetic drum; a computer storage medium in which data is stored on rotating metal cylinders

drum storage, data storage on a magnetic drum

dry run, a review of each step of a program prior to running it on a computer; testing a program with a computer run using no data or dummy data

DSK, Dvorak Simplified Keyboard

DSS, decision support system; the computerized analysis of information to assist in the decision making process

DSW, device status word; a computer word in which the bits indicate the status of a device

DTE, data terminal equipment; any device where a transmission path begins or ends

DTP, desk top publishing

dual channel controller, a tape controller which allows reading and writing at the same time

dual disk drive, two floppy drives in the same cabinet

dual in-line package, (DIP) a package of integrated circuits with two parallel rows of leads which plug into the circuit board

dual intensity, a view screen display or printout with boldface and regular characters

dual mode printer, a dot matrix printer which has the capability of printing in draft mode (low quality and high speed) and in NLQ or near letter quality (high resolution and low speed)

dual processors, two processors in a computer as mutual backups, for task sharing or to run different types of software

dual processor system, a computer system which incorporates a second processor as an emergency backup

dual system, a system which runs the same program on two computers and compares the results to confirm accuracy

dumb terminal, a terminal which has no memory or processing capability and is completely dependent on the host computer

dummy, an artificial element in a program whose only function is to fulfill program specifications or to hold space for future use

dummy address, an address which has no effect on machine operations, inserted only to attain a fixed word or instruction length

dummy argument, an argument which represents a variable to be replaced by a quantity or symbol when a macro-operation is executed

dummy character, a pad character; a character inserted to fill time or space

dummy instruction, a do-nothing instruction; a line in a program whose only purpose is to mark a space as to fulfill a program structure requirement or to hold it for future use; also, do-nothing instruction

dummy load, loading a program without running it to verify that the program is ready to be run

dump, to transfer the contents of memory to the printer without regard to its significance, in effect, to dump the memory; a large-scale transfer of data from memory to a storage device or peripheral

dump, ac, to remove power from a system or component by design, accident, or program conditions

dump and restart, a special routine which dumps the contents of memory in case of failure and is able to restart the program at the dump point

dump, binary, the contents of all or part of memory displayed or printed out in binary form

dump, change, a printout of the memory locations in which contents have changed

dump, DC, the removal of direct current power from a computer system or a component

dump, disaster, a dump to the printer triggered by a non-recoverable program error

dumping, the copying all or part of a computer's memory to storage or printer

dump, memory, copying the contents of a storage device to a printer or display screen

dump, monitor control, a programmed juncture in a routine when the program and its data are written to backup storage

dump point, the programmed juncture in a monitor control dump

dump printout, a printout of the contents of memory, usually in binary or hexadecimal form

dump, rescue, the programmed periodic recording of the entire contents of the computer so that the program can be rerun from the last dump in the event of failure

dump, screen, a transfer of the data appearing on the screen to the printer or to storage

dump, selective, a printout of certain sections of memory

dump, storage, a printout of the contents of memory; a memory dump or dump printout

duplex, any combination of two things; simultaneous communication in both directions

duplex channel, a channel which is able to transmit in both directions at the same time

duplex, half, the ability to communication in one direction at a time

duplexing, using two pieces of equipment as security against the failure of one

duplicate, an exact copy; to copy without altering the original, as data files, program files, etc.

duplication check, a monitoring operation in which two separate executions of the same operation or program are compared

Dvorak simplified keyboard, (DSK) a keyboard with an arrangement of keys designed to be more efficient than the more familiar QWERTY keyboard

DVST, direct view storage tube; a high resolution screen which maintains a constant image, used with CAD, DTP or other graphics programs

DWM, destination warning marker

dyadic, based on or relating to the number two; binary

dyadic Boolean operation, a Boolean procedure using operators such as AND, OR, etc, which act on pairs of operands

dyadic operation, any operation which require two operands such as addition, multiplication, subtraction, etc.

dynamic, describing a quantity which is changeable or unstable

dynamic cell, a memory location storing data which requires refreshing to maintain the data

dynamic circuit, a memory circuit made up of dynamic cells

dynamic control, an interactive program which can alter its instructions while computing or executing commands

dynamic data base access, a routine which uses several means of accessing a data base during the same operation

dynamic instructions, a sequence of computer instructions performed in a real-time or simulated environment

dynamic loading, loading a program on instructions from another program

dynamic memory, semiconductor memory which must be refreshed in order to retain its contents

dynamic printout, a printout of data which is part of a program

dynamic RAM, (DRAM) random access memory using capacitors which must be refreshed to retain data

dynamic relocation, changing the location in memory of a partly executed program without affecting the execution of the program

dynamic response, the specific output of a device dependent on the time of the input as well as on the input

dynamic scheduling, scheduling changes made according to varying demands or conditions

dynamic stop, a stop in a program caused by an instruction which branches to itself

dynamic storage, dynamic memory; memory which can be altered

dynamic storage allocation, the system of assigning storage to the first space available in order to make the best use of disk space

dynamic storage, permanent, storage of data which can be altered but which is not lost when power is turned off, such as tape, fixed disk or floppy disk storage

dynamic subroutine, a subroutine

which the computer adjusts to suit the data being processed; a subroutine containing relatively coded variables to adjust processing; a **parametric subroutine**

E

e, a mathematical constant, approximately 2.71828; the base of the system of natural logarithms

EAM, electronic accounting machine; punched card processing equipment which is predominantly electromechanical

EBCDIC, extended binary coded decimal interchange code, an eight-bit communications code

echo, to repeat (or echo) on a printer or monitor, data being entered or transmitted

echo check, a routine to verify a transmission by sending the data back to its source to be compared with the original

ECL, emitter-coupled logic; a type of bipolar integrated circuit which offers advantages in speed, packing density and low power

edit, to make changes in data, text, a document or a program; to test data for probable accuracy

edit commands, commands in a program which alter the appearance of data output; commands or menu selections in an application program which alter appearance or change text on a monitor or printer

editing, data, reviewing data to confirm formatting and probable accuracy prior to or immediately after inputting; correcting and updating data in the system

editing terminal, a terminal with text editing functions, such as insert, delete, etc.

edit key, one of the special keys on an editing terminal used to edit text

editor, a program used to write and change program code on a line by line basis

editor, link, a program which combines separately assembled or compiled routines

editor, program, a type of text editor designed for use in the coding of programs

editor, text, a program with minimal word processing functions and without the ability to format printout usually in ASCII

edlin, a text editor provided with MS-DOS which allows efficient line by line editing, but is not user friendly and is especially inconvenient for large text files

EDP, electronic data processing; the gathering, maintenance and manipulation of information with the help of a computer

effective address, address actually used to execute a computer instruction; the address which results from converting a relative or symbolic address

effective byte, the byte currently accessed during a computer operation on a byte string

effective byte location, the actual location of a byte in storage

effective instruction, the instruction containing effective addresses which actually executes a command initiated by a relative or indexed instruction

effective transmission speed, the rate at which information is transferred based a large sampling of total lapsed time for transmissions, as contrasted to maximum transmission speed

effective word, the word actually accessed when a computer operation is performed on a single word

efficiency, computer, a comparison of actual hours of effective operation compared to the total hours a computer is available or scheduled

EFT, electronic funds transfer; financial transactions by electronic media with no recourse to cash or other physical means

EFTS, electronic funds transfer system

EGA, enhanced graphics adapter; a color monitor display in 16 colors with a resolution of 640 pixels across by 480 pixels down

EIA, Electronic Industries Association

EIA interface, the specific characteristics of the signal and the physical coupler for connection of terminals to modems as specified by the EIA

EIA RS-232, a standard 25-pin connector for interfacing computers and peripheral devices

EIA standard code, any code which conforms to EIA standards

eight-bit, a computer word size; often, one byte

eight-bit microcomputer, a small computer which uses an 8-bit data word

eight-bit microprocessor, an integrated chip using an 8-bit data word

eight-level code, an eight-bit character code with additional elements to start and stop asynchronous transmission

electroluminescence, the light emission of a phosphor within an electrical field

electroluminescent screen, a type of computer display screen, used mainly for portable microcomputers, which offers high contrast, light weight and durability

electromagnetic relay, a relay which completes a circuit through the use of a magnetically activated switch

electromechanical, referring to a device which incorporates both electrical and mechanical principles

electron, a subatomic particle with a negative charge

electron beam, a narrow stream of electrons moving under the influence of an electric or magnetic field

electronic, pertaining to electrons; operating by the movement of free electrons

electronic bulletin board, a computer message center, accessed by modem, which can be called up from a remote terminal to get information and exchange messages or programs

electronic circuit, a assemblage of electronic components which function together as a unit

electronic data processing, (EDP) the gathering, maintenance and manipulation of information with the help of a computer

electronic data processing system, the assortment of hardware, software and people which together perform electronic data processing

electronic funds transfer, (EFT) financial transactions by electronic media with no recourse to cash or other physical means

electronic hash, electrical interference on a communications line

Electronic Industries Association, (EIA) a professional society which sets various technical standards

electronic library, a general information library in which cataloging information and all texts are stored on computers; a computer center's collection of programs, manuals and other computer related material

electronic mail, the exchange of messages through the computer, either within an organization's private network or through an external, public carrier

electronic mail packet, a block of messages with its own addressing and control information

electronic pen, an electronic stylus

electronic spreadsheet, a computer data manager comprised of rows and columns of cells into which may be entered an absolute value or a formula to calculate a value based on other cells in the current spreadsheet or cells in another spreadsheet to which it is linked

electronic stylus, a pen-shaped device used for inputting graphics from a special board or selections from the monitor screen

electronic switch, an electronic circuit which emulates a mechanical switch in its capacity to be set to one of two stable states

electronic switching system, a telephone switching system which is controlled by a digital computer

electronic typewriter, an electric typewriter which contains some semiconductor memory which allows text editing before printing

electrostatic printer, a printing process in which ink adheres to charged portions of paper or other receiver

element, a basic part; a component

element, data, a combination of items which forms a unit of information; a data field or unit of information such as name, employee number, etc.

element, decision, a circuit which performs a logical operation

element, logic, a device which performs a logic function

elimination, zero, a program device to eliminate printing of zeros to the left of a stored number

embed, to put an object from one file or document into another document, such as an element from a graphics library or created by a graphics program into a text document

embedded command, characters in word processing text which control their appearance on screen or printed, such as bold face, underlined, indented, etc.

embedded object, an element created in one document or file which is inserted into another document or file

embedded pointer, an indicator within a record of its association with or relationship to another record or records

emergency button, a button or switch which stops a computer operation in the event of a malfunction

emergency off, an automatic control switch which cuts off all power to a system in the event of a spike, severe equipment malfunction, etc.

emergency switch, a control switch which disconnects all power from a computer system

emulate, to imitate or to duplicate

emulation, the simulation by a device of a different device, with the help of special hardware or software

enable, to signal to restore a suppressed interrupt

enabled, the state of a device which has been given a signal permitting it to operate

encode, to redefine data in a particular code, such as decimal to binary; to code, or write, a program

encoder, a device which translates data from one system or language to another

encoder, keyboard, a device which converts the striking of a key into binary signal

encryption, coding sensitive data for the purpose of security

encryption algorithm, an algorithm which implements a cipher

END, the program statement indicating the end of a source program

end card, the final card in a punched card deck, the card which indicates the end of a program

end data symbol, a code which indicates the end of a data set

endless loop, a program loop with no logical exit

end mark, an indicator of the end of a unit of data, a record, file, etc.

end of data marker, a code which indicates the end of a data set

end of file, (EOF) a marker which identifies the last record in a set of sequenced records

end of message, (EOM) a code or pulse which indicates the end of a transmission

end of page indicator, an embedded code which marks the end of the copy to be printed on a particular page and signals the printer to eject the sheet of paper or to advance to the top of the next sheet of continuous feed paper; a mechanical indicator on the printer which signal the end of a sheet of paper

end of run routine, a housekeeping procedure which is run at the end of a set of program instructions or when an applications program is shut down

end of tape marker, a machine-readable mark on a magnetic tape indicating the end of the tape is imminent

end of tape routine, a routine which updates the heading and other pertinent data when a magnetic tape has run to the end

end of tape warning, an end of magnetic tape marker

end of transmission, (EOT) a code or pulse which indicates the end of a transmission

end user, the person or organization which actually makes use of the computer, one of its peripherals or its output

end value, a value contained in a program which is to be compared with the current count or value to see if a condition has been met

engine, casual term for a processor

ENQ, enquiry character

enquiry character, a communications control character which checks for the presence of a remote station

enter, to type in data or programs to a computer

enter key, a keyboard function key, also called *carriage return,* which is used to move the cursor to the beginning of the next line or, in some programs, to direct execution of a selected command; in some word processing application programs, inserts an end-of-line or paragraph marker

entry, a statement in a program; a cell in a spreadsheet; input received from a terminal; an item on a list

entry block, a block of main memory that is assigned to an entry when it occurs and remains assigned until that entry ends

entry, data, recording information in a data file by typing from a terminal, by reading from an input source such as punched cards or microfilm, or by direct access such as shop floor collection

entry instruction, the first instruction to be executed in a subroutine

entry point, the address of the first instruction executed in a computer program or branch of the program

envelope feeder, a printer attachment which feeds envelopes for addressing

environment, the aggregate of all internal and external conditions; the hardware configuration and software capabilities available to the programmer or user; the aggregate capabilities of a particular operating or control system, as in a DOS® environment or Windows® environment

EOF, end of file; a marker which identifies the last record in a set of sequenced records

EOM, end of message, a code or pulse which indicates the end of a transmission

EOT, end of transmission; a code or pulse which indicates the end of a transmission

equality, the condition of being equal; having the same value

equation, a statement of equality between two expressions, variables or constants

equipment, a general reference to computer hardware

equipment, auxiliary, equipment which is not controlled by the CPU

equipment compatibility, the capability of two computers or devices to share data without conversion or translation

equipment, peripheral, any equipment which is added to a computer or system

erasable optical drive, a storage device for backing up compute files and programs with a capacity of up to 1 GB, one gigobyte or 1,000,000,000 bytes, per cartridge

erasable storage, a storage medium which can be erased and used again, such as disks or magnetic tape

erase, to delete or remove from storage

error, a deviation from the correct value; the magnitude of deviation

error, ambiguity, an error, often fatal to a program run, which may cause the formation of incorrect data or an abend

error, catastrophic, a series of errors or a single error with such far reaching effects that the job must be terminated

error checking, testing data to ascertain its validity in terms of type, range, etc.

error, composition, an error which is detected as soon as it is entered and can be immediately corrected

error condition, a situation which occurs when a program attempts to execute an illegal command or to manipulate invalid data

error control, a set of procedures maintained to detect and correct errors at the earliest possible point in the data flow

error correcting codes, codes transmitted with data which provide the means to detect and correct errors

error correction, the detection and correction of errors originated by transmission

error correction, automatic, techniques employed to detect and correct errors which occur during the routine operation of a system without involving the user or interfering with that operation

error correction, transmission, the accurate repeat transfer of data which initially contained transmission errors

error, data, a mistake in data being processed or to be processed such as numeric data in an alpha field, non-numeric data in a numeric field, an invalid date in a date field, data outside the limits posed by the field specifications, etc.

error detecting code, a system whereby errors produce a forbidden code combination

error detection, automatic, techniques which discover errors in the operation of a program or system, display the source of the error and, sometimes, correct them

error dump, program, a dump to the printer, or printout, of the computer state and memory contents at the time an error occurs

error, fatal, an error which causes a halt to the execution of a program

error file, a file created during pro-

cessing which lists any errors discovered by the system

error, intermittent, an error which surfaces at irregular intervals and, often, with no apparent cause

error interrupt, an interrupt which occurs as the result of an error condition

errorlevel, a numeric value in some programs which can be tested to signal a branch

error, logic, a program error caused by a faulty logic statement

error, machine, an error produced by a computer malfunction

error, memory, an error which occurs when data is read incorrectly from memory

error message, any message transmitted to a printer or to a monitor which declares an error condition, and often, the nature and probable cause of the error

error message, assembler, a message displayed by the assembler when an error in the source program is detected

error, parity, the loss of a bit or bits in the transmission of a computer word

error, permanent, an error which is not removed when data is reprocessed, usually the result of a programming error

error, program, a mistake made by the programmer in the process of writing a program

error range, the limits of the values which a given error can assume

error rate, the number of errors transmitted for a given number of transmissions or during a given time period

error ratio, the number of errors in proportion to the number of actions, usually expressed as errors per million or per billion bits

error reset key, a button on the computer which is pushed to acknowledge recognition that an error occurred and to reset the error detector

error, round off, the error introduced by rounding off numbers in the course of several calculations

error, sequence, an error caused by an instruction or a data record which is out of order

error, transmission, the loss or distortion of data during transfer from one location to another

Esc, the escape key

escape, to exit from the current state, such as canceling an operation in progress or, in an applications program, to back up to a previous menu or exit the program; a non-printing control character which signals the computer that the character which follows is a control or command; to cancel a command which the system or program cannot complete

escape character, ASCII control character 27, often used to distinguish the beginning of a series of characters which represent a command

escape key (Esc) a key which is used to exit from the current state or to cancel a command which the system or program cannot complete

escape sequence, a series of characters beginning with the escape character which indicates that they are to be interpreted as a command

ESS, electronic switching system, a telephone system controlled by a digital computer

etched circuit, a printed circuit

ETX, end of text; a control character which indicates the end of text in a text file

evaluate, to find or determine the value of

evaluation, data, to examine and analyze data; a program procedure which examines data for validity before processing

evaluation, performance, a comparison of the effectiveness of a program in meeting initial objectives

even parity, the condition which exists when there is an even number of 1's, including the parity bit, in a byte or data word

even parity check, testing for dropped bits during transmission by making parity in all words even and checking parity after transmission

exception principle system, a scheme in which only results differing from the norm are reported

exception report, a report which lists only those events or conditions which differ from the norm

exchangeable disk, a disk pack

exclusive-NOR, a logical operator which sets to one if two bits being compared are the same and 0 if they are different

exclusive-OR, a logical operator which sets to 0 if two compared bits are the same and to 1 if they are different

executable, a program statement which is to be performed immediately; a program which has been translated into machine language and is ready to run

execute, to act on a command or

instruction

execute phase, the part of a program cycle when an operation is being performed

execute statement, a job control instruction which specifies the operations to be performed

execution, performance of operations in the programmed sequence

execution cycle, the time during which a machine instruction is interpreted and accomplished

execution instruction, the statement which specifies the operations to be performed

execution time, the time required for an operation to be completed, without regard to memory access time or time devoted to other operations

executive, in a computer system, a master program which controls operation of the system utility routines

executive control language, the set of commands used in an executive system

executive instruction, a command which controls the operation of other routines or programs

executive overlay, an executive program environment from which other programs can be run, and which resumes control upon completion of the run

executive program, same as **executive system**

executive system, a set of routines which manages the sequencing and executing of programs; an operating system which provides for the running of several programs at one time or multi-tasking

exit, the time or place in a routine where control is returned to the

calling routine; a way out of a loop

expansion card, a computer add-on which supplies additional memory, functions, etc.

expansion slots, edge card connectors in the computer which hold expansion cards

explicit address, absolute address; an address that is specified by constants

exponent, a number or variable, printed in superscript to the right of a base number or variable, which expresses a power (the number of times the base number is to be multiplied by itself) to calculate the value of the expression

exponential notation, a system of using exponents to represent very large numbers which would be awkward to write out in full

exponentiation, raising a number to a power

expression, a set of symbols which can be evaluated or calculated to have a particular meaning or value

extended address, an operation code followed by two bytes which specify an absolute address

extended addressing, addressing which can directly access any part of memory; the technique of adding two bytes following an operation code to specify an absolute address

extended binary coded decimal interchange code, (EBCDIC) an eight-bit communications code

extended VGA, same as **super-VGA**

extension, file, a code which follows a file name, separated from it by a period, which often is an indicator of the type of file such as .bat for a batch file, .com for a command file, .txt for a text file, .sys for system file, etc.

external data file, a data file stored in a location other than that of the program which is processing it

external delay, down time caused by something outside of the computer system such as a power outage

external device address, an address which specifies which external device is being referenced

external interrupt, an interrupt originating in a peripheral device

external memory, a storage device which is not an integral part of the computer

external reference, a path or directions to a symbol, name, data, etc. outside the confines of the current routine or program

external register, a register which is addressable by the program

external sort, the merger of two partially sorted data strings

external storage, external memory; a storage device which is not an integral part of the computer

extract, to select specific items from a larger group using a filtering technique, that is, a routine which selects or rejects records based on the presence or absence of certain attributes

extraction, the selection and recording of specific portions of records

extrapolate, to estimate values beyond those of known values

F

fabricated language, any formal structure of terminology created as a relatively simple to express program instructions; any programming language of a higher order than machine code

face, a particular design of a type character set, such as Times Roman, Helvetica, etc.; see also, **font**

facsimile (fax), an exact reproduction; the transmission of documents, hard copy to hard copy or hard copy to computer, between detached locations via telephone lines; the machine used in such transmissions which optically scans copy for sending and creates a reproduction of copies received

factor, blocking, the number of records per fixed block; the ratio of logical records to physical records on tape or disk

fail-safe disconnect, the provision for an automatic disconnect from transmission lines in the event of an abnormal condition

fall-safe system, a computer system designed to record and periodically move changes to a special backup file which can be retrieved after a power or system failure

fail soft, a computer system which is designed to warn the user and continue running in the event of partial failure so that data can be saved and the system shut down in an orderly fashion; **graceful degradation**

failure, catastrophic, a total failure in which the computer shuts down and any data not in storage is lost

failure logging, a procedure in which the computer automatically records the detection of errors of any kind

failure, mean time to, the average length of time a computer works without failing

fallback, a contingency operating plan; the use of another computer or manual system when the primary computer system malfunctions

fallback procedure, the assignment of tasks in the event of computer system malfunction or failure and the plan for recovery of data processed off line during fallback

fallback recovery, restoring a system, including capturing data processed by other means during a fallback

false code, a character which is not accepted as valid by the computer

family, computer, a group of CPUs which all have essentially the same architecture but vary in such things as efficiency, size and speed; a group of computers which use the same operating system and software

fan-fold paper, continuous paper divided into uniform pages separated by a perforation and folded along the perforations in an accordion-like style; continuous forms

fan-in, the number of devices which can be joined to a circuit without degrading its function

fan-out, the number of circuits which can be furnished with input from a single output

fatal error, an error which causes a halt to the execution of a program

fault, a condition which causes a device to fail

fault current, the maximum current which can flow in a particular circuit without producing a short

fault location program, a procedure which locates and identifies defective equipment or components

fault, permanent, a constant or repeated failure of a device to perform properly

fault time, the period of time during which a computer is not functioning properly due to internal failure

fault tolerant, a program or system which continues to operate in spite of an isolated failure in the system

fax, facsimile; an exact reproduction; the transmission of documents, hard copy to hard copy or hard copy to computer between detached locations via telephone lines; the machine used in such transmissions which optically scans copy for sending and creates a reproduction of copies received

fax card, a device, mounted in a computer, which allows the transmission and receipt of facsimile copies

FDC, floppy disk controller; the hardware and software required to control a floppy disk drive

FDM, frequency division multiplexing; dividing the available transmission frequency range into narrower bands which can each be used as a separate channel

feasibility study, analysis of a new or modified computer system in relation to its intended application to determine if it is suitable and cost effective

feed, to supply with material or information, as paper to a printer or data to a program; a machine or device which feeds another

feedback, response to a query, such as information about the current state of the system to a control device; using output from a device as input back to the device in order to self-correct the next output

feedback control, feeding output back to input to adjust it

feedback loop, a closed signal path in which output is used to modify input

feed, friction, a printer device which feeds paper by pressing it between the platen and another roller, as in a standard typewriter

feed holes, the holes along the sides of continuous printer paper or forms which are engaged by sprocket wheels

feeding, cyclic, automatically feeding documents at a constant rate through a document reader

feeding, form, using the printer feed mechanism which feeds continuous paper or forms by the use of a pin feed, as contrasted with single sheets

feed, pin, the paper feed mechanism on a printer which aligns and drives the paper with pins which fit in holes on the sides of the paper

feed, tractor, a part of the paper feed mechanism on a printer which helps move continuous form paper through a printer

ferromagnetic, a classification of certain metals which can easily be magnetized and are used in electromagnetic devices

fetch, obtain data or instructions from memory storage

fetch cycle, the process of locating and obtaining data or instructions from memory storage

fetching, demand, introducing program elements into memory only when they are called for

fetch instruction, an instruction that directs the location and retrieval of material from a memory location

FF, form feed; the control character which instructs the computer or printer to move to move ahead one full page; a button on the printer which moves the paper forward one full page or to the beginning of the next page depending on its state

fiber loss, the reduction in the strength of light as it flows through an optical fiber

fiber optic bit rate, the maximum bit rate of an optical fiber without regard for dispersion

fiber optic capacity, the effective bit rate of an optical fiber after allowance for dispersion

fiber optic cladding, material which protects optic fiber from external light

fiber optic communications, the use of fiber optics instead of wires for transmitting data

fiber optics, the transmission of information in the form of light pulses through hair-thin glass strands

fiche, a sheet of microfilm; microfiche

field, a unit of information in a database record, such as a name, address, employee number, etc.

field-effect transistor, (FET) a unipolar transistor which performs the same switching and amplification functions as a bipolar transistor and can be more densely packed on a chip of silicon

field length, the number of bits, characters or columns in a field

field mark, a code which identifies the beginning or end of a field

field name, the name of a database record field, usually descriptive of its content

field programmable logic array, (FPLA) a logic array which can be programmed by the user

field, protected, areas on a terminal screen which cannot be altered from the keyboard

field, sort, the field, specified in a program, on which records are to be sorted

FIFO, (first in, first out) the order in which elements are stored and retrieved

FIFO buffer, a buffer which reads data only in the sequence it was received

figures, significant, the digits place in a number which may not be rounded without a loss of accuracy

file, an accumulation of related records or information; a unit of storage on a disk or tape

file, active, a file which is in use and which may be referenced or modified

file attributes, information about a file which indicates if it is read-only, a hidden file, a system file, etc.

file-control block, a location in main memory which keeps a record of files in use

file conversion, changing records from one form to another, as from hard copy to magnetic disk; changing the format of the contents of a file from one type to another, as spreadsheet data to a document file or a word processor formatted file to ASCII, etc.

file, data, an accumulation of data records all of which contain the same data fields usually pertaining to the same informational objective

file, dead, a data file which is no longer used, but has not been deleted

file, destination, the file to which data is being transmitted after processing

file, detail, an update file containing data which is to be added to a master file

file extension, a code which follows a file name, separated from it by a period, which often is an indicator of the type of file such as *.bat* for a batch file, *.com* for a command file, *.txt* for a text file, etc.

file gap, the space on magnetic tape which indicates the end of a file

file, inactive, a file which is no longer used, but has not been deleted

file locking, on a network, the denying access to a file by more than one user at a time

file, logical, an accumulation of records associated by content without consideration of physical location

file maintenance, updating a file to include the most recent changes in the information pertinent to that particular file

file management system, the part of a disk operating system which controls the use of disk files; a set of operational procedures for the creation and maintenance of an organization's files; a software program which assists in the organization and maintenance of files

file manager, an executive program created to simplify the organization and use of files; file management system software

file mark, a code or record which indicates the end of a file; **end of file**

file, master, a relatively permanent data record or file; a file which contains relatively permanent information which is linked to other files for transient and updated data; also an archive file

file name, the characters which identify a particular file

file-name extension, a code which follows a file name, separated from it by a period, which often is an indicator of the type of file such as *.bat* for a batch file, *.com* for a command file, *.txt* for a text file, etc.

file organization, the structure of data or records in a file; the physical ordering of files on disk, tape, etc.

file processing, the periodic updating of master files

file protection, a hardware or software device to prevent overwriting sections of a file

file server, computer control of file access; a computer whose only function is storage and file management, usually to serve a group of microcomputers which need to access common data files

file slack, the percentage of the space on a disk or other storage medium, occupied by a file, which does not contain data

files, protected, read-only files; files which may not be altered; files which can be accessed only by authorized users through the use of a password

files, shared, data which may be simultaneously accessed by two or more users

file, stream-oriented, a file containing unstructured data such as a text document which is recorded in the sequence it is entered

file, transaction, a register of transactions used to update a master file

film, a thin layer of magnetic material used for logic or storage elements

filter, a device which sifts data, signals, etc. to separate certain elements for elimination or retention; a device which passes only a desired portion of a signal; a machine word which selects certain parts of other machine words, also called mask; to sift data base records for those which have certain information in a particular field

financial planning language, an applications language used with electronic spreadsheets and financial programs

financial planning system, a software package which permit the user to explore and rate options before making an investment decision

finite, a limit which can be reached; having bounds

firmware, software programs permanently coded into ROM

firmware monitor, an executive or control program stored in ROM

first-in/first-out, (FIFO) memory management in which the items which were first entered are the first items accessed

first level address, a direct address; an address in a computer instruction which is explicit; the precise storage location of an operand

fixed area, a storage area set aside for specific files or data and which may not be changed or used by any other files or data

fixed-cycle operation, a computer operation allocated a fixed amount of time for completion

fixed disk, a disk which is permanently mounted in its drive

fixed form coding, program coding in which every part of an instruction has to be in a certain field

fixed head, a stationary read/ write head on a disk drive

fixed-head disk unit, a disk drive in which each track is accessed by a stationary head

fixed length field, a data field which contains a specific number of character spaces

fixed length record, a record format in which the number or size of fields cannot be altered

fixed point, a recording system in which the decimal point is assumed between two specific characters in the field or always in the same position in reference to one end of the numeric string

fixed point representation, numbers displayed with an assumed radix point in a fixed position

fixed position addressing, a recording system which dictates a specific location in a record for a field of a set size so that alteration of data does not alter the position of adjacent data

fixed program computer, a computer with a permanently set program which cannot be altered

fixed radix notation, a system of numeric notation in which the value of each digit in a number is determined by its position

fixed size record, a fixed length record

fixed storage, ROM

fixed type bar, a long, narrow bar holding the font used by a printer which cannot be changed by the user

flag, an indicator set to mark a par-

ticular condition which requires special attention

flag bit, a single bit in a computer word which indicates some quality of that word, such as the sign of a number

flag indicator, a signal which denotes whether a flag has been set or reset

flat-bed plotter, a plotter in which the paper is fixed on a flat surface while the pens move vertically and horizontally over the surface

flicker, a visible refresh cycle of a raster scan display

flip-flop, an electronic circuit which can flip between one state representing zero and another state representing one

flip-flop storage, binary data stored on a device which uses bistable elements to record its state

flip-flop string, a series of flip-flops in a row

float, to shift a character in order to conform to a data structure, as a dollar sign or an arithmetic sign

floating decimal arithmetic, floating point arithmetic

floating point arithmetic, numerical calculation in which the location of the decimal point is variable

floating point number, a number characterized by a base value raised to a power

floating point processor, an arithmetic device which is a support chip or an integral part of a CPU and performs floating point operations

floppy disk, an external device which can be read to and from the computer; also, a diskette

floppy disk controller, the hardware and software required to control a floppy disk drive

floppy disk drive, the part of the computer which holds, drives, and reads a magnetic disk or diskette

floppy disk track, a concentric ring on which data is recorded

flow, a sequence of events

flow chart, a graphic illustration of the logic flow of a program

flow chart, detail, a flow chart which shows the step by step execution of a series of operations

flow chart, functional, a flow chart which outlines functional operations without distinguishing specific operations or steps

flowcharting, using the flowchart to summarize any set of successive and conditional activities

flow chart, logical, a detailed flowchart displaying each logical step, each procedure, all arithmetic, and all input and output

flowchart symbol, a graphic representation whose shape describes the operation illustrated

flow diagram, a graphic representation of the relationships between the hardware components of a system

flow line, the line which connects flowchart symbols to show the flow of control

font, a specific size and style of a type face, such as Time Roman, 12 point, italics

font cartridge, a font, or fonts contained in a small device which plugs into a printer

font, scalable, a software program which contains a definition of the characteristics of a type face from which it can produce a font of any size within a given range

font, soft, a font which is stored in

the computer and sent to the printer as needed; also called a downloadable font

fonts, printer, fonts which are stored in the printer, a device attached to the printer, or which are formatted by the printer based on data sent from the computer

forecast, an attempt to predict future events based on past events or conditions

foreground, programs or operations of first priority in a multitasking environment; that portion of processing which is accessible to and often interacting with the user

foreground processing, overtly active processing usually visible on screen and under the direct control of the user; the execution of routines of first priority

foreground program, a program which is operating under the direct control of the user and which has higher priority than any other processing taking place at that time

form, a preprinted document with spaces for insertion of information; a facsimile of a document, projected on the monitor screen, which is designed for insertion of information for data entry or direct printout

form control, the device on a printer which allows for adjustment of the platen to accommodate multi-part forms

formal logic, the consideration of the structure of sound reasoning without regard to the content or subject

format, generally describes configuration or arrangement of something, such as the arrangement of fields in a record, the configuration of the image on a monitor, the placement of data on a printed letter or document, etc.; the configuration and arrangement of computer files in storage; the process of defining the configuration of files or data; the process of initializing a floppy disk to accept data

format, address, the specific arrangement of the parts of an address in a computer instruction

format control, the management of the organization of data as it is stored or displayed

format, instruction, the configuration of an instruction within a program according to the rules of the language in which the program is written

format mode, a screen display mode in which a difference in intensity distinguishes between protected fields and entry fields

format, packed, a system of storing two decimal digits to a byte

format, symbolic coding, the rules which govern the way in which various elements of a program are written according to the syntax of the language used

form feeding, using the printer mechanism which controls the flow of continuous paper or forms, as contrasted with single sheets

form feed key, a button on the printer which moves the paper forward one full page or to the beginning of the next page depending on its state

forms design, the process of creating the layout of a form designed for the convenient entry or display of data either on screen or on the printer

forms file, a library of forms for use in display or data entry, either in actual use by an organization or generic forms which can be adapted for a particular use

forms, screen, forms designed for use on a monitor screen either for data entry or display of information

formula, a rule or principle expressed in symbolic form

FORTRAN, (formula translator), a widely used programming language designed for engineering and scientific applications

FORTRAN, commercial, a programming language combination of FORTRAN with elements of BASIC and/or COBOL, designed for business use

Fourier analysis, the decomposition of a signal to its simplest harmonic curves

fox message, a message containing all alphanumerics which is used to test printers

FPLA, field programmable logic array; a logic array which can be programmed by the user

fragment, a part of a document, program, or routine

fragmentation, disk fragmentation; file fragmentation; a condition which occurs when files are updated frequently and various parts of the file are scattered in pieces throughout the disk

frame, on a monitor, a single screen of data or graphics; a group of bits on magnetic tape

frame, main, the central processing unit of a large computer

free format, input which carries no formatting codes

frequency, a measurement of the number of cycles per second of alternating current or an audible tone

frequency, clock, the cycle of pulses generated by a clock to regulate signals

frequency division multiplexing, (FDM) dividing the available transmission frequency range into narrower bands which can each be used as a separate channel

friction feed, a printer device which feeds paper by pressing it between the platen and another roller, as in a standard typewriter

front end minicomputer, a small computer which operates as an interface between other computers

front end processing, using small computers or microprocessors to interface between communications terminals and a host computer

front end processor, a small computer which is a link between communications terminals and a larger host computer

full adder, a logic device with three inputs, two addends and a carry from a previous addition, and which produces two outputs, a sum and a carry

full ASCII keyboard, a keyboard which has both lower-case and upper-case characters

full duplex, refers to the ability to transmit data in two directions at the same time

full duplex operation, a routine in which data is transmitted in two directions at the same time

full page display, a screen display of about 80 characters wide and 55 lines deep which approximates a full sheet of letter size paper

full screen, descriptive of applications such as word processors which allow data entry anywhere on the screen of a monitor

full screen terminal, a terminal which allows data entry anywhere on the screen as contrasted to a terminal which allows typing only on the bottom line of the display

function, a set of instructions which generates a unique output; a special code which is part of an instruction set

functional diagram, a diagram similar to a flowchart which shows the relationship between parts of a system or process

functional interleaving, a situation wherein computer processing and input/output functions are operating at the same time, but independently and sharing memory by alternating or interleaving their calls

functional specifications, the design requirements of a computer system based on its intended use

function code, a code which directs the operation of a peripheral device

function element, any device which performs a logic function

function generator, a computing element which produces an output that is a nonlinear function of its input

function key, one of a set of special keys which, alone or in combination with another key or keys, transmits a command

function key, programmable, one of a set of function keys which can be set or altered by the user to transmit a specific command

function multiplier, a device designed to produce an analog output which is the product of two analog inputs

functions library, the set of mathematical or logical functions available through a computer or a programming language

functions, utility, ordinary system operations such as printing, reading keyboard input, etc.

fuzz, a difference in value between two numbers which is less than a specified tolerance

FX, fixed area; a storage area set aside for specific files or data and which may not be changed or used by any other files or data

G

gain, an increase or amplification of a signal; a ratio between output and input signals

game theory, the mathematics of probability, related to decision making, and strategy

gang punch, to code a number of punch cards with identical data at the same time; a device which punches multiple cards

gap, an interval, usually referring to space or time

gap, block, the space on magnetic tape which separates blocks of data

gap digit, a digit used only to fill the position of a word and which does not represent data

gap, file, the space on magnetic tape which indicates the end of a file

gap, head, the space between the read/ write head and the magnetic medium

gap, interblock, the space on magnetic tape which separates blocks or physical records

gap, interrecord, (IRG) the space

which separates records on a magnetic tape to control stopping and starting

gap, interword, the time or space permitted between computer words to allow control switching, and searching

gap length, the space separating the poles in a read/write head; the space permitted between elements on magnetic storage

gap, record, the space on magnetic tape which separates records

garbage, a general reference to the quality of certain data; unedited or poorly edited input; unreadable or unreliable output; undesirable interference on a transmission line

garbage collection, a routine which deletes obsolete data or files from memory; the task of purging obsolete or unreliable data

garbage in, garbage out, (GIGO) an oft used phrase to express the sentiment that the quality of output depends on the quality of input

gate, a circuit which produces a single output from one or more input signals; a logic circuit whose output depends on its function, such as AND gate, OR gate, etc.

gate array, the pattern of gates on a chip which can be interconnected to perform specific functions

gate, logic, a circuit which evaluates one or more input values and produces output based on its function

gate, NOR, a logic circuit which produces an output of 0 if any of its input values are 1

gate, NOT, a logic circuit which produces an output value which is the reverse of its input value

gate, timed, a gate which produces

output at specified intervals

gating circuit, a circuit which functions as a gate

generalized routine, a routine designed to handle a variety of tasks within an application

general program, a program which can solve a particular type of problem and, based on input specifications, will solve a specific problem

general purpose computer, (GPC) a computer which is not limited to a specific application; a computer which can be used for a number of broad applications depending on its software

general purpose interface, (GPI) an interface which comprises all essential registers, handshaking, and interrupt control circuitry

general purpose interface adapter, (GPIA) a device which allows communication between different types of interface connections

general-purpose LAN, a local area network which is not limited to a specific application

general purpose register, a CPU register which is able to perform several functions

generate, to create or produce; to create a new computer system or program; to produce new reports or information from updated data

generated address, an address obtained by running a program or routine which operates on a relative address

generations of computers, the evolutionary stages of computer development defined in terms of technological achievements such as vacuum tubes (first generation), transistors (second generation), and integrated circuits (third generation)

generator, a program which creates a portion of other programs

generator, character, the chip which stores the pixel patterns for characters displayed on a screen

generator, font, a program in the computer or printer which creates the patterns which allow printing for special type fonts on a dot matrix or laser printer

generator, pulse, a circuit which produces a timing signal

generator, random number, a routine which is used to produce random numbers for statistical analysis

generator, report program, an application program which automates or simplifies the task of creating a customized report from a database or spreadsheet file

get, a program instruction to bring into processing a record, a file, specific data, etc. from another location inside or outside the program

gibberish, nonsense; meaningless data passed to the screen or printed out as the result of a machine or program error; often the remnants of a file recorded on a damaged or faulty medium

giga, one billion; 1,000,000,000

gigabyte, one billion bytes

GIGO, garbage in, garbage out; an oft used phrase to express the sentiment that the quality of output depends on the quality of input

glitch, a minor error or malfunction, usually temporary

global, pertaining to an entire program or file, or a set of programs or files; a default value which applies to all files created within an application

global search, a routine which finds every occurrence of a character string within a file or group of files; a file name search which includes all drives and directories in the system

global search and replace, a routine which seeks out a character string in a file and replaces it with another specified string, usually offering the user a choice of automatic replace or a prompt before replacing

global variable, a variable which is available to the entire program; in an applications program, a variable which is available through all files created with the program

glossary, a list of the definitions of words related to a particular subject

GOTO statement, an instruction in FORTRAN, BASIC and other programming languages; in general, descriptive of an unconditional branch

GPC, general purpose computer; a computer which is not limited to a specific application; a computer which can be used for a number of broad applications depending on its software

GPI, general purpose interface; an interface which comprises all essential registers, handshaking, and interrupt control circuitry

GPIA, general purpose interface adapter; a device which allows communication between different types of interface connections

graceful degradation, a computer system which is designed to warn the user and continue running in the event of partial failure so that data can be saved and the system shut down in an orderly fashion; **fail soft**

graceful exit, to terminate a program in an orderly fashion by closing all open files and exiting the program before shutting down the computer

grammar checker, a program, either stand alone or part of a word processing application, which reviews a document for grammatical errors

grammatical mistake, an error in spelling or the rules of syntax for a particular programming language

grandfather cycle, the time period during which outdated records are retained before erasing so that partial data can be recovered in the event of loss of the active file

grandfather file, formerly a father file, the file remaining when a new father file was created by an update

graph, a pictorial representation of the relative value of numerical data in the form of lines, bars, etc.

graphic display, a monitor which projects drawings, graphs, etc. on screen as well as alphanumeric characters

graphic panel, a control panel which shows the lines of communication between the components controlled

graphics, the representation of graphs, charts, pictures, and other non-alphabetic or non-arithmetic data

graphics, bit-mapped, computer graphic images on screen or printed in which each pixel is represented by a bit in memory and can thus be manipulated; a system which creates high resolution graphics

graphics, business, representation of business data as graphs, charts, etc.; software used to enable such representation; audio-visual presentation and the enabling software; desktop publishing and the enabling software; CAD, CAD/CAM, engineering drawings, schematics etc., and the enabling software

graphics capability, in a monitor, the ability to display graphics as well as characters; in a printer, the ability to print graphic patterns as well as characters

graphics, computer, graphs, charts, pictures and animation created on the computer, contrasted with word processing characters; the generation and processing of visual elements by the computer with peripherals such as scanners, paint and draw programs, type generation programs, etc.

graphics digitizer, a device which converts line drawings and other forms of pictorial representation into digital data

graphics mode, a printer configuration in which signals sent to the printer are interpreted as graphic elements rather than character symbols, usually selected by a toggle or DIP switch on the printer

graphic solution, problem solving with the use of pictorial forms

graphics resolution, the relative quality of the reproduction of graphics on the printer, expressed as **dpi**, or dots per inch

graphics routine, a routine which transforms digital data into a graphic display

graphics tablet, a drawing surface which converts the position of an electronic stylus into digital data which can be displayed on a monitor screen

graphics terminal, a terminal with graphics input capabilities

graphics, three-dimensional, line drawings which use perspective to create the impression of a third dimension

graphics transformation, the alteration of a graphics display by changing size, position, or perspective

gray code, in graphics, a numeric code in which each number inside a finite range differs from the previous number by one digit

gray levels, in a continuous-tone black-and-white photograph or illustration, the digital values which represent shades of gray

gray scale images, the use of patterns of dots to simulate the gray tones of a black-and-white photograph or illustration

grid, an array of horizontal and vertical parallel lines used to measure and position the features of characters in optical character recognition

grid spaced contacts, electrical contacts arrayed in equally spaced rows and columns on connectors and printed circuit boards

grouping, dividing data into sets which are related by shared attributes

group mark, a symbol or code which denotes the end of a word or unit of data

guard bit, a file protection device; a bit contained in a computer word to denote that the contents of memory cannot be altered

gulp, a slang expression for a small group of bytes

H

hacker, a slang term for a person proficient in the use of computer hardware and software

half-add, a computer command to do bit-by-bit additions

half adder, a circuit which inputs two addends and outputs a sum and a carry; see also **full adder**

half duplex, the transmission of data in one direction at a time

half duplex line, a communications line limited to transmission in one direction at a time

half duplex operation, a routine in which data is transmitted in only one direction at a time

half shift register, a type of flip-flop used with an AND gate to create a shift register for performing multiplication

half word, a series of bits which is half the length of a computer word and addressable as a unit

halt, termination of a program before the end by an instruction, an error or an interrupt

halt condition, termination due to a HALT instruction which leaves all flags and pointers unchanged from the last instruction

halt, dead, a cessation in processing from which the system cannot recover to continue

halt, drop dead, a cessation in processing from which the system cannot recover to continue; a dead halt

halted processing state, a condi-

tion which indicates non-recoverable hardware failure

halt indicator, a light which indicates that the computer is in the halt mode

HALT instruction, an instruction which stops the execution of a program

halt mode, a suspension of operation to permit the computer to receive commands from the control panel

halt, non-programmed, any stoppage of computer operation which is not attributable to a program command

halt, programmed, a deliberate stoppage of the computer processing by a command in the program

hand held computer, a computer with limited memory and a small display, adequate for a phone or appointment directory

hand print data entry terminal, a special digitizer tablet which accepts data printed by hand as its input

handshaking, exchange of data regarding equipment and line status between two pieces of equipment

hanging indent, a paragraph format in which all lines indent except the first which is the style of this paragraph

hanging loop, a **hang-up**

hang-up, a cessation of processing in which the computer cannot recognize input usually because of its inability to escape from a loop created by a fault in the program

hard carriage return, a carriage return inserted when the CR or Enter key is pressed: in word processing, it signals the end of a paragraph and any special text formatting associated with that paragraph

hard copy, information or data on a permanent, portable, physical medium such as paper

hard disk, a form of magnetic storage medium which in a large disk system is contained in a removable cartridge or pack and in a microcomputer is permanently fixed in the computer housing

hard disk cartridge, a single removable hard disk as contrasted to a disk pack

hard disk controller, the electronic component which controls the computer's disk drive

hard disk pack, two or more disks joined by a spindle and mounted in a packet for insertion into a hard disk drive

hard disk system, the components required for disk management including drives, heads, support chips, and software

hard error, a fault in a computer run induced by a malfunction in the hardware

hard sector, a disk data sector which is distinguished by punched holes

hard sector disk, a floppy disk on which the sectors are distinguished by punched holes

hardware, computer equipment, including the CPU and any peripheral devices which are part of the system as contrasted to software

hardware assembler, an assembler program which is stored in ROM

hardware-based language, any program language stored in ROM

hardware handshaking, any exchange of data between the CPU and peripheral devices

hardware pipelining, a technique entailing the staggering of sequential operations implemented by special circuits

hardware resources, a measure of the capacity and capability of hardware in a computer system

hard-wired, descriptive of circuitry which is wired into the computer

hard-wire logic, programming logic comprised of hard-wired circuits in contrast to a software program

hash, useless data; data which is no longer of use; filler for a fixed size block of data

hash clash, an error which occurs when two different commands are assigned to the same function key

hash, electronic, electrical interference

hash total, a number which is meaningless except for control; the sum of the numbers in a field which is compared with a like sum from a previous processing step to verify the accuracy of the processed data

head, the device on a disk or tape drive which reads data from storage and writes it to storage

head crash, the result of the read/write head of a disk drive coming into contact with the surface of the disk causing fatal damage and, usually, complete loss of data

header, the first record in a database file; the database record which identifies a file; information or graphics at the top of a printed page; a **heading**

header card, the first card in a deck of punched card which identifies the contents of the deck

header label, a block of data at the

beginning of a magnetic tape which identifies the contents of the tape

head, fixed, a stationary read/write head on a mass storage device

head gap, the space between the read/write head and the magnetic medium

heading, data at the beginning of a message which specifies its routing, destination, and format; on a printed page, the information at the top of the page, such as title, page number, etc.; also called a **header**

head, movable, a movable read/write head on a mass storage device

hello program, a program which runs automatically when a computer is turned on, allowing the user to sign on

help, assistance available to the user of an applications program, usually on demand and often context sensitive, to explain the workings of the program

help, context sensitive, a program feature wherein the response to a request for help is directly related to a highlighted menu item, dialog box or error message

help screen, on screen instructions under the control of a software package explaining how to use the features of that software

hertz, (Hz) cycles per second

heuristic, a method of problem solving through trial and error in which decisions are based on learning during the process

heuristic program, same as **heuristic routine**

heuristic routine, a system in which the computer examines and tests a number of possible solutions, evaluates them at each step and selects the best

HEX, hexadecimal

hexadecimal, the numbering system to the base 16, with the 16 integers represented by the numbers 0 through 9 plus the letters A through F

hexadecimal byte, an eight bit byte referenced as a two-digit hexadecimal number

hexadecimal digit, any one of the characters 0, 1, 2, 3, 4, 5, 6, 7, 8, 9, A, B, C, D, E, F

hexadecimal number, a number represented in base sixteen

hexadecimal point, the radix point in a hexadecimal number

hierarchical, descriptive of a structure in which elements are classified and accessed by general categories which are broken down to ever more specific categories moving down through the structure

hierarchical data base, a data base structure in which related data files are arranged in sets which are further subdivided into sets which represent closer relationships

hierarchical file system, a file system which allows cataloging files in directories and sub-directories depending on their relationship

hierarchy, an arrangement of items in a descending series of increasing specificity

hierarchy, data, data organized into sets and subsets so that data in a subset is of a lower order than the data of the set to which it belongs

hierarchy, memory, the classifying of computer memory by size or speed

high-level language, (HLL) a programming language somewhat resembling English which does not require the programmer to have a working knowledge of machine language

highlighted, an element on a monitor screen which is set apart from the rest of the screen in some fashion, such as reverse video, contrasting color, underlined, etc.; in some application programs, elements which have been selected for modification

high, logical, the voltage level which the processor interprets as one, or high, aside from the actual voltage value

high order, applies to elements of relatively greater importance

high order bit, applies to the far left bit in a computer word

high-order column, applies to the far left column of a punched card

high order digit, applies to the more significant digit; the far left digit in a number string

high order language, (HOL) a high level language

high resolution, refers to the relative quality of screen graphics; graphics which are displayed using a relatively large number of picture elements, or pixels, in order to represent fine detail

high speed printer, a draft printer which operates at speeds compatible with the speed of processing

high speed reader, (HSR) a scanner of magnetic or text input which converts scanned data into digital signals at a rate which does not perceptibly slow computer operation

high speed storage, memory with faster access time than disk or tape storage

hit, a successful match of two data items

HLL, high-level language; a programming language somewhat resembling English which does not require the programmer to have a working knowledge of machine language

HOL, high order language; a high level language

hold, the retention of information in one location after transferring a copy to another; the temporary halt of an operation to allow user examination of input or output

hold button, a switch on an analog computer which temporarily halts operation to permit user examination of the Input

hold instruction, an instruction which retains information in its original location after being copied to another location

Hollerith card, a punch card containing eighty columns and twelve rows of punching positions

home, a reference position which varies depending on the application and context; the left end of a line of text, the upper left corner of the monitor screen or the beginning of a document in a text file

home computer, a computer system intended primarily for home use and recreation often bundled with a set of software applications such as an address book, appointment calendar, checkbook manager, household budgeting system, etc.; often, refers to a system with minimal expansion capability

home key, a function key which moves the screen cursor to the beginning of a line, the upper left corner of the screen or the beginning of the document, depending on the application program

home record, the first record in a string of records which are linked by pointers

home security system, a system for the home, controlled by a computer, which can control and monitor the operation of burglar alarms, smoke detectors and lights as well as locks for windows and doors

hopper, the device which feeds punched cards to a punch or card reader

horizontal scrolling, shifting the screen image to the right or left to expose text beyond the borders of the screen

host computer, the main computer in a system which controls other computers, peripherals and terminals

hostile environment, a computer or system which can not run a particular piece of software

hot key, a key or key combination which executes a command, such as bringing a memory-resident utility to the foreground or executing a macro

hotline, a phone number provided by the supplier of hardware or software to provide the user assistance in the use of the supplier's products

housekeeping, routine overhead operations performed by the computer before and after running a program

housekeeping operation, any operation required before processing begins and after a run has finished, in preparation for the next

user

HSP, high speed printer; a draft printer which operates at speeds compatible with the speed of processing

HSR, high speed reader; a scanner of magnetic or text input which converts scanned data into digital signals at a rate which does not perceptibly slow computer operation

human engineering, designing a computer system and programs to accommodate the user rather than requiring the users to adapt to the machine

hunting, in automatically controlled systems, repeated attempts to find a desired equilibrium condition

hybrid computer, a computer which accepts analog signals and processes them digitally

hysteresis, a lag in response caused by a change in the strength of a signal

Hz, hertz; cycles per second

I

IBM card, the generic term for any punched card; a Hollerith card

IC, integrated circuit; a mass produced solid state circuit containing a number of elements designed to work together

IC mask, a pattern or stencil used in the manufacture of integrated circuit chips

icon, a graphic symbol depicting an object, device, or operation used to communicate non-verbal information to the user

icon, application, a graphic element which represents a computer program

identifier, a symbol or name used to identify data

identifier word, a computer word which is compared to stored information in a search

identify, to assign a unique code or name

identity gate, a logic gate which produces a value of true when all inputs are the same

idle characters, control characters used to synchronize data transmission

idle time, the period of time when a computer is available but not in operation

IDP, integrated data processing; data processing in which all elements are coordinated so as to maximize efficiency

IEEE, Institute of Electrical and Electronics Engineers

IEEE 488, a bus controller standard for general purpose interfacing

IF statement, a program statement which assigns control to an alternate instruction or series of instructions when the IF condition is true

IF THEN ELSE, a programming logic statement which branches to one of two routines depending on whether of not the IF condition is true

illegal character, a character which is not recognized within the context it is being used in a program; a combination of bits not accepted as valid by the computer

illegal code, a character or symbol which is not part of a defined alphabet or instruction set

illegal control message error, an error produced by reading a control message which has not been defined

illegal instruction, an instruction which is not recognized by the CPU

illegal operation, an operation which the computer cannot execute or which will be executed incorrectly

image processing, computer manipulation of photographs or illustrations; any of the operations involved in processing graphic images with the use of a computer such as scanning, optical character recognition, creation of type fonts, screen paint and draw programs, etc.

image restoration, enhancement of a photograph or illustration by manipulating groups of pixels

image sensors, devices which convert light into digitized signals

imaging, the creation or modification of visual elements from nonoptical data sources

imaging, digital, creating graphics from information which is stored in digital form

immediate access, the ability to quickly obtain data or place data in memory

immediate address, (zero level address) an address of data which is included in the instruction which operates on that data

immediate addressing, the inclusion of the address of data in the instruction which operates on that data

immediate instruction, an instruction which processes data contained in the instruction itself as contrasted to calling data from memory

impact printer, a printer in which an image is transferred by striking the paper with the printing element through an inked ribbon such as in a daisy-wheel printer or a dot matrix printer

imperative statement, a statement which is converted into a machine-language instruction

implementation dependent, features of a programming language which can only be utilized on a system designed to accommodate them, such as special graphics commands for computers which have graphics capabilities

implicit address, an assembler address which is converted to an absolute address by a displacement or offset value

implied address, an address derived from other data or reference to specific registers

implied addressing, a system whereby an address is derived from other data or reference

impulse, a pulse or change of value of extremely short duration

impulse noise, output noise which is not transmitted from the input but from the circuit itself or from some other outside source

inactive file, a file which is no longer used, but has not been deleted

in-circuit emulator, a device which is plugged into a system for examination and debugging in real time

inclusive OR, a Boolean operator which returns true if either or both of two inputs are true

increment, a fixed value, usually a value set by a program to modify a variable

incremental compaction, a routine which transmits only the initial value and subsequent changes in value

incremental compiler, a compiler which compiles a program one line at a time allowing on-line editing

incremental data, data which describes the difference between two or more elements in a series

incremental plotter, a plotter which draws lines as a series of finite steps rather than as a smooth curve

index, a number or symbol which identifies a particular element in an array; a file which contains a list of references to information such as records or files

index, cycle, the number of times a routine has been or is to be executed

indexed addressing, data addressed through an index

indexed array, an array in which individual items can be accessed through the use of a subscript

indexed file, a file which provides access through a record identifier

indexed sequential access method, (ISAM) a system for storing data records consecutively and retrieving them quickly with the use of an index

index file, a table of record identifiers

indexing, locating records in a random access file by the use of index keys; modifying an address through reference to an index register

index key, a field within a record which is used to find the record

index, permutation, a document index which lists each key word in each title so that the document may be searched by those words

index register, a hardware register

which holds the index value of an element in a table or array; a hardware register which counts down the number of times a loop should be performed; a register in a loop which accesses consecutive locations in memory; a register containing a value used to modify an address

indicator, a device which displays a condition in a computer such as whether a device is on or off

indicator, priority, characters, codes or other information which determine the order of transmission or execution

indirect address, an address in computer instruction which references another address

indirect addressing, an instruction wherein the address cited references another address

induce, to produce or change a condition

induced failure, equipment failure caused by elements other than a fault in the equipment itself

inductance, the measure of the strength of a magnetic field

induction, the creation of a charge, current, voltage, or magnetic field in one body by proximity to another

inductor, a coil of wire which can store energy in the form of a magnetic field

inequality, the relationship between two elements which are not equal

inequivalence, the Boolean exclusive-OR operator which returns true if only one of two inputs is true and returns false if both are false or both are true

inference program, an application of artificial intelligence in which

decisions are inferred from the available data

information, a compilation of data; the conclusion drawn or meaning assigned to data

information bits, bits which carry pure data in contrast to control or check bits

information channel, the lines, modems, and other equipment which carry data between two terminals

information management, the access and control methods used in a data base system

information management system, a system designed to collect, organize, store, and retrieve data; the collection of hardware and software available to perform all data processing functions within a particular organization

information processing, generally, used to describe any type of computer processing; specific manipulation of data such as selecting, sorting, etc.; the production of information and reports from stored data

information processing center, the location within an organization where the bulk of the data processing equipment, operating personnel and administrators are located; an organization which provides data processing services to other organizations

information retrieval, the branch of computer science concerned with the mechanical devices and the logical methods required to deal with the storage and recovery of data

information system, the procedures for storing and retrieving data in a particular situation or organization and making it available to those who need it

information word, a computer word which expresses data as contrasted to controls or instructions

inherited error, an error value brought in from a reference or carried over from a previous operation

inhibit, to prevent

inhibiting input, an input which may prevent output

inhibiting pulse, a signal which prevents reversal of state in a magnetic core

initial condition, the value of a variable before it is altered by processing

initialization, the process of setting up a computer, program, or storage medium for operation

initialize, to purge extraneous data from a computer before running a program; to format magnetic media for recording data; to set the initial values of variables in a program

initial program loader, a program which loads the operating system into the computer when it is first turned on

ink jet printer, a printer which shoots tiny charged drops of ink at the paper, capable of forming a high resolution dot-matrix image

ink, magnetic, ink containing material capable of holding a magnetic charge

in-line coding, a portion of program instructions in the main part of a program

in-line processing, direct processing of data as it comes in without editing or sorting

in-line subroutine, a program subroutine which is inserted into the

main program wherever it is needed

input, information put into a computer for processing; to put information into the computer

input area, the part of computer memory where input is received

input block, the input area; a block of instructions or data to be entered into the computer

input buffer register, the register which accepts input and transfers it to computer storage

input channel, a channel which conveys signals to the computer

input converter module, an analog-to-digital converter

input data, data which is to be processed

input device, any device which accepts data from a user and enters it into the computer

input editing, reformatting raw input to provide more effective storage and handling

input limited, program processing which is restricted to the speed with which input data can be processed

input/output, (I/O) a general reference to data moving to and from the computer as well as the techniques and devices required for the operation

input/output area, a storage area set aside for holding input (data coming into the computer) and output (data going out of the computer)

input/output buffer, the temporary storage area for computer input and output; a buffer which permits the transfer of data without interrupting other processing; a buffer which compensates for the variation in speed of different devices

input/output, buffered, input-output which is buffered to permit concurrent operations at optimum speed

input/output bus, a collection of wires or paths for data, address, commands, control codes, etc. on which information is moved between I/O devices

input/output cable, a cable which connects I/O devices and the main computer

input/output channel, the physical path between a peripheral device and the computer

input/output chip, an integrated circuit which executes I/O functions

input/output control system, (IOCS) a set of routines for managing I/O operations

input/output medium, the material on which data is recorded for input or output such as punched cards, magnetic disk, etc.

input-output port, the connection between a computer and the data path to another device in the system

input/output processor, a processor which handles input and output, thus relieving the CPU for other tasks; same as **peripheral processor**

input/output symbol, a flowchart symbol which indicates I/O operations

input program, a program which controls the reading of data and programs into a computer

input routine, a hardware or software routine which controls the reading of data into the computer

input storage, temporary storage of

input which is waiting to be processed

input stream, the control statements and data which are entered to the computer from a terminal

input, synchronous, input which is accessible only in time with a clock signal

input translator, the portion of a program which converts entries from the keyboard into machine operators

inquiry application, a computer routine which enables scanning and selecting records from stored data such as a data base

inquiry program, a program which allows information in a data base to be accessed by the user

inscribe, the reading of data from a document and writing it back in a form acceptable for optical scanning

inserted subroutine, a subroutine in a program which is positioned in the place where it is to be used, in contrast to being accessed by a jump

installation, a computer system and the personnel required to operate it

instantaneous access, the ability to quickly obtain data or place data in memory

instruction, a command to the computer to perform a task

instruction, absolute, a command in absolute coding which specifies the execution of a computer operation

instruction address, the location of an instruction in computer storage

instruction address register, the register in a CPU where the address of the next instruction to be executed is stored

instruction area, that area of storage set aside to hold program instructions

instruction, arithmetical an instruction which directs that an arithmetic operation be performed

instruction, blank, an instruction whose only function is to advance the program counter

instruction, breakpoint, a command which causes the computer to interrupt execution unconditionally, based on certain conditions or as a result of conditional branching

instruction characters, characters which can start, stop, or change a control operation

instruction code, the list of instructions, symbols, names, etc. which are understood by a particular computer

instruction, control, an instruction which manages data, memory and other instructions in a program

instruction counter, a counter which points to the location of the next instruction to be executed

instruction cycle time, the time required to fetch, decode, and execute an instruction

instruction decoder, a part of the CPU which translates instructions into control signals

instruction digit, unallowable, a character or set of bits which are not recognized by the CPU

instruction, dummy, an instruction which performs no function except to fill or hold space for future use

instruction execution time, the sum of the instruction cycle time, the address fetch time, and the destination output time

instruction, executive, a command which controls the operation of other routines or programs

instruction format, the configuration of an instruction within a program according to the rules of the language in which the program is written

instruction, hold, an instruction which retains information in its original location after being copied to another location

instruction, illegal, an instruction which is not recognized by the CPU

instruction, logic, an instruction which performs a logic operation, such as AND or OR

instruction, look-up, an instruction which references arranged data such as a table of values

instruction, machine, an instruction in the language which the machine can read and execute

instruction modification, a change in an instruction prior to execution so that repeats will perform different operations

instruction, multi-address, an instruction which contains more than one address

instruction, no-op, an instruction which performs no operation, but is included to provide space for the addition of an instruction in the future or to advance the program counter

instruction, privileged, a machine instruction which is accessible only to the operating system

instruction register, the register which holds the current instruction or the address of the next instruction

instruction set, all of the machine level operations which a particular

CPU can perform

instruction, supervisory, an instruction which controls the execution of routines or programs

instruction time, the time necessary for a command to be fetched from memory and executed

instruction word, a computer word which contains, or is, an instruction

instruction, zero address, an instruction which includes the address of the data to which it applies or on which it will operate

insulator, any material which does not transmit electricity

INT, interrupt

integer, a whole number

integer arithmetic, performance of mathematical operations on whole numbers only, ignoring fractions

integer programming, programming in which the value of variables is restricted to whole numbers

integer, single precision, an integer which can be depicted by a single computer word

integral, referring to the portion of a number represented by integers; the part of a number to the left of the decimal point

integral boundary, a position in memory where a fixed length field must be located

integrated circuit, a mass produced solid state circuit containing a number of elements designed to work together

integrated component, a group of electrical elements which cannot be disassociated without disabling the component's function

integrated data processing, (IDP) data processing in which all elements are coordinated so as to maximize efficiency

integrated software, applications packages which offer the user several, usually interactive, capabilities in a single package, such as a word processing, data base manager and spreadsheet

integrated system, a method of combined processing which provides that data need not be reentered to be used in succeeding operations

integration, the development of computer applications programs which work together in that they can share data and the user can switch from one to another with a minimum of effort

integrator, a device which produces an output representing the integral value of the input

integrator, limited, an integrator which will not accept input exceeding a certain level

intelligence, the ability of a computer or program to alter command parameters or criteria based on past performance

intelligence, artificial, a reference to the characteristics which make a computer more self-sufficient in terms of problem-solving, learning, adapting, etc.; the amplification of human intelligence through the use of the computer's ability to organize and assemble a mass of data in a short period of time

intelligent breadboard, a breadboard which can be connected to a console for development and testing

intelligent controller, a control device which accepts and acts on feedback from the device controlled

intelligent terminal, a terminal with built in input/output and other processing operations which to some extent free it from dependence on the host

intelligent work station, a work station terminal which can perform all of the operations of a microcomputer although it is connected to a host computer for mass storage and certain specialized functions

interactive, referring to a system in which the user can communicate with the computer through a terminal; a program which responds to user input while running; referring to two or more applications programs which can be called from within each other, as a drawing or painting program called from within a word processing application

interactive compiler, a program which compiles another program one statement at a time as it is received; a compiler which allows on line editing while producing a compiled program

interactive debugging, debugging a program while it is in progress by analyzing a memory dump

interactive debugging system, a program which allows examination of a program line by line by simulating a run of the program and providing an accompanying hexadecimal display of memory states

interactive processing, data processing in real time which allows the user to edit data or the instructions operating on the data

interactive program, a program which accepts and acts on user input while it is running

interactive system, a system which allows the user or a peripheral device to communicate with the computer and alter its actions during processing

interactive terminal, a terminal equipped with a keyboard for data entry

interblock gaps, blank areas which separate blocks of data records on magnetic tape

interchangeable type bar, a type bar which can be replaced by a different font

inter-computer communication, transmission of data from one computer to another for processing or storage

interface, the hardware or software which comprises a communication link between two devices and allows them to exchange information

interface adapter, general purpose, (GPIA) a device which allows communication between different types of interface connections

interface, analog, a device which allows a digital computer to accept analog input

interface, DMA, direct memory access interface; a device which controls a bus for the direct transfer of data between memory and a peripheral

interface, EIA, the specific characteristics of the signal and the physical coupler for connection of terminals to modems as specified by the EIA

interface, general purpose, (GPI) an interface which comprises all essential registers, handshaking, and interrupt control circuitry

interface, general purpose adapter, (GPIA) a device which allows communication between different types of interface connections

interface, interrupt, a circuit which addresses an interrupt routine

interface latch chip, a device which does not allow loading the system bus with input until an enabling signal is received

interface, parallel, a multi-channel connection which permits transfer of a full computer word at a time

interface, people/machine, any device or technique which permits communication between a user and a computer

interface, peripheral, an interface card which plugs into one of the computer's card slots; a plug which connects a computer and a peripheral device

interface, RS-232, a standard 25-pin connector for interfacing computers and peripheral devices

interface, serial, a single channel connector between a computer and a peripheral which handles data one bit at a time

interface, standard, an interface which matches one of the industry standards for connecting a computer and peripherals

interference, any undesirable disturbance which degrades the signal quality

interleave, a technique used to merge parts of two programs so that they can both be run at the same time

interleaving, functional, the process of alternating input/output and processing information so that their operation is independent, but simultaneous

interleaving, memory, the process of alternating memory calls to speed up memory access

interlock, a control arrangement which coordinates signals to prevent any device from interfering with another which is in operation

interlude, a computer subprogram which performs preliminary calculations and which may be written over after use

intermediate memory storage, a section of memory used to temporarily hold data

intermittent error, an error which surfaces at irregular intervals and, often, with no apparent cause

internal arithmetic, calculations performed by the ALU in the CPU of a computer

internal clocking, bit-timing in communications provided by the computer rather than by a modem

internal code, the structure of data representation in a computer, such as 8 bits per computer word, byte or character

internal interrupt, an interrupt caused by the computer's detection of a non-standard condition; a peripheral routine which causes a stop to perform a designated program subroutine

internally stored program, a program which is stored in the computer's internal memory

internal memory, main memory or RAM; the computer's working memory

internal sort, the sequencing of records within the computer's main memory

internal storage, the memory which is directly accessible to the CPU

interpret, the translation of a programming language into machine instructions; the translation of a coded command into the action which the code dictates; the translation of computer words into characters

interpreter, a program which translates a programming language into machine instructions, executing each instruction as it is translated

interpretive code, a code which is translated and executed immediately in contrast to being compiled

interpretive debugger, a routine for debugging programs which allows the examination of memory in varied formats and moving through the program one instruction at a time

interpretive routine, a routine which translates and executes instructions as they are entered

interpretive tracing, a debugging system which simulates the operation of a program by interpreting each step

interrecord gap, (IRG) the space which separates records on a magnetic tape to control stopping and starting

interrupt, (INT) a control signal which stops the normal flow or a program or routine; a halt in the normal flow of a program to perform another operation with control returning to the main program after the operation is completed

interrupt control routine, a routine which stores the status of an interrupted program so it can be reentered when the interrupt is completed; a routine which stores the status of the computer at an interrupt to determine the cause

interrupt device, a peripheral

which may generate interrupts that require the attention of the CPU

interrupt enable, an instruction which permits an external device to interrupt a processor

interrupt, error, an interrupt caused by an error condition

interrupt, external, an interrupt produced by a peripheral device

interrupt interface, a circuit which holds the address of the subroutine called for by an interrupt

interrupt, internal, an interrupt caused by the computer's detection of a non-standard condition; a peripheral routine which causes a stop to perform a designated program subroutine

interrupt, involuntary, an interrupt which is caused by external conditions

interrupt logging, the recording of interrupts in the process of testing and debugging a program

interrupt mask, an instruction designating which external devices are allowed to interrupt processing and which will be ignored

interrupt mask bit, a software controlled interrupt disable

interrupt, multiprogramming, an interrupt which permits the efficient running of more than one program at the same time

interrupt, override, an interrupt which cannot be disarmed or disabled

interrupt, parity, an interrupt which is caused by a parity error

interrupt priority, the indication of the relative status of possible interrupts, that is, which operations may be interrupted by which other operations

interrupt, priority, a temporary

halt of the highest level which may not be interrupted by another

interrupt, processor, a temporary halt called by hardware to allow handling of other functions

interrupt request lines, (IRQ) the lines over which signals indicating that a device is ready to send or receive are sent

interrupt signal, the control signal which calls an interrupt to the CPU

interrupt, software, an interrupt called for in a program

interval, significant, the time within which a representative item is, or should be, transmitted

interval timer, an internal clock which keeps track of the time of day and has the ability to interrupt if specified to do so

interword gap, the time or space permitted between computer words to allow control switching and searching

inventory management, a system which, with the help of a computer, is designed to maintain records including inventory quantities, additions and withdrawals, unit costs, total value, reorder levels, etc. and to produce reports which assist in prudent purchasing, etc.

inversion, the process of changing the state of binary bits; the Boolean NOT operator which returns true if the input is false and false if the input is true

inverted file, a file which can be accessed by the characteristics of its records

inverter gate, a NOT gate; a logic circuit whose output is the opposite of its input (inversion)

inverting circuit, a circuit which functions as a NOT gate

involuntary interrupt, an interrupt which is caused by external conditions

I/O, acronym for input/output

I/O bound, refers to a state in which the processing time is decided by the speed with which input and output operations can be performed

I/O buffer, the temporary storage area for computer input and output; a buffer which permits the transfer of data without interrupting other processing; a buffer which compensates for the variation in speed of different devices

I/O bus, a collection of wires or paths for data, address, commands, control codes, etc. on which information is moved between I/O devices

I/O bus lines, the lines which make up an I/O bus

I/O cable, a cable which connects input/output devices and the main computer.

I/O channel, the physical path between a peripheral device and the computer

I/O chip, an integrated circuit which executes input/output functions

I/O command word, a computer word which controls an I/O device

I/O communications device, any device which controls the transmittal of information in a data communications system

IOCS, input/output control system; a set of routines for managing I/O operations

I/O instruction, a command which directs the transmittal of data to or from the computer

I/O interface, any device which

translates the signals of peripheral equipment and the computer to allow the exchange of data

I/O interrupt program, a subprogram which interrupts the main program when an external device produces input and which determines under what circumstances such interrupt may is allowed

I/O, memory-mapped, a system of accessing peripheral devices by addressing memory locations in contrast to addressing the device itself

IOP, input/output processor; a processor which handles input and output, thus relieving the CPU for other tasks

I/O port, the physical connection between a CPU and peripheral devices

I/O status word, a computer word which reports the status of an I/O device

IPL, information processing language; a programming language; initial program loader, a program which loads the operating system into the computer when it is first turned on

IRG, interrecord gap; the space between records on a magnetic tape to control stopping and starting

IRM, information resource management; the techniques for retrieving data and providing meaningful information from that data

IRQ, interrupt request lines; the lines over which signals indicating that a device is ready to send or receive are sent

ISAM, indexed sequential access method; a system for storing data records consecutively and retrieving them quickly with the use of an index

ISO, international standards organization; an organization which coordinates the efforts of national committees and organizations to establish worldwide standards for computer codes

ISR, information storage and retrieval; reference to the mechanical devices and the logical methods required to deal with the storage and recovery of data

item, a field or set of fields of related data; information connected with one part of a single thing

item, line, an element of data or a record field which could logically be included, or printed on the same line, with other related elements of data or record fields

iterate, to repeat or do again

iteration, repetition of an instruction or series of instructions

iterative operation, a routine which automatically repeats the same operation with different values, as in a **loop**

J

jack, a connecting device

jack, data, a jack or plug which connects a modem direct to the telephone lines

jacket, the stiff, plastic casing which protects a floppy disk

JCL, job control language; a series of control statements which establish communications with the operating system and identify the equipment on which the program is to run, source of data files and conventions for identifying them within the program, etc.

job, a program sent to a computer

to be run; a series of tasks for the computer to perform

job control language, (JCL) a series of control statements which establish communications with the operating system and identify the equipment on which the program is to run, source of data files and conventions for identifying them within the program, etc.

job control program, a program which contains a series of JCL statements which direct the preparation and running of a job or program

job control, stacked, the execution of programs in the sequence in which they are received

job entry system, remote, a system which provides for job entry from a remote terminal

job input stream, initial input to an operating system which contains information which the computer needs to execute the jobs which follow

job library, modules which load the data sets for a specific job

job oriented terminal, a terminal which is designed for a specific application

job processing, the steps involved in executing a program; accessing job instructions, loading data files, executing the program and printing out the results

job processing, master file, accessing the programs which are necessary for job processing, such as input/output drivers, system control and management, utility routines and library subroutines

job queue, a list of programs being processed and waiting to be processed

job step, one of the assortment of tasks which make up a job

job stream, the aggregate of jobs submitted for processing in turn by the computer

JOVIAL, Jules' Own Version of the International Algorithmic Language; a programming language developed for real-time command and control applications

joystick, an input device used for playing computer games which consists of a handle that controls the movement of objects on the monitor screen

Julian date, a date expressed as a five digit number of which the first two digits are the year and the last three the days since the beginning of the year, for example, January 5, 1993 is 93005

jump, a branch; the process in which the normal sequence of operations is interrupted to begin processing from a different location in the program

jump, conditional, an instruction to move control to a new section of the program if a certain condition is met

jumper, selectable, a switch or control device which changes a feature of a computer or peripheral; usually, a DIP switch

jump instruction, a branch instruction; an instruction which directs the computer to interrupt processing and to move to another part of the program, usually as the result of certain conditions

jump operation, the performance of a jump instruction

jump routine, a jump instruction

jump, unconditional, an unconditional branch; an absolute or unqualified instruction to move control to a new section of the program

junk, garbled data, usually received in transmission

justification, in typesetting, the alignment of characters along the right and left margins

justified, left-hand, in typesetting, the alignment of characters along the left margin; also described as *flush left*

justified margin, in typesetting, a margin in which all the characters are aligned both right and left

justified, right-hand, in typesetting, the alignment of characters along the right margin; also described as *flush right*

justify left, the formatting of printed text with the left margin aligned

justify right, the formatting of printed text with the copy aligned to the right margin

juxtaposition, the placement of items side by side

K

k or **K,** kilo; one thousand; in reference to computers, often used to represent 2^{10} or 1024, approximately one thousand

Kansas City standard interface, a criterion for encoding data on standard audio cassette tape using regular cassette recorders

KB, kilobyte; 1024 bytes

KCS, one thousand characters per second, a unit for measuring transmission rate

kerning, in typesetting, proportional spacing of certain characters so that the white space between them is not excessive in relation to other characters

key, a group of characters or symbols used to identify or locate an item; the field on which a set of records is sorted

keyboard, a device comprised of a set of keys similar to those on a typewriter, used to input data to a computer, monitor screen, etc.

keyboard, ANSI, American National Standards Institute keyboard; a standard typewriter keyboard featuring a choice of upper-case letters only, or of upper-case and lower case

keyboard, ASCII, a keyboard with keys representing the printable ASCII character set, and a control key for accessing the extended character set and non-printing control characters

keyboard computer, a computer which has a keyboard as its primary or only source of input

keyboard control keys, keys on a keyboard which perform special functions such as control, shift, escape, etc.

keyboard, detachable, a keyboard which is connected by a cable to a computer or terminal, contrasted to being built into the same housing

keyboard, display console, a keyboard attached to the computer or workstation whose entries are displayed on a monitor

keyboard encoder, a device which converts the striking of a key into binary signal

keyboard label, the label on a key which identifies the character transmitted by the key or its special function

keyboard, live, a keyboard which

allows interaction with the program while it is running

keyboard lockout, a feature in an interactive program which prevents the input of further data from the keyboard while certain functions are being performed, such as a database sort, document repagination, etc.; a physical lock on a computer which prevents entry from the keyboard and thus access to the computer

keyboard overlay, a flexible film designed to fit over the keys of a particular keyboard, either used only to protect the keys or to label keys which have been reprogrammed for special functions

keyboard processor, the device which translates the pressing of keys into signals which are sent to the computer

keyboard, QWERTY, a standard typewriter keyboard arrangement of alpha characters, so-called for the order of the row of letters at the top left hand side of the keyboard

keyboard ROM, read only memory which stores the character codes associated with specific keys

keyboard send/receive set, (KSR) a communications system in which transmission is from a keyboard and reception is direct to a printer; a teletype system

keyboard shift, to change between the normal keyboard which produces numbers and lower case letters to the shifted keyboard which produces special characters and upper case letters

keyboard, touch-sensitive membrane, a flexible membrane printed to look like the standard keyboard which it replaces and which sends the appropriate signals to the computer when touched

key, control, a shift key on the keyboard, labeled CTRL, which, when pressed in conjunction with another key, modifies its signal to one recognized by the computer as a control code

keyed sequential access method, (KSAM) a system of sequential file structure which permits the direct access and reading of records based on the content of key fields

key, index, a field within a record which is used to find the record

keypad, an auxiliary keyboard which contains a limited set of characters, usually for control

keypad, numeric, an extra set of number keys on some keyboards, similar to those on a calculator, which allow fast entry of numbers and numeric operators and usually toggle between numeric and cursor movement functions

keypunch, a device which punches data onto punch cards

keypunching, the process of transferring data into a keypunch machine to produce punched cards

key, sequencing, the field in a record which is the basis for a sort; in instruction which directs the order of a sort

keystroke, the pressing of one key on a keyboard

key switch, the switching element of a key which sends a signal to the keyboard processor

key verification, a process for confirming the accuracy of keypunching by rekeying the data on a machine which simultaneously reads the punched cards and sounds an alarm if the signals do not match

keyword, a word in a programming language statement which indicates the operation to be performed; the most significant word in a title, usually one which gives the best indication of content

keyword-in-context, (KWIC) a cross index which lists the key word or words in each title

kilo, (K or k) a prefix which represents one thousand

kilobit, commonly, one thousand binary digits; 1024 bits

kilobyte, commonly, one thousand computer words of eight bits each; 1024 bytes

kilocycle, one thousand cycles per second

KSAM, keyed sequential access method; a system of sequential file structure which permits the direct access and reading of records based on the content of key fields

KSR, keyboard send/receive set; a communications system in which transmission is from a keyboard and reception is direct to a printer; a teletype system

KWIC, keyword-in-context index; a cross index which lists the key word or words in each title

L

label, a name in a program which identifies an instruction or subroutine; a name in a JCL given to a file, program, device, etc.

label, keyboard, the label on a key which identifies the character transmitted by the key or its special function

LAN, local area network, a limited number of workstations connected to each other or to a common host

or file server

LAN, general-purpose, a local area network which is not limited to a specific application

language, a clearly defined system of vocabulary and syntax for coding instructions, routines, programs, etc. which are run on a computer

language, absolute, the form of instructions understood directly by a computer without additional translation; machine language

language, artificial, a language with very specific vocabulary and syntax developed for the purpose of writing computer programs which can be subsequently translated into machine language

language, assembly, a low-level programming language which is computer-specific and requires detailed instructions for the computer to process

language, command, a procedural syntax for directing performance of basic functions

language, common business oriented, COBOL, a business-oriented programming language

language, computer, machine language; a language understood directly by the computer

language, computer oriented, a low-level language which translates quickly into machine language

language, direct-execution, a programming language which is designed for use on a computer which executes its commands directly, without compilation

language, hardware-based, any program language stored in ROM

language, high-level, a programming language somewhat resembling English which does not require the programmer to have a working knowledge of machine language

language interpreter, a program which translates a programming language into machine instructions, executing each instruction as it is translated

language, job control, a series of control statements which establish communications with the operating system and identify the equipment on which the program is to run, source of data files and conventions for identifying them within the program, etc.

language list, assembly, a printout showing both the symbolic and the machine form for elements of an assembly program's instructions

language, low-level, a language which is structured in a fashion similar to machine language, but is much more detailed than a high-level language and therefore more difficult to use in writing a program

language, machine, the absolute form of computer instructions, that is, a series of binary signals represented by zeros and ones, as utilized by a CPU and unique to that particular type of processor

language, native, the machine language understood by a particular type of processor

language, natural, a spoken language; not a computer language

language, non-procedural, a language which indicates only what is to be done and not how it is to be done

language, object, machine language specific to a particular computer, usually the output of an assembling or compiling operation; **native language; machine language**

language, programming, any language which is used to furnish instructions to a computer

language rules, the discipline which must be followed to insure that a compiler will not misinterpret or reject in instruction

language, source, a high-level language in which a program is written, such as COBOL, Pascal, BASIC, etc.

language, special purpose, a language created to work a specific type of problem or perform a special function

language, structured, a computer language which is suited to structured programming

language subset, parts of a computer language which can be used independent from the rest of the language

language, symbolic, any computer language which must be translated to machine language before running, hence, any language of a higher order than machine language; the use of symbols to represent logic instructions

language, system, a language in which instructions relate directly to machine language statements

language translation, converting a program from one language into another, as from BASIC to Pascal

LAN, single purpose, a local area network dedicated to a single application

laptop computer, a computer which is small enough to be held in the lap, often as powerful as a desktop and which can usually be connected to other computers and peripherals such as printers, etc.

large scale computer, a computer with complex and powerful programmable logic designed for the performance of extremely complex tasks

LASER, light amplification by stimulated emission of radiation; focused light of a single wavelength

laser printer, a printer which uses laser technology to create an image on paper or film

laser scanner, a device which uses laser technology to copy an image which is translated into digital data for processing by the computer

last in, first out, (LIFO) describing a buffer or queue routine in which the last element entered is the first element accessed

latch, a circuit which remains in a given state until changed by an external signal

latch chip, interface, a device which does not allow loading the system bus with input until an enabling signal is received

latency, delay time; the time gap which separates the end of one task and the beginning of another

laundry list, a list of items related to a particular application or action from which the user may make a selection

LCD, liquid crystal display; a form of monitor screen which relies on changes in the refractive qualities of liquid crystal

lead, a cable connecting electronic components

leader, a gap of non-recordable tape at the beginning of a reel of electromagnetic tape

leapfrog test, a program used to detect computer malfunctions

learning, computer, a self-adjusting routine in which the parameters of a function are modified to suit conditions such as the density of a scan for OCR recognition; the modification of program or data by a computer based on its experience while executing the program

least-significant bit, the bit of least importance in setting the value of a computer word; the rightmost bit in a computer word

least significant character, the character of least importance in setting the value of a word or string; the rightmost character in a word or string

least-significant digit, the rightmost digit in a number, therefore, the digit of least consequence in determining the value of the whole number

LED, light-emitting diode; a semiconductor which emits light, used in displays such as clocks, calculators, etc.

left-hand justified, in typesetting, the alignment of characters along the left margin, also described as *flush left*

left shift, in a shift register, the process of moving the bits of a binary word one position to the left to effect a multiplication

length, the number of bits or characters in a computer word

length, block, block size expressed in bytes, characters, words, records, etc.

length, field, the number of bits, characters or columns in a field

length, interrecord gap, the space which separates records on a magnetic tape to control stopping and starting

length, record, the number of words, bytes, or characters in a single data record

length, register, the number of positions in a register; in effect, the number of bits, digits, etc. which a register can store

length, string, the number of positions or characters in a string

letter, one of the set of symbols which are combined to form words

letter quality, a printing standard based on quality comparable to the image produced by a typewriter

letter-quality printer, a printer which uses formed character impact elements such as a daisy wheel, or a high resolution dot matrix printer

letter shift, to change between lower case and upper case letters

level, relative status; comparing programming language based on ease of use, an element of storage in relation to position in the file hierarchy of directories and sub-directories, programs and peripherals based on their allocation of processing time and access to the CPU, etc.

level, nesting, the level at which a program element exists, especially important when testing for a condition in which an improper sequence of tests can inadvertently eliminate valid data; the level at which a macroinstruction is processed

lexicon, a word list with definitions

LF, line feed; a control character which moves the print head to a new line; new-line character; the button on the printer which moves the paper ahead one line

library, a collection of programs, routines, data files, etc.

library case, a physical file for the storage of floppy disks

library, job, modules which load the data sets for a specific job

library, macro, an assortment of macros available to be called as needed

library, program, a collection of programs available to the computer

library routine, a program which can be called up from the library

library subroutine, a subroutine on file which can be called up as needed

library tapes, a collection of programs and routines saved on tape

library track, the data track on a magnetic disk which stores information about the files on the disk

library, user, general purpose routines or subroutines available to the user

LIFO, last in, first out; describing a buffer or queue routine in which the last element entered is the first element accessed

LIFO stack, data stored in such a way that the last item entered is the first item to be accessed

light emitting diode, a semiconductor which emits light, used in displays such as clocks, calculators, etc.

light pen, a device which is used to select elements or modify the display on a monitor screen

light, ready, a light which indicates that a device is prepared for use

light sensitive, referring to materials which produce a chemical or electrical response when exposed to light

light stylus, a **light pen**

limited, used to describe the activity which, because of its slower processing speed, restricts the operation of all other activity, such as **input limited, output limited, printer limited,** etc.

limited integrator, an integrator which will not accept input exceeding a certain level

line, a character string in a single on the monitor or printed; a communications band which links two devices

linear equation, an equation which represents a straight line on a graph

linearity, the relationship between two values in which a modification of one produces a proportional adjustment in the other

linear program, program instructions written in the order in which they are to be executed; also known as an unstructured program; see also **structured program**

linear search, the examination of a file by reading through all records sequentially until the search object is located; also called sequential search

line code, one computer instruction written on one line

line control, the process of controlling communications by informing each terminal of the proper time to begin transmitting

line control block, a memory area which contains data required for the control of a transmission line

line coordination, the process of ensuring that two devices are able and ready to communicate

line, dedicated, a communication line set aside for a specific purpose

and no other

line dot-matrix printer, a dot-matrix printer which prints a complete line at a single stroke

line drawing, a graphic representation using lines as contrasted to dots or half-tones

line drawing, three-dimensional, a line drawing in perspective to simulate a three dimensional, or solid, object; a graphic representation used in computer aided design; **three dimensional graphics**

line drawing, two-dimensional, a graphic representation of a single plane or side of an object

line driver, an amplifier which receives a signal, augments and retransmits it

line feed, a control character that moves the print head to a new line; new-line character

line feed code, a command which causes the paper in a printer to be moved up one line

line feed key, the button on the printer which moves the paper ahead one line

line height, the measure of a printed line of type; the number of lines of type per inch of a printed page; the measure, in inches, picas or points between the base of two lines of type

line item, data which logically belongs on the same line as other related data

line number, the number of an individual line of type or of code in a program; a reference number used to locate a line of type or program code

line noise, interference or undesirable signals in a transmission line

line of code, a program statement

which represents a single command or instruction which may extend over more than a single physical line

line printer, (LP), an impact printer which forms a complete line of characters at a single stroke

line printing, the printing of a complete line of characters at a single stroke rather than character by character sequentially across the line

line, program, a single command or instruction which may actually extend over more than a single physical line; a **line of code**

line speed, the rated speed of signal transmission expressed in baud or bits per second

line status, the state of a communications line, whether able to send, receive, etc.

line surge, an unexpected momentary increase in the voltage of a power line

line surge suppresser, a device which protects equipment from line surges

link, any connection between hardware or software elements; a physical connection between two hardware devices; a code or instruction which connects or references documents, files, applications, etc.

link bit, a special bit flag in a register which allows its contents to be combined with another register to form a double-length computer word

linked documents, document files connected by a transparent bond so that information held in common is updated in all of the documents whenever it is changed in one document

linked files, files connected by a transparent bond which allows them to share formatting or data

link editor, a program which joins separately assembled or complied routines into a single unit

linked list, a data structure in which each item contains a pointer to the next item

linker, a program which joins separately assembled or complied routines into a single unit; a **link editor**

linking loader, a program which connects separate subprograms as they are loaded into memory

liquid crystal display, (LCD) a form of monitor screen which relies on changes in the refractive qualities of liquid crystal

LISP, (List Processing) a programming language used in artificial intelligence research

list, a series of related items; to write or print out lines of program code; to print out the contents of a data file; a set of data elements which are to be accessed in a given sequence

listing, a computer printout of program instructions

listing, assembly language, a printout showing the binary equivalents of symbolic instructions as an aid to debugging a program

list processing, a programming technique which uses linked lists to order data

list processing language, a programming language such as LISP, developed to manage complex data structures

list, push-down, a data set in which

new data is added at the beginning so that existing data is "pushed down" to a new position

list, push-up, a data set in which new data is added at the end so that existing data maintains its position

list structure, the configuration of a list which describes linking to sub list elements, etc.

list, waiting, a queue; a list of programs or data awaiting processing as for printing, transmission, etc.

literal, in a computer program, a symbol or group of symbols which represent a specific, constant value, such as A=5; or which are to be presented exactly as written, such as "The total is "

literal operand, an operand which represents a constant value such as A=5.

live keyboard, a keyboard which allows interaction with the program while it is running

load, to transfer a program or data into the computer's main memory; to activate an application and ready it for use

LOAD, a reserved word or command in some computer languages such as BASIC which directs that a program or data be transferred to the computer's main memory

load and go, a technique which translates a programming language directly into machine language for immediate execution

loader, a program which loads another program into the computer's main memory for execution

loader, bootstrap, a program which loads the operating system when the computer is turned on

loader, initial program, a program which loads the operating system into the computer when it is first turned on

loader routine, a program element which calls up other programs or routines

loader, system, a program which places assembler or compiler output into computer memory

loading, block, a technique for loading sections of a program into contiguous sections of the computer's main memory

loading, bootstrap, loading a program or routine from a program built into the computer

load on call, a technique for loading sections or subroutines of a program as they are needed

load sharing, using two or more computers in tandem to share the processing of data

local, referring to equipment which is located at the user's site, as contrasted to *remote*

LOCAL, load on call

local area network, (LAN) a limited number of workstations connected to each other or to a common host or file server

local format storage, the storage of regularly used formats at a remote terminal to reduce transmissions from the main computer

local memory, RAM contained in a remote terminal to speed processing operations

local variable, a variable used by a subroutine and not available to the rest of the program

locate, to search the directories and sub directories of a disk or disks to find a file by name or content; to search a file for the next occurrence of data which matches a specific criteria

LOCATE, a reserved word or command in certain programming languages which directs the search for data which matches a specified model

location, the position in memory where an element is stored

location counter, a register which holds the address of a particular element of a program or data

location identifier, a label assigned to an element in computer memory or to the register which holds the address of a particular element; the label which describes a specific field in a database record

lock code, an identifier which prevents the alteration of a program; a password which limits access to a program or data

lockout, any prevention of certain functions, usually for security or to expedite execution of other functions

log, logarithm

log, a list of events or activities; to make an entry to such a list; a record of date and times a computer or file is accessed and by whom

logarithm, the exponent or power to which a base number must be raised to produce a given number

logger, a device which records the date and time of activities as they occur

logging, failure, a procedure in which the computer automatically records the detection of errors of any kind

logging, interrupt, the recording of interrupts in the process of testing and debugging a program

logic, the formal principles of reasoning; the principles of binary

calculation in which all relationships are expressed as true or false

logical, subject to relational testing by the principles of binary calculation

logical add, combining quantities in base two as contrasted to an arithmetic add in base ten

logical circuit, a set of logic operations gates, such as AND, OR, etc.

logical comparison, analyzing elements to establish coincidence or difference

logical connectives, in programming, the select or reserved words IF, AND, OR, etc. which direct a logical comparison

logical decision, selecting one of two possible choices

logical diagram, a graphic representation of the interconnection of logic elements in the computer

logical file, an accumulation of records associated by content without consideration of physical location

logical flow chart, a detailed flowchart displaying each logical step, each procedure, all arithmetic, and all input and output

logical high, the voltage level which the processor interprets as one, or high, aside from the actual voltage value

logical instruction, a program line which requires the use of Boolean logic

logical product, the conclusion derived by use of the AND operator

logical record, data related by content without consideration of physical location

logical relation, coincidence or difference between elements

logical sum, the conclusion derived

by use of the exclusive OR operator

logical symbol, a symbol which represents a logical operator

logical value, the product of a logic operation; true or false, 0 or 1, yes or no, etc.

logic, Boolean, problem solving with variables which may represent either of only two possible values; problem solving using the logical operators AND, OR and NOT

logic bug, a computer program error caused by faulty logic in a program statement or statements

logic card, one of several circuit boards in a computer containing electrical components and wiring

logic chart, a program flow chart which shows the logical steps applied to solve a problem

logic chip, a circuit chip which performs logic functions and, in conjunction with other chips, is used to create more complex circuits

logic circuit, a circuit which performs logic functions, such as AND, OR, etc.

logic, combination, an arrangement of circuits to determine output by subjecting input to a number of logic tests

logic device, any circuit in the computer which performs a logical operation such as a gate

logic diagram, a graphic representation of the interconnection of logic elements in the computer

logic element, a logic device; any circuit in the computer which performs a logical operation such as a gate

logic error, a program error caused by a faulty logic statement

logic flowchart, a detailed flowchart displaying each logical step,

each procedure, all arithmetic, and all input and output

logic, formal, the consideration of the structure of sound reasoning without regard to the content or subject

logic gate, a circuit which evaluates one or more input values and produces output based on its function

logic instruction, an instruction which directs the performance of a logic operation, such as AND or OR

logic operation, a non arithmetic operation executed by the computer, such as a comparison, branch, etc.

logic operator, the operators used in Boolean or symbolic logic, such as AND, OR, etc.

logic shift, a non-arithmetic shift

logic symbol, a symbol which represents a logical operator

log in, to identify oneself by password in order to gain access to computer time, programs and data; same as **log on**

log off, to close program or data files as required by the system and clear ones password to exit from the system; to end a computer session; same as **log out**

log on, to identify oneself by password in order to gain access to computer time, programs and data; same as **log in**

log out, to close program or data files as required by the system and clear ones password to exit from the system; to end a computer session; same as **log off**

look ahead, a system which permits scanning the program ahead of the current instruction in order to load files, subroutines, etc. in anticipation of need while executing the current instruction

look-up a technique for locating the value of a variable stored in a table

look-up, binary, a technique for finding an item in an ordered list by dividing the list in half and discarding the half that does not contain the search item

look-up instruction, an instruction which references arranged data such as a table of values

look-up table, data stored in referenced columns and rows which allows easy access when the value of a variable is required

look-up, table, the use of a known value to locate a variable in a referenced data array

loop, a device which permits the repeated execution of an instruction or series of instructions without the necessity of repeated iterations of code; program instructions which are repeated until a specific condition is met; to execute a loop

loop breaker, a program routine which monitors the iterations of a loop and exits when a maximum value is reached; a control routine to prevent clogging the system with unnecessary repetitions of an unplanned closed loop

loop checking, a system of confirming the accuracy of data transmission by resending back to the source for verification

loop, closed, a set of instructions from which there is no logical exit; a set of instructions repeated indefinitely; a programming error in which the output from the execution of a set of instructions is the input for the next execution of the same instructions; a technique involving data feedback for verification

tion

loop code, the computer language syntax for programming a loop; a segment of a program contained in a loop

loop counter, a register which monitors the iterations of a loop; see **loop breaker**

loop, feedback, a closed signal path in which output is used to modify input

loop feedback signal, loop output which is relayed back to cause the loop to be repeated

loop, hanging, a cessation of processing in which the computer cannot recognize input usually because of its inability to escape from a loop created by a fault in the program

loop, modification, a loop which modifies addresses or data in the program instruction

loop, nesting, a loop that contains an inner loop; an **outside loop**

loop, open, a loop which pauses after each iteration, usually with operator access to output, in order to allow user input such as to continue, alter instructions or exit

loop operation, instructions which are restored or modified prior to each iteration of the loop

loop stop, a loop monitor used in programming to indicate an error to the programmer; see also, **loop breaker**

loop termination, ending the iterations of a loop when a certain condition is met, whether programmed or an error condition

loop, outside, a series of instructions comprising a loop, part of which contains one or more secondary loops

loosely coupled, computers which are connected, but which are able to function independently

loss, transmission, a decrease in signal power during transmission

low end, a reference to any device or application which is among the less sophisticated of those available, such as a slow printer or processor, a limited data base or spreadsheet application, etc.

low-level language, a language which is structured in a fashion similar to machine language, but is much more detailed than a high-level language and therefore more difficult to use in writing a program

low order, the rightmost digits in a number, or those bits of the least significance

low order column, the rightmost column in a punched card

low order digit, the rightmost digit in a number

low resolution, descriptive of a monitor screen in which the display is characterized by rough, uneven edges

LP, line printer; linear programming

LSI, large scale integration; referring to integrated circuits which contain a large number of transistors and components on a single chip

M

machine address, direct address; a group of characters which indicate the location of specific data stored in memory which can be accessed directly by the computer

machine check, an audit, either automatic or programmed, of machine functions

machine check interrupt, a halt which occurs when a machine error is discovered

machine code, instructions written in machine language

machine code instruction, a command which expresses a basic operation in machine language

machine cognition, a type of artificial intelligence; the recognition by a computer of patterns which are then stored for use in future decision making

machine cycle, the time required for the computer to complete one operation

machine dependent, a program or application which is designed for use with a particular computer or type of computer

machine dependent language, a low-level computer language in which each statement corresponds to one machine language statement and which is usable only on a particular computer or type of computer

machine error, an error produced by a computer malfunction

machine independent, a program or application which can be run on a variety of different computers

machine independent language, a programming language capable of use on any computer with the proper compiler or interpreter

machine instruction, an instruction in the language which the machine can read and execute

machine language, the absolute form of computer instructions, that is, a series of binary signals represented by zeros and ones, as utilized by a CPU and unique to that particular type of processor; the language into which any other language must be translated before the computer can process them; **absolute language**

machine language compile, to translate a program written in a source code into machine language

machine learning, a self-adjusting routine in which the parameters of a function are modified to suit conditions such as the density of a scan for OCR recognition; the modification of program or data by a computer based on its experience while executing the program

machine operator, the person responsible for operating a mainframe computer as contrasted to a programmer or user

machine oriented language, (MOL) a language which is specific to a particular computer and usually more closely resembles assembly language than a high-level language

machine readable, a language or instruction which can be understood by the computer; hard copy which is suitable for scanning and saving by the computer as graphics or OCR

machine-readable characters, stylized characters which can be interpreted by humans or by scanners such as OCR or MICR

machine-readable data, data in a form which can be read by a computer, such as that recorded on tape or disk

machine run, the execution of one or more machine program routines

machine, scanning, a machine which reads printed matter or magnetic ink and inputs the data to the computer

machine sensible, data which is in a form readable by a computer.

machine translation, the conversion of programs or data from one form to another, such as from OCR to a data file, one program language to another, etc.

machine word, a fixed-length sequence of bits manipulated as a unit in processing and memory storage; a unit of data in a computer; a **computer word**

macro, a group of program instructions which are executed by a single key word to which they are attached; in some application programs, a series of user defined keystrokes executed by calling up the macro or pressing a combination of keys

macro assembler, an assembler which translates key words in a program into executable instructions

macro code, a key word which represents a group of computer instructions

macro coding, the creation of a group of instructions activated by a key word

macro command, a single command which activates a group of individual commands

macro definition, the assembly language commands which are designated by a macro

macro definition library, a list of macros with their key words

macro generating program, a program which is used to create macros, either by writing code or recording the keystrokes which make up the macro instructions.

macro generation, the creation of a group of machine language instructions from one macro instruction in a source program

macroinstruction, a predefined set of instructions executed in an assembly language program by a key word

macro library, an assortment of macros available to be called as needed

macro processing, the translation of macro instructions into machine code by a macro assembler; the execution of macro instructions by use of a combination of keys

macro processing instruction, a program command which calls the macro assembler

macro program, a group of instructions activated by a key word; in some applications, a series of key strokes activated by a shortcut key or a key combination

macro programming, writing a computer program using macro instructions

macro recorder, a device which records keystrokes for inclusion in a macro

magnetic bubble memory, a type of random access memory which uses movable magnetic fields in a solid state device

magnetic card, a card containing a magnetic strip on which data can be stored

magnetic character, a character printed with magnetic ink

magnetic character sorter, a machine which scans and sorts documents by reading printed magnetic characters on the documents

magnetic disk, a magnetic storage medium; in large computers, a disk pack, which consists of a number of disks joined together on

a spindle; in microcomputers, a hard disk (also called a fixed disk or a hard drive) or a floppy disk (also called a diskette)

magnetic drum, a computer storage medium in which data is stored on rotating metal cylinders

magnetic head, the device on a disk or tape drive which reads data from storage and writes it to storage

magnetic ink, ink containing material capable of holding a magnetic charge

magnetic ink character recognition, (MICR) the process of reading and recording data printed with magnetic ink

magnetic ink scanner, a machine which reads characters printed in magnetic ink

magnetic memory, computer storage on electromagnetic media, such as drum, tape or disk

magnetic storage, mass storage on magnetic media, such as drum, tape or disk

magnetic strip, a band of electromagnetic sensitive material applied to a card or document for the purpose of storing data

magnetic tape, recording tape used for the storage of computer programs and data

magnetic tape cartridge, magnetic tape for mass storage contained in a plastic case

magnetic tape cassette, self-contained package of reel-to-reel magnetic tape, such as that used in stereo systems and video recorders which can be used to store computer data

magnetic tape density, the compactness data on magnetic tape;

the number of characters per inch which can be or is recorded on magnetic tape

magnetic tape drive, a device for manipulation of tape reels while data is transferred to and from the magnetic tape

magnetic tape reader, a device which reads the data stored on tape

magnetic tape storage, mass storage on magnetic tape, often a backup system

magnetic tape unit, a magnetic tape drive with read/write heads and controllers

magnetic track, the part of a magnetic recording device to which data is written

magnitude, the size of a value without regard to sign

mail merge, the technique of combining a database of names and addresses with text such as a letter to print out for personalized mass mailings

main frame, the central processing unit of a large computer

main memory, the computer's working memory, or RAM (random access memory); internal memory

main path, the principal course or direction of a program; the path which defines the location of the operating system

main program, a program which controls the basic functions of the computer, such as reading input from the keyboard, visual display on the CRT monitor, function of the disk drives and printer, etc.; **operating system;** a primary program designed to perform a specific task and which controls routines and subroutines

main routine, the **main program** or **operating system**

main storage, the RAM memory or working storage of a computer; **main memory**

maintainability, the comparative ease or difficulty with which a system may be kept in operating condition

maintenance, the process of keeping hardware in working order, whether through preventive maintenance before repairs are necessary or through making necessary repairs; periodic review of files and programs to purge or archive outdated material

maintenance, software, reworking and improving a program to keep it current and working properly; reviewing data files to archive or purge outdated information

maintenance time, the regular operating hours lost due to machine failure

major control data, data used to regulate other records, files, operations, or data

majority, an operation which returns *true* if more than half the data evaluated are true

major state, the computer's control state

malfunction, failure of the computer or a peripheral device

management, data base, a data base management system; an individual responsible for controlling access and security for data files

management information system, (MIS) the procedures for storing and retrieving data in a particular situation or organization and making it available to those who need it

management services, assistance supplied by a management consulting firm

management support system, the computer analysis of information to assist management in decision making

management system, the organizational structure of the personnel who direct the operations of an organization

management, task, instructions in a control program which allocates the use of system resources

manifold, multiple part forms

manipulated variable, a variable which is altered in order to regulate a condition

manipulation, altering or reordering data and data formats

manipulation, string, the technique for processing or manipulating data or character strings

man-machine dialogue, the interaction or communication between man and machine in data processing

mantissa, the decimal or fractional part of a logarithm

manual address switch, an external switch which allows the computer operator to select a specific address for storage

manual backup, making duplicate copies of program or data files on demand as contrasted with an **automatic backup**

manual control, the use of physical switches to control a computer function

manual entry, the input of data from a keyboard

manual input generator, a device which records input and retains it until called up

manual link, an update link between documents or files which is controlled by the user, that is, linked elements are updated to reflect changes only at the user's direction

manual read, computer reading of the settings of manual switches

manufacturer's software, utilities provided by the manufacturer of hardware for use with their equipment, such as printer or scanner drivers, etc.

many-for-one language, a computer language assembler which converts one source instruction into several object instructions

map, a list of the contents in storage

map list, memory, a listing by addresses of a memory map

map, memory, a listing or graphic representation of the location of various functions in memory

mapped memory, blocks of memory assigned to specific users who each have access to their own block

mapping, moving a section, or page, of memory from one medium to another, such as from a storage disk to RAM

mapping, data base, outlining the interrelationship of data base files such as fields in common and interdependent fields

margin, the (usually) unprinted area surrounding copy on a printed page; the difference between two values; an allowance or provision for contingencies

marginal, notes or copy placed within the usually unprinted area reserved for a margin; of limited value or almost lacking utility

marginal cost, the difference in cost between alternatives compared to what that cost will buy; the cost of improved quality or greater quantity expressed as the premium paid related to the quality or quantity obtained for that premium

marginal testing, the testing of hardware to ascertain which components are most likely to fail under stress; **bias checking**

mark, a symbol which acts as a pointer for future reference; a communications pulse; **end of message; end of transmission**

mark detection, sensing and recognition of character elements in optical character recognition

mark, end, an indicator of the end of a unit of data, a record, file, etc.

marker, a pointer which indicates the beginning or end of a data set, page or file; a named reference point within a document or set of documents which can be accessed through the use of a hot key; **end data symbol; end of data marker; end of file; end of page indicator; end of tape marker; end of tape warning**

marker, beginning-of-information, an indicator on magnetic tape which indicates where recording may begin

marker, destination warning, (DWM), a reflective spot on magnetic tape which is sensed photoelectrically to indicate proximity to the end of the tape

marker, end of data, a code which indicates the end of a data set

marker, end of file, (EOF) a marker which identifies the last record in a set of sequenced records

marker, end of message, (EOM) a code or pulse which indicates the end of a transmission

marker, end of tape, a machine-readable mark on a magnetic tape indicating the end of the tape is imminent

marker, end of transmission, (EOT) a code or pulse which indicates the end of a transmission

mark, file, a code or record which indicates the end of a file

mark matching, in optical character recognition, comparing the elements of input with a matrix in order to identify a character

mark reader, a device which senses and translates dense impressions in specific locations on a document, such as those made with a soft pencil on a multiple choice test sheet

mark, record, a character or symbol which separates records in a database

mark, record storage, a character in the record storage unit of a punched card reader which limits the length of the record read into memory.

mark, segment, used in magnetic storage to delineate each section of a file

mark sensing, apprehending by machine, marks on special cards or documents; **mark reader**

mark, word, a character or symbol which indicates the beginning or end of a word

MASER, microwave amplification by stimulated emission of radiation; a device which generates electromagnetic waves of precise frequency, used in communications to amplify signals

mask, a pattern of bits in a machine word which limits the parts of another word which can be processed, used in comparison operations; a pattern or stencil used in the manufacture of integrated circuit chips, also called **IC mask**

masked, refers to the state of an interrupt feature which has been repressed or **disabled**

masking, the utilization of a pattern of bits in a computer word for control or recognition of another computer word

mask, interrupt, an instruction designating which external devices are allowed to interrupt processing and which will be ignored

mask matching, in optical character recognition, a system of matching the elements of an input character with those of a matrix for the purpose of identifying the input character

mass data, data files which are held in mass storage

mass data multiprocessing, a system whereby various levels and types of processing are performed simultaneously; processing of a single database by two or more computers in tandem

mass storage, devices, such as disk or tape, used for somewhat permanent storage of programs and data

master, the main copy of a program or data file, to which changes are made only after verification and from which new working copies are made; a relatively permanent data record or file

master card, a punched card which contains pertinent data about a card deck

master clear, a switch or command which clears all registers; **clear**

master clock, the device which controls the timing signals in a

computer; **clock**

master clock frequency, the pulses per second or the interval between pulses produced the computer clock; **clock frequency**

master control interrupt, an interrupt which returns program control to the master control program

master control program, a program which controls all phases of a job including equipment functions, data flow, instructions to the operator, etc.; also the **operating system** or **main program**

master data, the contents of a master file; relatively permanent data

master file, a relatively permanent data record or file; a file which contains relatively permanent information which is linked to other files for transient and updated data; also an archive file

master file job processing, accessing the programs which are necessary for job processing, such as input/output drivers, system control and management, utility routines and library subroutines

master program file, a record of all programs available to a system

master record, a relatively permanent record which is part of a master file

master/slave system, an arrangement of computers in which all are controlled by one

master synchronizer, a source of timing signals; **master clock**

master tape, a tape which contains the operating system program, the main program or control program of an integrated set of programs or a master data file

master terminal, the terminal in a

network which is controlling the computer, its peripherals and communications with other terminals in the system

match, the process of analyzing sets of data, records, etc. to determine if they are the same

math chips, dedicated circuits which perform arithmetic functions

math co-processor, a special device which operates in conjunction with a CPU and which performs high-speed arithmetic operations

mathematical check, analysis based on numeric functions

mathematical logic, the technique of manipulating numbers in a binary system

mathematical model, representation of a process or system in terms of numeric values

mathematical modeling, representing processes or systems in terms of numeric values

mathematical operator, a symbol which directs an arithmetic operation, such as add, subtract, multiply, divide, square root, etc.

mathematical power, a number, usually written as superscript following a base number, which indicates the number of times the base number is to be multiplied by itself to express the value of the representation

matrix, a two-dimensional array

matrix, dot, a rectangular array of dots from which characters and graphic symbols are formed on a CRT or on a printer

matrix printer, a dot matrix printer; a printer which forms characters and graphics from a rectangular array of dots

mb, megabyte

MCI, media control interface; a standard control interface for multimedia hardware and software

mean time between failures, a pattern of the reliability of a computer or a component

mean time to failure, the average length of time a computer or component works without failing

mechanical dictionary, a program which translates from one spoken language to another, word-for-word

media, (*sing.* **medium**) in relation to computers, the type of devices on which programs and data are stored, such as punched cards, magnetic tape, magnetic disks, etc.

media control interface, (MCI) a standard control interface for multimedia computer hardware and software

media file, a computer file which contains multimedia data such as animation or sound

medium, singular of **media**

medium, storage, the devices on which programs and data are stored, such as punched cards, magnetic tape, magnetic disks, etc.

mega-, one million

megabit, approximately one million bits, actually 2^{20} or 1,048,576 bits

megabyte, (mb) approximately one million bytes, actually 2^{20} or 1,048,576 bits

megahertz, (MHz) one million cycles per second

member, print, the device on a printer which transfers image to paper such as a type bar, daisy wheel, ink jet, etc.

membrane keyboard, a flexible membrane printed to look like the standard keyboard which it replaces and which sends the appropriate signals to the computer when touched; a touch-sensitive membrane keyboard

memory, the part of a computer where programs and data are held while being accessed (RAM or ROM); any device which stores data which can be accessed by the computer

memory access, direct, the direct transfer of data between memory and a peripheral

memory address, the location in memory, identified by name or number, where data is stored; the register in a CPU wherein an address is stored

memory addressing capacity, the amount of memory available for programs, data and other functions

memory address counter, the register which contains the address of the next command to be processed

memory, addressed, a memory area that contains a specific register

memory addressing modes, the various means for indicating the location of an address; **direct addressing; immediate addressing; implied addressing; indexed addressing; indirect addressing; multilevel addressing; relative addressing; symbolic addressing**

memory address register, the register in a CPU wherein an address is stored

memory allocation, the designation of specific locations in memory for certain programs, drivers, or blocks of data

memory annex, a small section of memory between the I/O and main memory reserved for temporary storage of data; a **buffer**

memory, associative, a high speed search based on memory content rather than memory address

memory, backing, memory in auxiliary or backup storage characterized by unlimited capacity and long access time

memory bank, a unit of main memory in a computer

memory, bootstrap, a protected section of memory in which loading instructions are stored

memory, bubble, a type of random access memory which uses movable magnetic fields in a solid state device

memory buffer register, a temporary register able to receive or send data at different I/O rates

memory bus, the communication lines between the CPU and main memory in the computer

memory, cache, a section of memory set aside to hold just-closed files and which uses read ahead procedures to anticipate future calls so that it usually has the next file ready before it is needed, speeding access time

memory capacity, the amount of data which can be held in memory, usually expressed in bytes

memory card, a card, similar to a credit card, containing one or more imbedded magnetic chips to which data can be recorded

memory, CCD, charge coupled device memory; random access memory using a semi-conductor characterized by high density storage and low power consumption

memory chip, semiconductor memory such as RAM or ROM usually mounted on cards to interface efficiently with the CPU

memory, content-addressable, a memory location which is identified by the data or type of data which it contains rather than by its address

memory cycle the time necessary to access and read or write data in memory

memory data register, a register which temporarily stores the last data word processed

memory, dedicated, a portion of memory set aside for a specific purpose

memory dump, copying the contents of a storage device to a printer or display screen

memory, dynamic, semiconductor memory which must be refreshed in order to retain its contents.

memory error, an error which occurs when data is read incorrectly from memory

memory expansion modules, memory boards which can be added to the computer

memory expansion mother board, a main circuit board in the computer to designed to accept additional memory

memory, external, a storage device which is not an integral part of the computer

memory fill, loading certain areas of memory with symbols or codes to prevent access to them; also called, *memory guard*

memory hierarchy, rating memory units according to size, speed, and cost

memory interleaving, the process of alternating memory calls to speed up memory access

memory, internal, main memory or RAM; the computer's working memory

memory, local, RAM contained in a remote terminal to speed processing operations

memory, magnetic, computer storage on electromagnetic media, such as drum, tape or disk

memory, main, the computer's working memory, or RAM (random access memory); internal memory

memory management, hardware and software techniques which regulate memory handling

memory map, a listing or graphic representation of the location of various functions in memory

memory map list, a listing by addresses of a memory map

memory-mapped I/O, a system of accessing peripheral devices by addressing memory locations in contrast to addressing the device itself

memory-mapped I/O bus, an I/O bus accessed by directions in main memory

memory-mapped video, a monitor display in which each pixel is assigned an address in memory

memory mapping, allocating functions such as input/output to specific locations in memory; allocating specific areas of memory to individual users

memory map, user, an area of memory available to an individual user, distinct from areas available to other users

memory, non-volatile, computer memory which retains its content when power is off

memory page, a logical section of memory, addressable by one byte.

memory, permanent, non-volatile storage which retains its content when power is off

memory, programmable, memory contents which are under program control

memory protection, any technique designed to prevent corrupting program or data files; coding program and permanent data files to prevent overwriting; dividing memory among individual users to prevent overwriting by another user or program; use of protectors to prevent corruption of storage media by power surges

memory, random access, (RAM) memory which allows data to be addressed independent of the last access

memory, read only, (ROM) special memory which can be read, but not altered

memory resident, referring to elements which have been loaded into the computer's main memory or RAM

memory resident program, a program, often a utility such as a scratch pad or reference chart, which has been loaded into the computer and can be called up as needed from within another program

memory, scratch pad, a memory area used for temporary storage of the intermediate results of calculations

memory, secondary, an external storage device, such as disk or tape

memory, serial, memory which must retrieve data by reading records in sequence until the search object is found, contrasted to random access

memory storage, intermediate, a section of memory used to temporarily hold data

memory typewriter, an electronic typewriter which stores text as it is typed and allows editing before printing

memory, volatile random access memory which blanks when the power is off

menu, a list of choices from which the user of an interactive program may select

menu driven, software which uses menus to list the choices for the user to select

menu, drop down, options menus which appear when subject headings are selected by the user

merge, the combining of two or more files or sets of records into a single set of records

merge, mail, the technique of combining a database of names and addresses with text such as a letter to print out for personalized mass mailings

merge sort, a technique for combining and arranging in order, two or more sets of records

message, in communication, a block of information with identification of the intended receiver and an end of message indicator; any significant group of characters which conveys information

message, automatic, the automatic rerouting of messages to another destination after receipt and analysis of the contents by the processing unit

message center, automatic, a center which routes messages according to the information they contain

message control flag, a flag, or

code, which indicates whether a transmission is data or control information

message, diagnostic, the error message displayed when an interpreter or compiler encounters errors in a program; an error message which usually includes the location and type of error such as incorrect syntax, data exception, etc.

message, end of, (EOM) a code or pulse which indicates the end of a transmission

message, error, any message transmitted to a printer or to a monitor which declares an error condition, and often, the nature and probable cause of the error

message format, the rules defining the placement of headings, address, text, start and stop codes, etc.

message, fax, facsimile message; the documents, transmitted hard copy to hard copy or hard copy to computer between detached locations via telephone lines

message, fox, a message containing all alphanumerics which is used to test printers

message header, the lead characters of a message denoting the source of the message, destination, etc.

message queuing, management of the sequence of processing and transmitting messages

message retrieval, the routine for accessing messages in the system

message routing, management of the transmission of a message through the system or from one system to another

message switch, the hardware and software routine which routes mes-

sages to their respective destinations; one of the routing stations in a message switching system

message switching, the automatic rerouting of messages to another destination after receipt and analysis of the contents by the processing unit

message-switching center, a center that routes messages according to the information they contain

metal oxide semiconductor, (MOS) a type of integrated circuit

MHz, megahertz; one million cycles per second

MICR, magnetic ink character recognition

MICR code, magnetic ink character recognition; a code developed to machine-read documents, often to control banking transactions

micro-, in metrics, a prefix denoting *one millionth* as in a microsecond or one millionth of a second; a prefix denoting a thing unusually or relatively small such as a microchip or microcomputer

microchip, a microprocessor chip

microcircuit, miniaturized circuitry

micro code, a system for coding subroutines in a program

micro command, a command which defines a basic machine operation

microcomputer, a computer in which the CPU consists of a single integrated circuit called a microprocessor

microcomputer architecture, the internal design of a microprocessor which defines its word size, registers, input/output operations, data paths, etc.

microcomputer bus, a collection of wires or paths for data, address, commands, control codes, etc. on which information is moved between the CPU, memory and I/O devices

microcomputer card, a printed circuit card for special devices which can be connected into the computer's motherboard

microcomputer chip, a microprocessor; an integrated circuit containing the complete CPU for a computer, such as the 8088 with a rated speed of 8 MHz or 8 cycles per second, the 80286 which operates at speeds up to 25 MHz, the 80386 with speeds rated up to 40 MHz and the 80486 with speeds of 50 MHz and climbing; a **computer on a chip**

microcomputer, 8-bit, a microcomputer which utilizes an 8-bit data word

microcomputer, 8/16-bit, a microcomputer which utilizes a 16-bit data word on an 8-bit bus

microcomputer, 16-bit, a microcomputer which utilizes a 16-bit data word

microcomputer, 16/32-bit, a microcomputer which utilizes a 32-bit data word on a 16-bit bus

microcomputer, 32-bit, a microcomputer which utilizes a 32-bit data word

microcomputer system, a complete computer system operated by a microprocessor including the CPU, memory, keyboard, CRT monitor, and any peripherals

micro controller, a control device comprising a microprocessor and any necessary sensors, output devices, etc.

microelectronics, the design and assembly of miniature electronic

circuits

microfiche, fiche; a sheet of microfilm

microfilm, a strip of film used to store photographically reduced text and graphics

microfloppy disk, a diskette; a magnetic disk 3 ¼ inches in diameter enclosed in a hard protective case

micro instruction, a simple command such as *delete* or *copy*

micromini, a microcomputer; usually a desktop computer

microminiaturization, the process of reducing to very small size, often microscopic, of photographs, circuits, etc.

micron, one millionth of a meter, hence one thousandth of a millimeter

microprocessing unit (MPU), a circuit board containing the CPU plus necessary support chips; a motherboard

microprocessor, an integrated circuit which holds the entire CPU on a single chip

microprocessor, bit-slice, a microprocessor containing several modular chips which have been joined to produce a CPU with a specified word size

microprocessor card, a circuit card containing a microprocessor and necessary support chips

microprocessor chip, an integrated circuit which holds the entire CPU, such as the 8088 with a rated speed of 8 MHz or 8 cycles per second, the 80286 which operates at speeds up to 25 MHz, the 80386 with speeds rated up to 40 MHz and the 80486 with speeds of 50 MHz and climbing

microprocessor, custom, a computer chip designed to meet a customer's requirements

microprocessor, 8-bit, a microprocessor which uses an 8-bit data word

microprocessor, 16-bit, a microprocessor which uses a 16-bit data word

microprocessor slices, modular chips which can be joined to produce a CPU of any specified word size

microprocessor, 32-bit, a microprocessor which uses a 32-bit data word

microprocessor word, a series of bits which are processed as a unit; a computer word

micro program, one of the programs which directly control the elements in a microprocessor, usually in ROM; spoken language or near-spoken language commands translated by hardware into machine subcommands; a program written in a computer's basic commands

micro program assembly language, a set of assembly language instructions defined by micro programs

micro program, bit-slice, the instructions which make up the machine code for a bit-slice microprocessor

micro program instruction set, the machine-dependent commands which are valid in an assembly language program

microprogrammable instructions, instructions which do not require access to main memory

microprogrammable ROM computer, a computer whose instruction set is retained in ROM

microprogrammed processor, a CPU with an instruction set which is contained in ROM, as contrasted to wired circuitry

micro programming, using the basic processor operations to define more complex tasks

microsecond, one millionth of a second

MIDI, musical instrument digital interface; a protocol for communication between a digitized musical instrument and the computer

MIDI sequencer, a program which records and plays music from a digitized musical instrument

milli-, a prefix meaning one thousandth

millisecond, one thousandth of a second

mini-assembler program, a program which allows entry of mnemonics from the keyboard, produces the object code and places it in memory

miniaturization, drastic reduction in the size of an element

minicomputer, a computer which ranks between a microcomputer and a mainframe in size, power and cost not normally based on a single processor chip and supporting ten to one hundred users

minidisk, a type of diskette; a 5 1/4- inch floppy disk

minimum access code, a code designed to reduce delays in the transfer of data or instructions between storage and other components

minuend, the result of a subtraction; the number from which another number has been subtracted

MIPS, millions of instructions per

second; a measure of the performance of a CPU

MIS, management information system; the procedures for storing and retrieving data in a particular situation or organization and making it available to those who need it

misfeed, the missing or incorrect feeding of punched cards, printer paper, etc.

mistake, a human error, often faulty logic or syntax in a program

mixed mode, the use of different types of variables in the same arithmetic expression in a program

mixed number, a number comprised of a whole number and a fraction or decimal

mnemonic, anything designed to aid the memory

mnemonic address, an address defined by a mnemonic abbreviation

mnemonic code, code devised with a built in memory aid; a code whose name is a reminder of what it represents, such as ACC for accumulator

mnemonic instruction code, instructions written in assembly-language mnemonics

mnemonic language, an assembly language

mnemonic operation code, operation codes written in assembly-language mnemonics

mnemonics, assembly language instructions designed to remind the programmer of the instruction's function

mode, a method of operation

mode, alter, a program mode which allows changes and updates to data in memory

mode, analysis, a computer operation in which statistical and analytical data is stored for later retrieval by the analyst

mode, burst, a mode of communication which involves reading or writing data without an interrupt

mode, byte, transmission of data one byte at a time

mode, conversational, a procedural mode in which the computer and user interact, usually an applications program

mode, format, a screen display mode in which a difference in intensity distinguishes between protected fields and entry fields

mode, graphics, a printer configuration in which signals sent to the printer are interpreted as graphic elements rather than character symbols, usually selected by a toggle or DIP switch on the printer

model, a graphic, mathematical, physical or verbal representation of a process or device

modeling, conceptual, creating a model which characterizes a result and experimenting to confirm the validity of the model

modeling, mathematical, representing processes or systems in terms of numeric values

modem, modulator/demodulator; a device which converts digital signals to telephone signals, permitting communication between computers via telephone lines

modem, acoustic, a modem which accesses a telephone line through an acoustic coupler, converts digital computer signals to sound for sending and encodes sound which it receives back to digital

modem audio loop back control, a control function which returns a received audio signal for verification

modem bypass, a cable which links a device directly to a modem communication port

modem check control, a procedure for checking data transmission by sending it back to the source to match it with the original data

modem communications, communications between computers and terminals using modems

modem connect-line control, a procedure which checks for availability, then connects the telephone line to the modem

modem, direct connect, a modem which is linked directly to a telephone line from the computer

mode, mixed, the use of different types of variables in the same arithmetic expression in a program

modem synchronization, the system of matching the speed and mode of two modems to function either asynchronous or synchronous

modem tester, a device which evaluates modem performance by simulated data communication functions

mode, operational, the computer operating mode which is in effect

mode, printer a hardware or software selection of the manner in which a printer interprets signals sent to it and which determines output from the printer, such as text mode, graphics mode, PostScript® mode, HP LaserJet® emulation mode, etc.

modification loop, a loop which modifies addresses or data in the program instruction

modify, to alter or change, as the

structure of a file, program instructions, etc.

modular, in computer programming, a program made up of smaller program units, each of which performs a specific function

modular construction, the concept of developing a computer system or program from modules; **building block principle**

modular programming, programs written as a series of units which can be tested individually, then strung together in the main program and called as needed

modulate, to change the frequency, phase, intensity, or amplitude of a signal

modulation, the modification of any of the characteristics of a signal

modulation, dipole, binary digits described on a magnetic medium

modulator, a device which translates digital data to analog signals for transmission by telephone lines

modulator/demodulator, a **modem**

module, a relatively independent unit of a larger system or program which is designed to perform a specific function

modulo, a procedure which yields only the remainder after executing a division

modulo check, verifying a process by matching the remainders of division operations

MOL, machine oriented language; a language which is specific to a particular computer and usually more closely resembles assembly language than a high-level language

monadic, singular; an operation which requires only one operand, such as finding the negative of a number

monadic Boolean operator, a Boolean operator which has only one operand

monitor, a display screen, usually a CRT or cathode ray tube, for a computer; to observe the activity of a program while it is running to check for errors

monitor control dump, a programmed juncture in a routine when the program and its data are written to backup storage

monitored instruction, an input/output or function transfer instruction which may be observed and interrupted

monitor program, a program which supervises the operation of another program

monitor system, a set of routines which supervise the order and execution of programs in a multitasking environment

monitor, time-sharing, a program which coordinates and controls time sharing

monochrome CRT, a console which displays in one color only, most often white, green, or amber

monolithic, a single piece; the single silicon substrate of an integrated circuit

monospaced, referring to a type font in which the space occupied by each character is the same width, as contrasted to **proportional spacing**

monostable, of a device which has only one stable state

Monte Carlo method, a system of problem solving which uses random numbers in repeated trial and error calculations until the best solution is reached

MOS, metal oxide semiconductor; a type of integrated circuit

most-significant bit, the bit which, if changed, would effect the greatest change in the value of a computer word; the leftmost bit in a computer word

most-significant character, the character which, if changed, would effect the greatest change in the value of a word or number; the leftmost character in a number or word

most-significant digit, (MSD) the digit which, if changed, would effect the greatest change in the value of a number; the leftmost digit in a number

motherboard, the main printed circuit board in a computer to which other boards and cards are connected

mouse, a hand-held input device which is rolled across a flat surface to produce corresponding movements of the cursor on the screen

movable head, a movable read/write head on a mass storage device

move, the command to move a selected block of text in word processing as a single unit

moving average, represents a statistical average based on a string of data which is updated by adding new data to the end of the string and deleting corresponding data from the beginning of the string; for example, a six month average which is recalculated by adding a seventh month and deleting the first month

moving domain memory, a nonvolatile semi-random storage system which uses arrays of magnetic bubbles in a microchip

moving head disk system, a disk drive in which the read/write head moves across the surface of the disk, in contrast to a fixed head

MP/M, Multiprogramming control Program for Microprocessors, an operating system

MPS, microprocessor system; a computer system designed for a specific task or a variety of tasks controlled by a microprocessor

MPU, microprocessing unit; a circuit board containing the CPU plus necessary support chips; a motherboard

MPU application, the task for which a computer has been designed based on its architecture

MPU support chips, chips which provide I/O and other capabilities to the main processing unit

ms, millisecond, one thousandth of a second

MSD, most-significant digit; the digit which, if changed, would effect the greatest change in the value of a number; the leftmost digit in a number

MS-DOS,® Microsoft Disk Operating System; one of the most widely used operating systems for personal computers

MT, machine translation; the conversion of programs or data from one form to another, such as from OCR to a data file, one program language to another, etc.

MTBF, mean time between failures; a pattern of the reliability of a computer or a component

MTF, MTTF, mean time to failure; the average length of time a computer or component works without failing

multi-access, descriptive of a system which is designed and equipped to accommodate many users simultaneously

multi-address instruction, an instruction which contains more than one address

multi-channel, a system which divides signal frequency into separately transmitted bands which are recombined at destination

multi-chip card, a multi-chip memory card

multi-chip integrated circuit, an integrated circuit comprised of two or more chips

multi-chip memory card, a memory card containing more than one memory chip

multi-chip microcircuit, a circuit comprised of two or more integrated circuit chips

multi-computer system, a computer system which operates with two or more CPU's

multi-drop line, a circuit which connects several workstations or terminals

multi-drop terminal, one of several workstations connected to a single line

multi-file sorting, the sorting of two or more files independent of operator involvement

multi-layer printed circuit, circuitry in which layers of printed circuits are isolated by layers of insulation

multilevel addressing, using an instruction that references the address which contains the data address

multilevel software, application programs in which the user interacts with the computer on one level other functions required to run the program are being handled on another level in the background

multimedia, referring to a combination of sight and sound

multimedia computer, a computer designed to create and run **multimedia programs**

multimedia PC, a personal computer coupled with the hardware and software to program and run **multimedia programs**

multimedia presentation, same as **multimedia program**

multimedia program, a computer program which blends graphics, animation and video cuts combined with sound to create a sales presentation, training program, etc.

multimedia software, programs for creating voice and music program files; programs for running multimedia peripherals such as recording and playback devices; the multimedia programs created with the help of multimedia software and hardware

multimedia system, a computer system which includes an audio system, visual display devices and all necessary programs to create and run a multimedia presentation

multi-pass sort, a sort program in which only part of the records are sequenced in a single pass through the data so that additional passes are required to complete the sort

multiple access, a system which is designed and equipped to accommodate many users simultaneously

multiple access computer, a computer which can handle input and output through several user terminals simultaneously

multiple address code, program code in which an instruction word is not limited to a single address

multiple address instruction, a computer instruction which contains more than one address

multiple computer system, a system with more than one CPU and other peripherals which are interconnected and functioning in harmony

multiple job processing, executing several data processing tasks simultaneously

multiple pass program, a procedure which needs more than one run to generate the required results

multiple precision notation, the use of two or more computer words to define a single number

multiple process operating system, an operating system which is capable of accessing more than one application and executing more than one function at a time

multiple programming, directing a computer to handle more than one operation at the same time

multiplex, to combine signals to or from multiple sources over a single line

multiplex data terminal, a terminal which processes data between two or more input/output devices

multiplexed bus, a bus wherein is combined address and data signals supported by independent control lines

multiplexer, a device which combines and separates signals from and to multiple sources and destinations

multiplexer, time division, a device which interleaves signals from several sources at timed intervals

multiplexing, sending multiple signals over a single line

multiplexing, byte, delegating time slots on a channel to different sources so that bytes can be interlaced in sequence

multiplexing, frequency-division, dividing the available transmission frequency range into narrower bands which can each be used as a separate channel

multiplexor, multiplexer

multiplicand, a number which is to be multiplied by another number

multiplication shift, moving binary digits in a register one place to the right which is the means of multiplying the number by 2

multiplication table, a numeric array used for a lookup during a multiplication process

multiplier, analog, a device which calculates a variable equal to the product of two or more variable input signals

multiplier, digital, a device which multiplies the representation of two digital numbers by shift and addition

multiplier, function, a device designed to produce an analog output which is the product of two analog inputs

multiply/divide package, a set of subroutines which execute single and double precision multiplication and division of binary numbers

multi-point circuit, a circuit which connects multiple time sharing terminals

multi-point data link, the station in a network which is designated as the controller to manage and monitor data flow to all other stations

multi-precision arithmetic, computer arithmetic in which two or more computer words are used to represent each number

multi-priority, referring to a queue containing items of varying priority

multiprocessing, executing two or more tasks simultaneously within a computer system

multiprocessing, mass-data, a system whereby various levels and types of processing are performed simultaneously; processing of a single database by two or more computers in tandem

multiprocessor, a computer with multiple arithmetic and logic units which can be used simultaneously

multiprocessor interleaving, the process of alternating memory calls for the most efficient use of a multiprocessor

multiprogramming, executing two or more programs simultaneously on a single computer

multiprogramming interrupt, an interrupt which permits the efficient running of more than one program at the same time

multiprogramming priority, the allocation of resources which are shared when running more than one program, whether allowing equal system time to all programs or a greater share to one

multiscan system, a monitor which can be scanned at rate within a given range, in contrast to a monitor limited to the 60 Hz standard

multitasking, simultaneous execution of more than one program, program segment or task on one computer

multi-user, referring to equipment

which may be available to two or more users at the same time

multi-user system, a computer system with multiple terminals, all of which may be used at the same time

multi-view port, a CRT image which is split into several viewing areas, each of which may be addressed independently

musical instrument digital interface, (MIDI) a protocol for communication between a digitized musical instrument and the computer

music synthesizer, a computer peripheral and software which enables a user to create music

N

n, used to signify a variable, often user defined

N, negative; often used as a prefix, as in *N-channel*

NAK, negative acknowledge; a control signal which indicates that a transmission error occurred in the last data block sent

name, a label which identifies a program, a routine, a data set, a data file, etc.

name, data, one or more words used to identify a record in a data base

named program, a program referenced from within another program

name, file, the characters which identify a particular file

name, field, the name of a database record field, usually descriptive of its content

name, procedure, a label used to call up a catalogued procedure

name, program, an alias or label which identifies a particular program

name, variable, the identifier of a program element which can assume a range of values

NAND, not and; the logical negation of AND

NAND gate, a logic gate whose output is 0 if all its inputs are 1 and is 1 in any other situation

nano-, a prefix meaning one billionth

nanosecond, one billionth of a second

nanosecond circuit, a circuit in which changes in state are measured in billionths of a second

narrow band, referring to a communication line similar to a voice grade line but operating at a lower frequency

native compiler, a compiler which is designed to produce code only for the computer on which it is run

native language, the machine language understood by a particular type of processor

natural language, a spoken language; not a computer language

natural language processing, the use of a spoken language to pass instructions to a computer

natural language system, a computer system that accepts a spoken language as contrasted to a machine language

NC, numerical control; controlling a machine using digital data

NC language processor, a numerical control program which creates a mathematical representation of a geometric shape

NC system, a device which uses programmed numerical data to control machine functions

NDR, non-destructive read; the process of copying information from storage with no alteration in the status or contents of the original

negate, to perform the logical NOT operation

negation gate, a device which converts a signal, condition, or state to its opposite

negative acknowledge, (NAK) a control signal which indicates that a transmission error occurred in the last data block sent

negative feedback, a negative acknowledge; a reverse feed which inhibits input until a condition is met, such as correction of a transmission error

negative-true logic, a system in which signals are reversed so that high voltage represents 0 rather than 1

nest, a program statement, a portion of a program or data which is contained within another program or data element

nesting, placing one program statement, routine or data element inside another such as nesting loops or nesting IF statements which direct that when a condition is met, another IF statement test for additional conditions, etc.

nesting level, the level at which a program element exists, especially important when testing for a condition in which an improper sequence of tests can inadvertently eliminate valid data; the level at which a macroinstruction is processed

nesting loop, a loop that contains an inner loop; an **outside loop**

network, the connecting of a number of computers and peripherals to function in harmony; the elements so connected

network, analog, circuits which represent physical variables in such a way that mathematical relationship between the variables can be examined by checking the relationship of the electronic signals in the circuit

network architecture, the configuration of a communications system

network awareness, a system in which the CPU is always informed of the state of the elements in a network

network bus, a communication line which connects the stations of a local area network

network, communication, the complex of channels, transmitters, and receivers required to carry data from one installation to another

network, data communications, the hardware components and the connections between them necessary for transferring data between one or more remote stations and the data base

network, distributed-processing, data processing shared by two or more host computers in a network of computers and terminals

network drive, a disk drive which is the main storage of data for users of a network; also called a file server

networking, enabling various processors and terminals to communicate within the same environment

network, local area, a limited number of workstations connected to each other or to a common host or file server

network, packet switching, a network which employs packet switching for communications

network, ring, a network in which terminals and computers are connected in series with the last member connected back to the first to form a loop

network server, a computer which manages programs and data for several other smaller computers or workstations connected to it

network, star, a network in which terminals and computers are each connected directly to a main computer

new input queue, a line of new messages waiting for processing

new-line character, a control character that moves the print head to a new line; a line feed

nibble, one half a byte, or a string of four bits handled as a unit

n key rollover, a keyboard buffer which allows typing faster than characters can be echoed to the monitor screen; a technique for holding entries from the keyboard to await processing up to n characters, n being a user-defined value; also called **type-ahead buffer**

n level logic, logic gates connected in such a way that a limited number of gates are in a series, with the number of allowable gates indicated by the variable n

no address instruction, a computer instruction which can be executed without the need to retrieve data from memory

node, any computer, terminal or work station in a network

noise, undesirable variation in an electronic signal; any disturbance or random signal which tends to interfere with normal operation or has the ability to corrupt data in transmission

noise, background, extraneous data which must be removed in the course of processing; extraneous material picked up by an optical scanner, especially troublesome in OCR processing; errors introduced into the system by electrical or other fluctuation; in general, any disturbance which interferes with operations

noise, carrier, undesirable variations in the frequency of a signal caused by the physical medium which is carrying the signal

non-arithmetic shift, a binary shift in which any digits dropped off one end of a computer word are moved to the other end

non-breaking hyphen, in word processing, a special hyphen, inserted by the user in a hyphenated word which is to be kept together on one line, as a hyphenated name

non-breaking space, in word processing, a special space, inserted by the user between two words or elements which are to be kept together on one line

non-destructive read, (NDR) the process of copying information from storage with no alteration in the status or contents of the original

non-equivalence element, a circuit which performs the exclusive-OR operation

non-equivalence operation, exclusive-OR; a logical operation which sets to 0 if two compared bits are the same and to 1 if they are different

non-erasable storage, storage elements or media which cannot be erased or changed, such as punched cards or paper tape; stored data which is coded as read-only such as ROM or protected files

non-executable statement, a program statement which sets up a program or procedure as contrasted to a command which directs the performance of a task

non-impact printer, a printer which produces an image by means other than directly striking the paper such as ink jet, electrostatic, electrophotographic, etc.

non-numeric programming, programming which does not entail any numeric calculations

non-operable instruction, an instruction which performs no operation, but is included to provide space for the addition of an instruction in the future or to advance the program counter

non-printing character, a control character

non-procedural language, a language which indicates only what is to be done and not how it is to be done

non-programmed halt, any stoppage of computer operation which is not attributable to a program command

non-switched line, a direct link between a terminal and computer which is always open

non-synchronous, not related by speed, frequency, or phase; **asynchronous**

non-volatile memory, computer memory which retains its content when power is off

nonvolatile storage, same as **non-volatile memory**

no-op instruction, an instruction which performs no operation, but is included to provide space for the addition of an instruction in the future or to advance the program counter

no-operation Instruction, same as **no-op instruction**

NOR, not OR; the logical negation of OR

NOR gate, a logic circuit which produces an output of 0 if any of its input values are 1

normalization routine, a system which standardizes floating point numbers for arithmetic operations

normalized form, the configuration of a floating point number which has been standardized so that the mantissa lies within a specified range

NOT, the logical NOT operation

notation, a system of symbols, mnemonics, reserved words, etc. used to represent instructions or quantities; the representation of instructions, quantities, etc. by symbols, reserved words, etc.

notation, fixed radix, a system of numeric notation in which the value of each digit in a number is determined by its position

notation, scientific, a system of expressing very large or very small numbers as powers of ten

notebook PC, a personal computer which combines small size with the capabilities of a desktop computer, operating with 286 and 386 processors, 2–4 MB RAM and storage in the range of 20–60 MB

NOT gate, a logic circuit which produces an output value which is the reverse of its input value

NOT operation, a Boolean operation which produces an output which is the opposite of the input, thus 1 becomes 0 and 0 becomes 1

ns, nanosecond; one billionth of a second

nucleus, part of a control program or operating system which must be always available in main memory

null, the absence of data, as contrasted to *zero* or *blank*

null character, a control character which fills space or time without having any other effect on an operation

null instruction an instruction which does not execute any commands

null modem, a cable which permits a device to be connected directly to a communication port

null set, a set which contains no elements, used for testing

null string, an empty data string

null suppression, a form of data compression which ignores all null characters

number, a character, word, or symbol which represents a numerical quantity

number base, the number of characters available for use in a numbering system; the base of a numbering system

number, binary, a number represented in base 2

number, check, a number which is transmitted to test data transmission equipment

number crunching, processing and displaying numeric data in a variety of formats and configurations for analysis, such as financial studies and reports; complex manipulation of a large volume of numerical data

number, decimal, a number represented in base 10

number, double length, a number requiring great accuracy which is represented by a binary number of double the binary digits that the computer's word length allows and uses two registers or storage locations; a double precision number

number, double precision, a double length number

number, floating-point, a number characterized by a base value raised to a power

number generator, a device which permits manual entry of a computer word

number, hexadecimal, a number represented in base sixteen, with the 16 integers represented by the numbers 0 through 9 plus the letters A through F

number, random, one of a series of unrelated numeric values selected from an orderless set

number, self-checking, a number which includes an extra digit, used to detect errors in transmission

number, sequence, a number attached to an item to indicate its relative position in a set

number, statement, the number of a line of code in a program used to locate it for debugging, etc.; synonymous with **line number**

number system, a technique for representing numbers using a fixed base, so that the relative position of an integer within the number determines its value, such as decimal, binary or hexadecimal

number theory, that part of pure mathematics which deals with the properties of and relationships between integers

number, positional, a number system in which each successive position to the left has a higher value, expressed as a power of the base, and each position to the right has a correspondingly lower value

number, radix, the base number or value of a numbering system

numeral, a symbol which represents a number; the figure 0 through 9 in a decimal system

numeralization, a system for representing alphabetic and symbolic data numerically

numerator, a quantity which is divided by another quantity

numeric, referring to digits, integers numbers, or numerals as contrasted to letters

numerical analysis, the analysis of a problem which has been reduced to or expressed in mathematical terms; the methods of computing answers to numerical problems

numerical control, (NC) controlling a machine using digital data

numerical integration, the method of finding the area under a curve by dividing the area into many small columns, adding the heights of the columns and multiplying the total by the width of the columns

numeric character, a digit, integer or numeral

numeric code, a code system which uses only numbers

numeric coding, coding which uses only numerals to depict instructions and data

numeric constant, a value which does not change; a self-defining numeric

numeric data, data which consists only of numerals

numeric keypad, an extra set of number keys on some keyboards, similar to those on a calculator, which allow fast entry of numbers and numeric operators and usually toggle between numeric and cursor movement functions

numeric processor chip, an auxiliary processor created to manage high-speed arithmetic and scientific functions

numeric word, a computer word comprised of numerals

O

object code, the code produced by a compiler or assembler translation from source code

object computer, the computer which executes an object program, which may be different from the **source computer** which assembles the program or stores input

object deck, a set of punched cards which contain an object program

object language, machine language specific to a particular computer, usually the output of an assembling or compiling operation; **native language; machine language**

object language programming, writing instructions directly to a computer in machine language

object linking and embedding, (OLE) a program device which allows an element created in one application to be inserted in an element created by another, so that when the imbedded element is modified, the user can elect to automatically modify it in every place it is being used

object machine, same as **object computer**

object module, an object program coupled with loading and linking instructions

object oriented programming, a programming technique in which the definition of a data type includes definitions of the operations which may be performed on the data

object program, a program which has been converted into machine language and is ready to run

OCR, optical character recognition; a technique for identifying typed or printed copy scanned into the computer, either of special characters designed for ease in recognition or of any typeface based on comparison with a set of standard matrixes

OCR data entry, data entry by means of optical character recognition, either through a device which reads and directly translates special characters from a source document or through a program which identifies and translates characters which have been scanned and imported as graphics

OCR program, a computer program designed to read copy scanned in as graphics and translate it to character bits for input to a word processor

OCR reader, a device designed to read and translate special printed characters for computer input

OCR source data entry, data entry by means of optical character recognition through a device which reads and directly translates special characters from a source document

octal, a number system in the base eight

octal numeral, a numeral in the octal system represented by the digits 0, 1, 2, 3, 4, 5, 6, or 7

octal point, the equivalent, in an octal number, of a decimal point

odd-even checking, a system for confirming the accuracy of an operation through an extra bit in a computer word which indicates whether the word had an odd or even number of 1's

odd parity, the condition which exists when there is an odd number of 1's, including the parity bit, in a byte or data word

odd parity check, a test for transmission accuracy which compares the sum of the bits in a computer word with a previously calculated bit sum which indicates an even or odd number of 1's in the original word

OEM, original equipment manufacturer; the company which manufactures or assembles a finished product for market, whether a component of a computer system or a complete system

off, emergency, an automatic control switch which cuts off all power to a system in the event of a spike, severe equipment malfunction, etc.

office automation, the use of computer systems to assist in the routine tasks of running a business such as accounting, inventory control, etc.

off-line, any function not integrated with the main system, although associated with it, such as an accounting system in which checks for payroll or accounts payable are written through a different program or machine than that which processes accounting data; a system or part of a system which is shut down

off-line operation, a task which is performed by a program or machine independent of the main program or machine

off-line processing, the execution of an off-line operation

off-line storage, storage which is not under the control of the computer

offset, a value added to a base address to get an effective address

off the shelf, hardware or software which is widely available and ready for use without alteration to suit the user

ohm, the measure of electric resistance

OLE, object linking and embedding; a program device which allows an element created in one application to be inserted in an element created by another, so that when the imbedded element is modified, the user can elect to automatically modify it in every place it is being used

one address instruction, a computer instruction which is limited to one command and involves one address

one chip computer, a computer in which all main components (CPU, RAM, ROM, clock, etc.) are on a single chip; **computer on a chip**

one-dimensional array, an arrangement of data consisting of a single row or line of elements

one element, a circuit which executes the logical OR operation

one-for-one, a relationship between sets in which each element in one corresponds exactly with the comparable element in another

one-for-one translation, in a computer program, producing one machine instruction for each programming statement

one-out-of-ten code, a ten-bit binary word in which a decimal digit value is represented by a 1 in the position which corresponds to that numeral, 0 through 9

one's complement, a binary number which is obtained by changing each bit to its opposite, 1's to 0's and 0's to 1's

one step operation, the execution of a computer program, one instruction at a time

one-to-one, a relationship between sets in which each element of one set relates to a single comparable element of another

on-line, a computer component, peripheral, program or process which is connected directly to the main computer; a computer or peripheral which is powered up and ready to run

on-line adapter, a high speed computer memory to memory link

on-line central file, the library of applications and data files which are readily available to the user

on-line compiler, a program which compiles a source code program one line at a time, allowing on-line editing while producing a fully compiled object program; an interactive, incremental compiler

on-line data base, a data base which can be continuously updated and is readily accessible, such as the reservations and seating database used by airlines or a fully automated inventory program

on-line data processing, data processing which is performed by computer, without user interaction

on-line diagnostics, running diagnostic routines which monitor the computer while it is performing other tasks

on-line documentation, information which is displayed as a program is being run or which can be called up by the user as needed

on-line equipment, any equipment or peripherals connected to the main computer and ready to run

on-line mode, the status of a computer, or peripherals connected to and controlled by the computer, in which they are ready to run

on-line processing, the processing of data as it is being entered into the computer, such as an **on-line data base**; processing which takes place in the computer or on peripherals under the control of the computer

on-line storage, non-volatile memory which is connected to and controlled by the computer

on-line system, a procedure whereby data is fed into the computer directly from its point of origin, as in some cash register, banking and airline systems

on-line testing, test equipment connected directly to the CPU for monitoring tasks as they are performed

op code, operation code; a symbol which directs the computer to execute an operation; a single instruction in assembly language

open, referring to a file which has been accessed and which may therefore be altered

open-ended system, a computer or computer system which may be modified or to which additional input/output devices may be added without disrupting the original system or the purpose for which it was intended

open loop, a loop which pauses after each iteration, usually with operator access to output, in order to allow user input such as to continue, alter instructions or exit

open loop control system, a routine for checking transmission without feedback, in which the check data is contained in the transmission data, such as a parity check

open routine, a routine which can be inserted into a program other than that for which it was originally designed

open shop, an installation in which the operation of computers is not restricted to specifically designated individuals or by job description

open subroutine, a subroutine which can be inserted where it is needed in a program

operand, a number or variable on which an operation is performed

operand, literal, an operand which indicates directly the value of a constant as contrasted to a relative value or an address for the value

operating code, a symbol which directs the computer to execute an operation; a single instruction in assembly language; **op code**

operating ratio, the relationship between total available time and the time during which data processing or other equipment is operating correctly

operating system, the program which handles the routine functions of computer operation such as reading the keyboard, accessing memory, managing input and output, etc.; **main program**

operating system, supervisory, same as **operating system**

operation, an activity which is directed by a single computer instruction; executing such activity

operational character, a special character code which controls a machine function, such as that of a line feed or clearing the monitor screen

operational mode, the computer operating mode which is in effect

operation code, a symbol which directs the computer to execute an operation; a single instruction in assembly language

operation cycle, the time lapse from the retrieval of an instruction to the completion and storage of the results of executing that instruction; **operation time**

operation, auxiliary, a task performed by equipment which is not under the constant control of the CPU; also peripheral operation

operation, dyadic, any operation which require two operands such as addition, multiplication, subtraction, etc.

operation, dyadic Boolean, a Boolean procedure using operators such as AND, OR, etc. which act on pairs of operands

operation, full duplex, a routine in which data is transmitted in two directions at the same time

operation, half duplex, a routine in which data is transmitted in only one direction at a time

operation, iterative a routine which automatically repeats the same operation with different values, as in a **loop**

operation, jump, the performance of a jump instruction; an instruction which directs the computer to interrupt processing and to move to another part of the program, usually as the result of certain conditions

operation, logic, a non-arithmetic operation executed by the computer, such as a comparison, branch, etc.

operation, loop, instructions which are restored or modified prior to each iteration of the loop

operation, peripheral, a task performed by equipment which is not under the constant control of the CPU; also auxiliary operation

•**operations,** the division of an organization responsible for maintenance of computer and information services

operations analysis, the use of data, manipulated and redefined by the computer to scrutinize operational problems; **numerical analysis**

operation, sequential, the execution of instructions in the order they are written, beginning one only after the previous instruction is completed

operations, logic, non-arithmetic operations executed by the computer, such as comparisons

operations manual, the detailed specifications and instructions pertaining to a given application

operation time, the time necessary to execute an operation; an **operation cycle**

operator, a person responsible for the operation of a computer or computer system; a symbol representing an arithmetic or logic function, such as +, -, *, /, >, etc.; the part of an instruction which indicates the action to be performed on the operand

operator console, the device which an operator uses to communicate with a computer, consisting of a control panel and usually a keyboard; a computer user's station consisting of a terminal or screen and a keyboard

operator control panel, the part of a console which contains manual controls and switches

operator, logic, the operators used in Boolean or symbolic logic, such as AND, OR, etc.

op register, a computer register which holds the code for the next instruction

optical bar-code reader, a scanner, either hand held or built into a checkout counter, which reads bar codes

optic cable, a set of optic fibers

optical character reader, a device which can read and translate printed characters, usually specially designed to facilitate reading by the computer

optical character recognition (OCR), a technique for identifying typed or printed copy scanned into the computer, either of special characters designed for ease in recognition or of any typeface based on comparison with a set of standard matrixes

optical detector, a device which converts signals from an optical fiber to electrical impulses

optical fiber, a hair-thin glass strand used for the transmission of laser light signals

optical fiber cladding, a material

that protects optical fiber from external light

optical mark reader, a device which reads dark marks, as those made with a soft pencil, from specific locations on a card or document

optical reader, any device which reads by optic scanning such as an optical character reader or an optical mark reader

optical recognition, same as **optical character recognition, optical scanning**

optical scanner, a device which scans images and converts them to digital data, whether directly entered to the computer as part of a database, for conversion by OCR to characters for word processing or as black and white or color graphics which can be altered and used in a variety of ways

optical scanning, scanning of an image into the computer for further processing

optical wand, a hand held optical scanner used to read bar codes or other similar codes

optic cable, a set of optic fibers

optimization, the continual monitoring and adjustment of an action in an attempt to improve performance

optimize, to alter conditions in order to achieve the best possible performance; to improve programs and data storage in order to minimize access and execution time

optimized code, the most direct solution to a problem; a program which contains no unnecessary instructions

optimum coding, coding of a program or routine to maximize efficiency, such as reducing access or execution time, using less memory, etc.

options, alternatives which may be selected by the user, such as type of screen display, printer output, relative time-sharing for background processing, etc.

OR, a logical operator which outputs 1 if either of two inputs is 1

OR circuit, an **OR gate**

order, to arrange in a particular sequence; the rank of an element in an ordered sequence

ordering, sorting and arranging data in a predetermined sequence

orderly close down, to shut down a system by first polling all stations for activity, then closing all open files and programs, so that there is no loss of data or interruption of work in progress

OR gate, a circuit which performs the logical OR operation

original equipment manufacturer, (OEM) the company which manufactures or assembles a finished product for market, whether a component of a computer system or a complete system

OS, operating system

oscilloscope, a device which displays graphically the value of voltage over time

out of range, a value higher or lower than that which is designated in an instruction

output, the results obtained by computer processing, made available to the user on screen, through a printer or to a storage file; information transferred between a computer and another device; to cause information to be transferred between the computer and another

device

output area, a section of storage reserved for the output of a computer; a buffer

output data, data which is sent out to the screen, printer, storage file, etc.

output device, any device displays the computer's output, such as a monitor screen or printer

output enable, the signal which controls output traffic, thus eliminating bus contention

output limited, program processing which is restricted to the speed with which output can be processed

output routine, a routine which controls the data output

outside loop, a series of instructions comprising a loop, part of which contains one or more secondary loops

overflow, arithmetic, a condition which occurs when the result of an arithmetic operation is larger than the space allocated to hold it; a condition often caused by an incorrect allocation of a fixed position address in the program; the bits or numerals which exceed the space allocated for them

overflow check indicator, a device which indicates that an operation has produced a number too large for the system to handle

overflow indicator, a flag which is set when an overflow occurs

overflow position, an extra location in a register to which an overflow digit can be written

overhead, the storage space on a disk which is lost due to formatting; the RAM space lost to the operating system, TSR's, working environment, etc.

overhead bit, a bit which carries control information, such as a stop bit, parity bit, etc.

overlap, to have more than one operation in process at the same time; **multi-tasking**

overlay, to use the same area of memory for different routines at different times; a program or part of a program which is placed over another program in memory

overlay, executive, a program from which other programs can be run, and to which control is returned when the run is completed

overlay, keyboard, a flexible film designed to fit over the keys of a particular keyboard, either used only to protect the keys or to label keys which have been reprogrammed for special functions

overlay load module, a load module which is divided into segments to facilitate the loading of program segments as they are needed

overlay program, a program which is designed to use the same areas of memory for different parts of the program at different times

overlay region, a special section of memory into which programs can be loaded and overlaid as needed

overlay supervisor, a routine which controls and manages the overlaying of program segments

overload, a condition caused by an input which is faster or more concentrated than the computer can handle

overload level, the level at which a system or component ceases to function properly due to a hardware or software failure

overprint, to print a second, identical character over one already printed to simulate bold face type

override interrupt, an interrupt which cannot be disarmed or disabled

overstrike, indicating deletion by overprinting text with a strikeout character; to print a second, identical character over one already printed to simulate bold face type

overwrite, to enter new data over data previously stored in memory and thereby deleting or destroying the original data

P

pack, to compress data by storing more than one datum in each computer word See also unpack

packaged software, commercial application programs designed for specific purposes, such as word processing, data base, etc., offered for lease in retail establishments or by mail order; see also **proprietary program**

package, program, a collection of programs relating to a single application, such as the various parts of an accounting package; an integrated software package which includes several applications, such as a business package containing word processing, spreadsheet and database functions

pack, disk, a number of magnetic disks connected by a spindle and packaged for insertion in a hard disk drive

packed data, a technique for condensing files so that the amount which can be stored on a magnetic disk is greatly increased: it is necessary to **unpack** such disks before the computer can access the data

packed decimal, storing two digits or a digit and code in one byte; same as **packed format**

packed file, same as **packed data**

packed format, a system of storing two decimal digits to a byte

packet, in communications, an independent block of data which contains its own addressing and control information

packet, electronic mail, a block of messages with its own addressing and control information

packet switching, transmitting data in a communications network by breaking it down into uniform packets which reassembled by the receiving computer

packet switching network, a network which employs packet switching for communications

pack, hard disk, two or more disks joined by a spindle and mounted in a packet for insertion into a hard disk drive

packing density, the number of bits per sector or measured unit in mass storage, such as disk or tape

packing density, file, the ratio between data stored in a file and the amount of data the file can hold

packing factor, same as **packing density**

pad, the metallic area on a chip to which leads are attached; to fill empty spaces in a fixed length block with dummy characters

pad character, a character which is inserted only to fill time or space

padding, filling the empty spaces in a fixed length block with dummy characters

page, a fixed-length block of memory which is the unit a system or program uses when transferring data from storage to RAM; a single sheet of output from the printer

page addressing, accessing large sections of memory by dividing the memory into pages, or sections which the computer can handle efficiently

page frame, the area in memory to which a page is copied when it is requested by a program

page heading, on a printed page, the information at the top, such as title, page number, etc.; also called a **header**

page printer, a device which composes a full page in memory and then prints the entire page at one time

page reader, a scanner which captures the image of a physical document page; a scanner which reads the marks in fixed locations from a page, as of a multiple choice test, etc.

page size, in computer memory management, the number of bytes in a page, ranging from 256 for early microcomputers to 16,000 (16K) in MS-DOS® 5.0; referring to a printer, the physical dimensions of a printed page or the page size which a printer can accommodate

pagination, formatting a document to be printed into individual pages; the page numbering of a printed document

paging, transferring memory pages between storage elements; same as **mapping**

PAL, programmable array logic; a grouping of logical OR and AND circuits which can be programmed to execute specific tasks; also called programmable logic array

panel, control, the part of a console which contains manual controls and switches; a removable board which can be wired to control equipment operation

panel, graphic, a control panel which shows the lines of communication between the components controlled

panel, operator control, the part of a console which contains manual controls and switches

panic button, an emergency button; a fictional alarm button which is pressed in emergency

paper, fan-fold, continuous paper divided into uniform pages separated by a perforation and folded along the perforations in an accordion-like style; continuous forms

paper feed, the unit on a printer which controls the flow of paper through the printer

paper tape, tape which stores data in rows of holes and spaces; also called **perforated tape** or **punched tape**

paper tape reader, a device which converts the holes in punched paper tape into binary signals

parallel, referring to operations or events which occur in synchronization with each other or at the same time

parallel access, concurrent access to all bits comprising a character or word

parallel adder, an adder which manipulates a series of digits as a group, or simultaneously

parallel arithmetic, a method of operating on more than one digit at a time, in contrast to **serial arithmetic**

parallel computer, a computer which processes data lines as units, in contrast to serially, or one element at a time

parallel conversion, the process of replacing an old system by running it along with the new system until the changeover is completed

parallel input/output interface, a device which permits simultaneous input and output of data to peripherals

parallel interface, a multi-channel connection which permits transfer of a full computer word at a time

parallel printing, printing a full row of characters at one time

parallel processing, simultaneous execution of two or more programs or routines

parallel run test, verifying a new system by running an old system at the same time using the same data

parallel storage, storage in which all bits of a word are processed simultaneously

parallel transfer, the transfer of all bits or characters of a word simultaneously

parallel transmission, a system communication in which all bits in a block or string are sent simultaneously

parameter, a variable which is set to a constant value for specific circumstances; a limit or guideline

parameter testing, using a parameter in a test routine to ensure that input produces the desired output

parameter word, a word which contains the parameters, or the address of parameters, which define or limit the action of a subroutine

parametric subroutine, a sub-routine which adjusts parameters passed from other parts of the program

parity, describing a quantity as even or odd

parity bit, the bit that is added to achieve **bit parity**

parity check, a test for transmission accuracy which compares the sum of the bits in a computer word with a previously calculated sum bit which indicates an even or odd number of 1's in the original word

parity check, even, testing for dropped bits during transmission by making parity in all words even and checking parity after transmission

parity check, odd, testing for dropped bits during transmission by making parity in all words odd and checking parity after transmission

parity error, the loss of a bit or bits in the transmission of a computer word

parity, even, the condition which exists when there is an even number of 1's, including the parity bit, in a byte or data word

parity flag, a flag which indicates whether the bit parity of a word is even or odd

parity interrupt, an interrupt which is caused by a parity error

parity, odd, the condition which exists when there is an odd number of 1's, including the parity bit, in a byte or data word

parse, to break an element down into its logical components; converting a high-level computer language statement into detailed machine language

parse, data, converting data from one file format to another, such as from a spreadsheet to a database, by breaking down the data strings which comprise the records from the source file to logical fields or columns to be entered into the target file format

parser, a program which translates or breaks down program statements according to the syntax of the language

partial program, a program which is not complete by itself; a subroutine

partition, a division or separation; a segment of the computer's main memory reserved for a particular function

partition sort, a sort which is accomplished by dividing a list into smaller lists which are ordered individually and then recombined

party line, a cable which connects a central computer to a number of terminals, workstations or peripherals

party line driver, a driver which controls terminals, workstations, etc. along the same line

Pascal, a structured, high-level language, commonly used for microcomputers, designed to encourage the use of modular programs

pass, one run through a set of data; complete execution of a cycle in a loop

pass, sorting, one access of each record in the process of reordering a series of records

password, an identification or security code which allows a user to access the programs and data in a system

patch, a routine added to a program

to make a change or correct an error

patching, correcting or altering a program by adding a routine

path, a logical course; the course taken by a computer in executing a subroutine; in a hierarchical file structure, the user-defined course along which the computer is directed to search for programs, subprograms, operating system commands and data files

path, main, the principal course or direction of a program; the path which defines the location of the operating system

pattern recognition, computer identification of shapes as definable elements as in MICR or OCR programs

PC, printed circuit; personal computer; program counter

peak transfer rate, the rate at which data is transferred, measured as actual transfer time only, disregarding gaps

PEEK, a command in BASIC and some other computer languages which allows the user to inspect the contents of a specific memory location

pen, light, a device which is used to select elements or modify the display on a monitor screen

pen plotter, a device controlled by the computer which creates graphics by manipulating one or more pens on paper

people/machine interface, any device or technique which permits communication between a user and a computer

perforated tape, same as **paper tape**

perforator, a device operated from a keyboard which punches holes in paper tape

peripheral, any device connected to, and usually controlled by, a computer

peripheral bus, a bus which interfaces with a peripheral device

peripheral compatibility, the ability to exchange peripherals of the same type, such as two printers from different manufacturers

peripheral device, programmable, any peripheral device which contains its own processor, eliminating the need for direct control by the computer

peripheral disk system, file storage on a disk system outside the computer

peripheral driver, an interface module between a digital device and a non-digital peripheral device

peripheral equipment, any equipment, not essential to the operation of the computer, which may be added to the computer system

peripheral interface, an interface card which plugs into one of the computer's card slots; a plug which connects a computer and a peripheral device

peripheral operation, a task performed by equipment which is not under the constant control of the CPU; also **auxiliary operation**

peripheral power supply, a power supply which is part of, or dedicated to, a peripheral device; a peripheral device which assures continuous power by sensing any drop in voltage to the computer and automatically taking over when such drop occurs

peripheral processor, a processor which handles input and output, thus relieving the CPU for other tasks; same as **input/output processor**

peripheral program, software which manages the operation of a peripheral device and its interface with the computer; a program which adds special features to another program although not critical to the operation of the main program, such as a grammar or spelling checker in a word processor program

peripheral slot, a card slot in the computer case which holds the controller of a peripheral device

peripheral storage, mass storage which is outside the computer case, such as a disk or tape unit

permanent dynamic storage, storage of data which can be altered but which is not lost when power is turned off, such as tape, fixed disk or floppy disk storage

permanent error, an error which is not removed when data is reprocessed, usually the result of a programming error

permanent fault, a constant or repeated failure of a device to perform properly

permanent memory, nonvolatile storage which retains its content when power is off

permutation, all possible changes of sequence within a group

permutation index, a document index which lists each key word in each title so that the document may be searched by those words

personal computer, (PC) a microcomputer, originally designed for a single user, now often linked to a mainframe or to a network of personal computers, used for a variety of applications, such as business accounting and management, learning, desktop publishing, preparing audio-visual presentations, monitoring and controlling manufacturing operations, home security, etc.

personal information manager, a utility program which offers a variety of options to the user for taking notes: essentially a combination word processor and data base, some are **TSR** and can be activated from anywhere in the computer, some will associate notes by subject or date and time, create outlines, search for notes by a key word, maintain a list of appointments, phone numbers, contacts, expenses, etc.

PERT, program evaluation and review technique; a system for the management of complex projects which involves analysis of the time frame for each step and its relation to the time frame for other steps in order to develop a critical path for the most efficient and timely completion of the project

phantom character, a character which can be produced by the printer, but which is not represented on the keyboard: some programs allow insertion of such characters by typing special codes or inserting from a special character menu

phase, a distinct stage or condition; a time-related condition, such as the position of the amplitude of a signal at a given instant; to operate two or more elements in harmony

phase, execute, the part of a program cycle when an operation is being performed

phase logic, the program logic

which switches a machine from one phase, or type of operation, to another

phase, run, the part of a machine cycle during which a compiled program is run

phase shift, a change in the relative time between parts of a signal wave form without change in the form of the signal

phase, sorting, the operations of a sort program: initialization, internal, and merge phases

phoneme, the smallest unit in the sound system of a language; a distinctive sound which is a component of a spoken word

phonetic system, a system of machine generated or voice sourced speech synthesis which constructs words from phonemes

phosphor, a material which emits visible light when stimulated by an electron beam

phosphor dots, spots on the screen of a cathode ray tube which are selectively stimulated to create images

phosphorescence, light emission which continues after stimulation is ended

photocell, a device which converts light into an electrical signal

photocell matrix, a photocell array used in optical character recognition

photoconductivity, electrical conductivity which is influenced by incident light

photoelectric reader, a device which reads data from a paper tape by sensing the light passing through holes punched in the tape

photo optics, a technique which produces an output signal from a light input

physical record, the data contained in a segment of memory including blanks, spaces, etc.

PIC, priority intercept controller; a chip which manages external interrupts

pica, a standard printing measure, equal to 12 point or one-sixth of an inch; a typewriter type font which measures six lines to the inch in height and produces 10 characters per linear inch

picture element, a **pixel**

pie chart, a graphic representation of parts of the whole as wedges cut from a circle

piezoelectric crystal, a crystal which vibrates at a specific frequency when an electrical current is applied to it and which generates an electrical charge when subjected to pressure

pilot, an original or test program or device

PILOT, programmed inquiry learning or teaching; a computer language designed for the development of computer aided instruction programs

PIM, personal information manager

pin feed, the paper feed mechanism on a printer which uses pins fitting in the holes on the side strips of continuous feed or continuous form paper to guide it through the printer

piping, a technique available in some operating systems such as MS-DOS®, wherein two or more programs are strung together so that the output of one becomes the input for another

pirated software, illegal receipt or transfer of proprietary software

pitch, the width of a character including the white space surrounding it, in characters per inch

pixel, picture element; the smallest unit of a graphic image which the computer can address

PLA, programmable logic array; a grouping of logical OR and AND circuits which can be programmed to execute specific tasks; also called programmable array logic

place, a position in a number which represents its value as a power of the base of that number

place marker, a device in some application programs which is a reference marker in a document to which a user may easily return with the use of a special code

platen, on a printer, the surface which supports the paper or other receiver as a printing mechanism strikes to form characters

PL/1, programming language one; a powerful programming language developed by IBM® for its System/360 mainframe computer

plot, to diagram or draw, as a graph; a graphic representation of data

plotter, a device controlled by the computer which creates graphics by manipulating one or more pens on paper

plotter board, the surface of a plotter which holds the paper on which the pens create a graphic image

plug board, a removable board into which wires can be plugged to set up a computer program

plug board computer, a computer programmed by wiring connections on a plug board

plug, cordless, a connector which

has no flexible portion

plug-in unit, a self-contained electronic component which can be plugged in as a unit

plus zone, the bit position in a computer word which carries the plus sign

PM, preventive maintenance; checking and servicing equipment before problems develop in an attempt to prevent unexpected failure

pocket computer, an extremely small computer, usually designed to function as an address book, appointment calendar and calculator, although some are powerful enough to download a spreadsheet or database

point and click, refers to moving an arrow on the monitor screen with a mouse and clicking a mouse button; a method of selecting options by clicking on a menu item or entering selected data by clicking on the insertion point, with the use of a screen pointer under the control of a mouse

pointer, an address which contains the address of the register which contains the location of required data

point, fixed, a radix point which always appears in the same position in a number stored in a particular field of a data record

point, floating, a radix point which can appear anywhere in a number whose value is determined by an exponent

point of no return, the juncture in the run of a program when a rerun is no longer possible

point of sale system, a scheme which computerizes the functions related to retail transactions including, but not limited to, recording and reporting transactions, summarizing activity, tracking and adjusting inventory, etc.

point of sale terminal, a cash register device connected to a computer

point, reentry, the address of the next instruction in a main program which is executed after a subroutine or branch command is completed

point, restart, the juncture at which a temporarily halted program can be restarted

POKE, a program instruction which allows the placement of a specific value to a specific memory address

polar, characterized by two states or conditions of opposite value

polarity, characterized by difference in a single respect between points in a system, such as positive or negative charge

polarizing slot, a slot in a connector which permits insertion in only one orientation

Polish notation, a method of algebraic expression without parentheses to indicate the order of operations, in which the operators precede the operands; opposite of **reverse Polish notation**

poll, the examination of communication lines in sequence to determine if any peripherals need attention or prepared to transmit

pop, to remove an item from the top of a stack which advances the remaining items up one position

pop-up program, a program which causes a message to appear on the screen as the result of a user-defined condition, such as an appointment reminder, notice of an incoming fax, etc.; also, a **TSR**

port, the place where a peripheral device connects to the system

portable computer, a computer in its own carrying case and rechargeable battery pack which can carried about with relative ease; **notebook computer; laptop computer**

portable program, a program which can be run on more than one type of computer

portability, a quality of software which can be run on more than one type of computer or data which can be accessed by more than one program

port, input output, the connection between a computer and the data path to another device in the system

positional notation, the convention of attributing a value to a number based on its position relative to the radix point

positional number, a number system in which each successive position to the left of the radix point has a higher value, expressed as a power of the base, and each position to the right of the radix point has a correspondingly lower value

post, to enter information to a record; a prefix word denoting *after*

post edit, to edit data generated by a previous operation

post mortem, the review and analysis of an operation after it is completed

post mortem dump, a printout of the memory after a program or operation has completed processing

post mortem routine, a programmed routine which dumps the content of registers and memory to the printer for analysis at the completion of a run

power, in mathematics, the value of an exponent; the number of times a quantity is to be multiplied by itself to express the actual value represented by a number and its exponent

power fail circuit, a circuit which initiates a routine to save volatile data when a drop in power level is detected

power failure interrupt, an interrupt which permits an orderly close down when power fails

power supply, a device which converts relatively high voltage AC current from to low voltage DC current to power the computer; a **transformer**

power surge, a sudden, undesirable change in the level of power coming into the computer or within the computer

power up, to turn on, or initiate power to, a computer or peripheral

precedence, the order in which mathematical operations are executed by the computer

precision, the accuracy to which a quantity is expressed; the number of digits in a number which can be expressed by the computer or program

precision, double, descriptive of data which requires two computer words for storage and computation

precompiler, a program which seeks out errors in a source program before compilation

precompiler program, same as **precompiler**

predefined process, a referenced process or subroutine in a program

which has been elsewhere previously defined

predefined process symbol, a flowchart symbol which represents a subroutine

predefined variable, those codes or symbols in an application programs which represent variables which may be inserted into a document, such as page number, date, time, etc.

prefix notation, a form of arithmetic expression in which the mathematics operators precede the operands

preparation, data, organizing data into a form suitable for computer input and processing

preprocessor, a program or routine which processes or formats data for further processing by the program

prerecorded tracks, formatting on tape or disk which provides timing, counting, and addressing information

preset, to fix initial conditions; to set a variable to a starting value

pressure sensitive keyboard, a flexible membrane printed to look like the standard keyboard which it replaces and which sends the appropriate signals to the computer when touched

preventive maintenance, checking and servicing equipment before problems develop in an attempt to prevent unexpected failure

primary storage, the computer's main RAM memory

primitive, basic; a fundamental unit of data or of a programming language

print-control character, any of a number of characters which control the operation of a printer

printed circuit, a circuit whose elements are linked by printed or etched conducting paths

printed circuit assembly, a printed circuit board to which components have been attached

printed circuit board, a board designed to hold chips and other devices with the connections between them printed on the board

printed circuit card, same as **printed circuit board**

printed circuit connector, the connection by which a printed circuit board is plugged into the computer

printed circuit, multi-layer, circuitry in which layers of printed circuits are isolated by layers of insulation

printer, a device which reproduces copy on paper or other carrier, such as film

printer, bar, a printer which uses a series of long, narrow bars each of which contains a font of type and supports one print position

printer, chain, a line printer whose characters are mounted on a moving chain

printer, dot matrix, a printer which forms characters and graphics from a rectangular array of dots

printer, electrostatic, a printing process in which ink adheres to charged portions of paper or other receiver

printer fonts, fonts which are stored in the printer, a device attached to the printer, or which are formatted by the printer based on data sent from the computer

printer, high-speed, a draft printer which operates at speeds compat-

ible with the speed of processing

printer, ink jet, a printer which shoots tiny charged drops of ink at the paper, capable of forming a high resolution dot-matrix image

printer, letter-quality, a printer which uses formed character impact elements such as a daisy wheel, or a high resolution dot matrix printer

printer limited, program processing which is restricted to the speed with which the printer can operate

printer, line, an impact printer which forms a complete line of characters at a single stroke

printer, line dot-matrix, a dot-matrix printer which prints a complete line at a single stroke

printer mode, a hardware or software selection of the manner in which a printer interprets signals sent to it and which determines output from the printer, such as text mode, graphics mode, PostScript® mode, HP LaserJet® emulation mode, etc.

printer, non-impact, a printer which produces an image by means other than directly striking the paper such as ink jet, electrostatic, electrophotographic, etc.

printer, page, a device which composes a full page in memory and then prints the entire page at one time

printer port, the circuits designated for the connection between a terminal or computer and the printer

printer, serial, a printer which prints one character at a time in sequence

printer speed, the optimum rate at which a printer can produce hard copy under ideal conditions, usually expressed as characters per second, characters per minute or pages per minute

printer-terminal interface, the type of coupler between a printer and a computer or terminal

printer, thermal, a dot-matrix printer which uses hot wires to form characters on heat-sensitive paper

printer, wire, a printer which forms characters by using an array of wires to strike the paper or ribbon; a **dot-matrix printer**

print member, the device on a printer which transfers image to paper such as a type bar, daisy wheel, ink jet, etc.

printout, the output from a printer; hard copy

print positions, the number of positions, or characters, which can be printed on a line

Print Screen, a function key on some keyboards which dumps the contents of the screen to a printer

print server, a computer which manages the operation of a printer so that more than one computer in a network can share a common printer

priority, precedence; the order in which events are to take place; the position of an element in relationship to that of other devices or routines

priority indicator, characters, codes or other information which determine the order of transmission or execution

priority intercept controller, (PIC) a chip which manages external interrupts

priority interrupt, a temporary halt of the highest level which may not be interrupted by another

priority, interrupt, the indication of the relative status of possible interrupts, that is, which operations may be interrupted by which other operations

priority, multiprogramming, the allocation of resources which are shared when running more than one program, whether allowing equal system time to all programs or a greater share to one

priority ordered interrupts, the managing of interrupts by assigning priorities to peripherals, programs, processes, etc.

priority processing, the processing of jobs by assigned priority, as contrasted to the order in which they are submitted

priority selection, choosing the next job to run based on its priority and the availability of system resources

privileged instruction, a machine instruction which is accessible only to the operating system

probability model, a mathematical model using probability theory to predict how, or how well, a thing will function under both normal and adverse conditions

probability theory, the mathematical routine for determining the likelihood of an occurrence

probable error, a statistical evaluation to determine the likelihood that an element or value is in error or the amount of error likely to occur in a set of data

problem, benchmark, a routine used to determine the relative speed and efficiency of a computer or peripheral; same as a **benchmark program**

problem definition, a logical description of the elements of a problem or task

problem description, a programmer's assignment; a statement of the problem to be solved or task to be performed by a proposed program

problem oriented language, a high-level language designed to address a particular problem or type of problem

problem, test, a routine designed to determine whether a computer or a program is functioning properly

procedure, the steps which must be followed to accomplish a specific task

procedure name, a label used to call up a catalogued procedure

process, any of the functions undertaken by the computer; to manipulate data or otherwise perform a computer function

process bound, a computer operation in which the time required for completion is determined or limited by the time to perform a particular task, with the implication that the task is slower than any other task or input/output function

process control, monitoring and managing industrial processes with the aid of a computer

process control block, data which defines a specific process

process control computer, a computer which monitors and manages industrial processes

processing, any of the functions handled by a computer

processing, background, refers to automatic processing not under user control which occurs using available resources while foreground or user-controlled tasks are being performed

processing, batch, a technique whereby a quantity of records is processed at one time without user involvement

processing, concurrent, performing two or more tasks at the same time

processing, continuous, on-line or real-time processing as contrasted to batch processing

processing, data, generally used to describe any type of computer processing; specific manipulation of data such as selecting, sorting, etc.; the production of information and reports from stored data

processing, demand, real-time processing; manipulating data as soon as it becomes available

processing, electronic data, the gathering, maintenance and manipulation of information with the help of a computer

processing, information, generally, used to describe any type of computer processing; specific manipulation of data such as selecting, sorting, etc.; the production of information and reports from stored data

processing, integrated data, data processing in which all elements are coordinated so as to maximize efficiency

processing, interactive, data processing in real time which allows the user to edit data or the instructions operating on the data

processing interrupt, batch, the suspension of batch processing to allow execution of a real-time transaction

processing, off-line, the execution of an **off-line operation**

processing, on-line, the processing of data as it is being entered into the computer, such as an **on-line data base**; processing which takes place in the computer or on peripherals under the control of the computer

processing, parallel, simultaneous execution of two or more programs or routines

processing, real-time, the processing of data as it is received from remote locations while the transactions producing it are taking place, such as shop floor data collection, automated bank teller transactions, etc.

processing section, the elements of the CPU which perform arithmetic and logic functions

processing, serial, processing file records in stored sequence, one at a time

processing symbol, a flowchart symbol which represents a process

processor, a microprocessor or CPU; that part of the computer which actually controls the functions which manipulate data

processor, arithmetic, a **math coprocessor**; a special device which operates in conjunction with a CPU and which performs high-speed arithmetic operations

processor, associative, a processor which accesses data according to memory contents

processor, attached, a CPU connected to the main CPU, acting as an extension of it, sharing software, memory and peripheral devices

processor, auxiliary, a processor which is a server to the primary processor, designed to handle a

specific task

processor, back-end, a computer devoted to data processing, as contrasted to computation or other routines

processor, distributed, a computer containing several processors which share the task of running a program

processor, floating-point, an arithmetic device which is a support chip or an integral part of a CPU and performs floating point operations

processor, front end, a small computer which is a link between communications terminals and a larger host computer

processor, input/output, a processor which handles input and output, thus relieving the CPU for other tasks; same as **peripheral processor**

processor, I/O, see **input/output processor**

processor interrupt, a temporary halt called by hardware to allow handling of other functions

processor, keyboard, the device which translates the pressing of keys into signals which are sent to the computer

processor, peripheral, a processor which handles input and output, thus relieving the CPU for other tasks; same as **input/output processor**

processor, satellite, a computer which supports the main computer, and which is at least partially under its control, in order to increase productivity

process, predefined, a referenced process or subroutine in a program which has been elsewhere previously defined

product, the result of multiplication

production run, the run of a program with live data, as contrasted to a trial or test run

productivity, an absolute measure of the quantity of work completed; a relative value expressing the quantity of work completed as compared to the quantity which was expected to be completed or which the equipment is capable of completing

productivity index, the ratio, expressed as a percentage, of a particular type of work completed or the work completed under particular conditions, compared to the work which could be competed under ideal circumstances

program, a set of instructions which directs a computer in the performance of a particular task; to write a set of instructions for the computer

program, application, a program or software package which uses the computer for a set of related tasks such as inventory control, word processing, spread sheet calculation, etc.

program, assembly, same as **assembler**

program, benchmark, a routine used to determine the relative speed and efficiency of a computer or peripheral; same as a **benchmark problem**

program, bootleg, a program created outside the purview of authorized operation; proprietary software illegally received or transferred; **pirated software**

program breakpoint, a breakpoint set by a programmer as an aid to debugging

program card, a punched card which contains a program step

program chaining, a program written in modules which are automatically called in order when the preceding module is completed

program, check, a short program which tests the validity of a part of a larger program; a hardware testing program run on a computer which does not have automatic or self-checking

program, coded, a program written in the syntax of a programming language (source code) or in machine language

program compatibility, the ability of programs to interact or to be integrated with each other

program, compiling, same as **compiler**

program, control, a process control system; operating system, the program which handles the routine functions of computer operation such as reading the keyboard, accessing memory, managing input and output, etc.

program controller, that part of a processor which controls the order and execution of instructions

program control transfer, the transfer of control from one program to another

program control unit, same as **program controller**

program counter, a register which contains the address of the next instruction

program deck, a set of punched cards which contain program instructions

program development system, the hardware and software used to design, write, test and debug software applications

program, diagnostic, a testing program which is run on a computer to identify and locate hardware malfunctions

program editor, a type of text editor designed for use in the coding of programs

program error, a mistake made by the programmer in the process of writing a program

program error dump, a dump to the printer, or printout, of the computer state and memory contents at the time an error occurs

program evaluation and review technique, (PERT) a system for the management of complex projects which involves analysis of the time frame for each step and its relation to the time frame for other steps in order to develop a critical path for the most efficient and timely completion of the project

program, executive, a set of routines which manages the sequencing and executing of programs; an operating system which provides for the running of several programs at one time or multi-tasking

program fetch, an instruction that directs the location and retrieval of material from a memory location; a **fetch instruction**

program file, a software library reference system

program flowchart, a graphic illustration of the logic flow of a program

program, heuristic, a system in which the computer examines and tests a number of possible solutions, evaluates them at each step and selects the best

program instruction, a statement in a program that directs the computer to perform a task

program, interactive, a program which accepts and acts on user input while it is running

program, internally stored, a program which is stored in the computer's internal memory

program, job control, a program which contains a series of JCL statements which direct the preparation and running of a job or program

program language, same as **programming language**

program library, a collection of programs available to the computer

program line, a single command or instruction which may actually extend over more than a single physical line; a **line of code**

program listing, a complete printout of the lines of code or instructions in a program

program loading, calling programs into memory by the user or by the program being run

program logic, the sequence of instructions which make up a program

programmable, a device or task which can be manipulated with a the aid of a program

programmable array logic, (PAL) a grouping of logical OR and AND circuits which can be programmed to execute specific tasks; also called programmable logic array

programmable calculator, a calculator which can store a sequence of mathematical operations for repeated use

programmable clock, a timing circuit which can be set to produce timing signals of a specified frequency

programmable function key, one of a set of function keys which can be set or altered by the user to transmit a specific command

programmable logic array, (PLA) a grouping of logical OR and AND circuits which can be programmed to execute specific tasks; also called programmable array logic

programmable memory, memory which is under the control of a program

programmable peripheral device, any peripheral device which contains its own processor, eliminating the need for direct control by the computer

programmable timer, same as **programmable clock**

program maintenance, the periodic review and update of a program to improve performance or make necessary changes to accommodate user requests

program, master control, a program which controls all phases of a job including equipment functions, data flow, instructions to the operator, etc.; also the **operating system** or **main program**

programmed check, a routine written into a program which tests its operation or parts of its operation

programmed halt, a deliberate stoppage of the computer processing by a command in the program

programmed input/output, input or output which is controlled by software rather than by the computer itself

programmed inquiry learning or teaching, (PILOT) a computer language designed for the development of computer aided instruction programs

programmed learning, classroom instruction which involves a presentation followed by questions, and branching to a repeat of the presentation or the next section, depending on the answer given

programmed logic array, a grouping of logical OR and AND circuits which can be programmed to execute specific tasks

programmer, an individual who writes instructions for a computer; a device which loads a program into the computer

programmer-defined macro, a section of assembly language programming which can be called by referencing a label

programmer's template, a card which contains traceable cutouts of symbols, used in preparing a flowchart

programming, writing a series of directives in a language understood by the computer, or which can be converted to a language understood by the computer, for the purpose of performing a task, or series of tasks which address a specific problem or need

programming aid, a program which aids in the development and debugging of other programs

programming analyst, a person skilled in the analysis of problems and the design of solutions designs applications for the computer

programming, applications, writing an interactive program which offers the user access to a number of tasks related to a specific application, such as inventory control, word processing, spread sheet calculation, etc.

programming, automatic, the ability of a computer to write some of its own code from minimal input by the user, as from a built in assembler or compiler

programming language, any language which is used to furnish instructions to a computer

programming language, automatic, a programming language which enables the computer to generate parts of a program

programming, linear, program instructions written in the order in which they are to be executed; also known as an unstructured program; see also **structured program**

programming, modular, programs written as a series of units which can be tested individually, then strung together in the main program and called as needed

programming, non-numeric, programming which does not entail any numeric calculations

programming, structured, program instructions contained in modules or routines which are selected as needed from a main or control routine

programming, symbolic, writing a computer program in a language which must be translated to machine language before running; the use of symbols to represent logic instructions

program module, a set of program instructions treated as a unit; one of the units which make up a modular program

program name, an alias or label which identifies a particular program

program, named, a program referenced from within another program

program package, a collection of programs relating to a single application, such as the various parts of an accounting package; an integrated software package which includes several applications, such as a business package containing word processing, spreadsheet and database functions

program, partial, a program which is not complete by itself; a subroutine

program, peripheral, software which manages the operation of a peripheral device and its interface with the computer; a program which adds special features to another program although not critical to the operation of the main program, such as a grammar or spelling checker in a word processor program

program, precompiler, a program which seeks out errors in a source program before compilation

program reference table, a section of memory used to store operands, array references, subroutines, etc.

program register, the register which holds the instruction being executed

program run, the execution of a program

program segment, a subprogram or routine which is designed to handle a specific task under the direction of the main program

program segmentation, the dividing of a program into segments or modules for ease in programming or to make the best use of main memory

program, segmented, a program

constructed in sections which can be brought into memory as needed, making the best use of main memory

program specification, a document which outlines the purpose of a program, the data to be used and the desired input and output

program stack, a routine used by a program for the temporary storage of data and instructions

program step, a single instruction in assembly or machine language

program stop, a processing halt called from the program

program stop instruction, an instruction to stop processing under certain conditions

program storage, the portion of memory where the program and its active routines are stored

program, support, a program which assists the user in the operation of the computer, file management, etc.

program switch, a program instruction to move to a new section of the program; a GOTO statement

program, systems, the program which handles the routine functions of computer operation such as reading the keyboard, accessing memory, managing input and output, etc.; **main program**

program tape, a paper or magnetic tape which contains program data

program testing, verifying the operation of a program by processing and monitoring the output of test data

program, trace, a program which has the capability to track the actions of another program for debugging

program, user, an interactive application program which is run by the user, in contrast to a program in which the user's primary interest is the output from the run; a program or routine written or modified by the user, as contrasted to a packaged program designed for a specific task and which cannot be altered

program, utility, a program which assists in the operation of a computer, such as a backup program, a disk compactor, etc.; a program which enhances the operation of another program such as a grammar or spell checker in a word processing program, etc.; a **peripheral program** or **support program**

prompt, a cursor symbol displayed on the monitor screen to indicate where the next entry from the keyboard will be typed in; a message displayed by a program informing the user of an existing condition, requesting input, etc.

proof listing, a printout of the command lines of a program and other pertinent data which may be used for checking and debugging

propagated error, an error in one programmed operation which also effects subsequent operations

proportional spacing, the spacing of typeset characters which relates to the width of each character, leaving an approximately uniform amount of white space between each, in contrast to constant spacing such as that from a typewriter

proprietary program, packaged software which is owned by a vendor and leased to a user; general purpose software, sold with the provision clearly stated that the user has not bought the program, but only the right to use it on a single machine, and that copying is limited to a backup, not for further distribution

proprietary software, same as **proprietary program**

protected field, a part of the monitor screen which cannot be accessed from the keyboard

protected files, read-only files; files which may not be altered; files which can be accessed only by authorized users through the use of a password

protected location, same as **protected storage**

protected memory, memory which does not lose its contents when power is off; sections of computer memory reserved for specific functions, not subject to overwriting by any other programs or data

protected storage, sections of computer memory reserved for specific functions, not subject to overwriting by any other programs or data; sections of storage set aside for specific users and which may be accessed only by a special code or password

protocol, the conventions which govern the transmission of data

protocol, bit-oriented, a data transmission technique which handles data bit by bit

pseudo code, a form of a machine-independent programming language designed to teach the principles of programming; a combination of spoken language and programming language, used as a convenience in preparing an outline of a program before writing the actual program

pseudo instruction, an instruction which is legal, but which performs no function except to hold a place for possible future additions to the program

public domain software, software to which no person or company lays claim of ownership and which can be freely used, copied, or modified

pull instruction, removal of an item from the top of a stack which advances the remaining items up one position

pulse, the change of an electrical current from one level to another

pulse counter, a device that records the number of pulses during a set time interval

pulse generator, a circuit which produces a timing signal

pulse rate, the incidence rate of the control signals of the computer

pulse string, a series of pulses occurring in time sequence

punched card, a card on which data is stored in the form of holes punched in columns

punched paper tape, same as **paper tape**

punched tape, same as **paper tape**

push-down list, a data set in which new data is added at the beginning so that existing data is "pushed down" to a new position

push-down stack, a stack whose data is loaded and unloaded from the top

push instruction, an instruction which calls for the entry of data to the top of a stack

push-up list, a data set in which new data is added at the end so that existing data maintains its position

push-up storage, storage in which the first item entered is the first item retrieved; same as **FIFO**

Q

Q test, a comparison of two or more units of quantitative data

quad, consisting of four elements or parts

quad capacity, a double density, double-sided disk which can hold four times the data of a standard disk

qualifier, a name which modifies another name to make it distinctive

quality control, the testing of a product by measuring it against a standard

quantity, vector, a quantity which has both magnitude and direction

quantization, representing a range of values as a finite number of distinct sub ranges

quartz oscillator, a timer whose frequency is controlled by the vibrations of a piezoelectric crystal

quasi instruction, an instruction which performs no function; a **pseudo instruction**

query, a request for data, as for a record from a data base file; a check for the status of a peripheral

query language, a language utilized for retrieving information from a data base

query program, a program which allows the retrieval of information from a data base

queue, a list of programs or data awaiting processing as for printing, transmission, etc.; a structure in which elements are added at one end and removed from the other end

queue, automatic, registers which automatically sort a LIFO or a FIFO stack

queue, push-down, a last-in, first-out queue

queuing list, a list of jobs in the queue, as awaiting printing

quoted string, a string of characters, enclosed by quotation marks, treated as a unit

quotient, the result of division

QWERTY keyboard, a standard typewriter keyboard arrangement of alpha characters, so-called for the order of the row of letters at the top left hand side of the keyboard

R

radial transfer, a technique for transferring data between peripheral equipment and main memory

radix, the base of a number system

radix notation, fixed, a system of numeric notation in which the value of each digit in a number is determined by its position

radix point, the point which separates a whole number from its fractional part

ragged right, in text formatting, non-justified or left-justified text; text which is aligned at the left margin and uneven on the right

RAM, random access memory; memory which allows data to be addressed independent of the last access

RAM dump, a printout of the contents of RAM; to copy the contents of RAM to a printout or disk file

RAM loader, a program which reads a program from input into main memory

RAM refresh operation, the rewriting of the contents of RAM memory back to itself

RAM refresh rate, the refresh cycles per second rate necessary to retain data in RAM

random access, refers to storage in which each site has a unique address so that the medium or the accessing device is able to move directly to any site specified; the ability to read and write data to any location in memory in a constant amount of time; a system which allows data to be addressed independent of the last access of data contrasted to **sequential access**

random access memory, (RAM) memory which allows data to be addressed independent of the last access

random access storage, storage whose contents can be accessed directly and thus very quickly

random files, files stored and retrieved directly, based on their address rather than position

randomness, referring to processes which are not sequenced and thus take place in random order

random noise, noise, or interference, which occurs without pattern

random number, one of a series of unrelated numeric values selected from an orderless set

random number generator, a routine which is used to produce random numbers for statistical analysis

random number sequence, a set of numbers in which each digit is as likely to occur as any other within the sequence

random processing, processing data in the order directed by the

system or program rather than by the order in which they are stored

random variable, a variable which can assume, with equal possibility, any value within the specified range

range, all of the possible values which a variable or function may assume

range, error, the limits of the values which a given error can assume

rank, to place in order according to value; the relative value of an item in a group or set

raster graphics, graphics produced on a CRT screen using raster scan image technology

raster scan, a display technique in which an electron beam projects lines of dots across the screen

rate, bit, the number of bits which are transmitted over a specific length of time

rate, error, the number of errors transmitted for a given number of transmissions or during a given time period

rate, scan, the frequency with which a computer verifies the process or condition it is governing

ratio, activity, the ratio of the records which have been accessed, used or changed compared to the total records in the file

ratio, operating, the relationship between total available time and the time during which data processing or other equipment is operating correctly

ratio, signal-to-noise, a comparison of the number of bad signals to the number of total signals over a transmission line

raw data, data which has not been processed in any way

reactive mode, an interactive communication mode in which each entry from a remote terminal causes the computer to perform some action

read, a term used to describe the receipt of information from input or from memory and the transfer of data from one place to another

read, destructive, a situation in which data read from a storage device causes the data to be erased from the device at the same time

reader, any device able to sense data and convert it to binary signals

reader, bar code, any device used to read bar codes and translate them for the computer

reader, character, a magnetic or optical device used to scan printed or written characters which it converts into digital data

reader, document, any device which can scan hard copy and translate the characters into digital data; a device which scan special codes for translation into digital data

reader, optical, any device which reads by optic scanning such as an optical character reader or an optical mark reader

reader, photoelectric, a device which reads data from a paper tape by sensing the light passing through holes punched in the tape

read error, a system interrupt created by the inability to read data from storage because of damage to the medium, a malfunction of the read/write head, etc.

read head, the device which senses data stored on magnetic tape or disk

read in, the process of transferring information to memory

read, manual, computer reading of the settings of manual switches

read, non-destructive, the process of copying information from storage with no alteration in the status or contents of the original

read only, storage medium whose content cannot be altered either due to the nature of the medium or by the setting of codes or switches which prevent access

read only memory, (ROM) special memory which can be read, but not altered

read-only storage, storage from which data can be read but which cannot be altered; **ROM**

readout, a display of information in memory or storage to the monitor screen or a printer

readout, destructive, a situation in which data read from a storage device causes the data to be erased from the device at the same time

read/write channel, a bi-directional data path linking main memory and a peripheral device

read/write counter, a register which stores the starting address and current address of data which is being transferred by a read/write channel

read/write cycle, the procedure necessary to execute a single read/write command

read/write head, the device in a disk or tape drive which reads data from storage and writes data to storage

ready light, a signal light which indicates that a device is ready to communicate

real time, referring to processing

which is not delayed, generally in an interactive program, accepting data as it is input and producing output as required

real-time batch processing, a real-time system which is programmed to handle batch jobs as computer resources are available

real-time clock, time maintained in conventional manner in order to execute program instructions which contain real-time commands

real-time control, control functions which manage real-time operations such as entries from a keyboard

real-time executive, a multitasking operating system manager

real-time input, the input of data as it is generated

real-time operation, computation and processing which takes place as soon as data and resources are available

real-time processing, the processing of data as it is received from remote locations while the transactions producing it are taking place, such as shop floor data collection, automated bank teller transactions, etc.

real-time processing communication, the receipt of data from remote locations while the transactions producing it are taking place, such as shop floor data collection, automated bank teller transactions, etc.

real-time system, a system which processes information so that the output can be used by the process supplying the information

reasonableness check, a testing of data to determine if it is within the predicted range

recognition, character, the ability

of a scanning device to recognize a printed or written character; reading characters with a scanner

recognizer, syntax, a program subroutine which interprets the syntax of a programming language

record, the basic element of a data file; a set of data elements or fields that contains information on one of the items in a file

record blocking, partitioning records blocks of data which can be manipulated as a unit

record, data, the basic element of a data file; a set of data elements or fields that contains information on one of the items in a file

record, fixed length, a record format in which the number or size of fields cannot be altered

record format, the size, data type and arrangement of fields in a data base record

record gap, the space on magnetic tape which separates records

recording density, the number of bits or bytes per unit of length or area on magnetic tape or disk

recording head, the device which writes data to magnetic tape or disk

record layout, same as **record format**

record length, the number of words, bytes, or characters in a single data record

record locking, a special routine which denies access to a record or file which is open, or currently accessed by a user

record, logical, data related by content without consideration of physical location

record mark, a character or symbol which separates records in a database

records management, the creation, storage, accessing and disposal of an organization's documents

record storage mark, a character in the record storage unit of a punched card reader which limits the length of the record read into memory.

recoverable error, a machine or program malfunction which can be corrected without shutting down the system

recovery, fallback, restoring a system, including capturing data processed by other means during a fallback

rectifier, a circuit which converts alternating current into direct current; a device which allows current to flow in one direction only

recursion, a process whereby a program statement or routine calls on or refers to itself

recursive, regarding a routine or statement which calls on or refers to itself

recursive function, a mathematical or logic process which is defined partly in terms of itself

recursive procedure, same as **recursive routine**

recursive process, an action in which each stage is not complete until succeeding stages have been completed

recursive routine, a routine which calls itself, either directly or indirectly through another routine or procedure

redirection symbol, the symbols, >, < and |, which are used on a command line to redirect output

reduction, data, using statistical analysis to produce intelligible information from raw data

redundancy, having, on line, two or more devices which perform the same function, for protection against the failure of one or the devices; transmitting the same data more than once in order to detect errors in transmission; repetition

redundancy check, a technique requiring the inclusion of extra data which is used only for checking purposes

redundant character, a character which is added to a word to allow a redundancy check

redundant code, a binary coded decimal number which contains a check bit

reel, a spool for magnetic tape

reel, take-up, the spool onto which tape is wound as it is being read for processing

re-enterable, referring to a routine which can be used repeatedly or shared by more than one process at the same time

reentry point, the address of the next instruction in a main program which is executed after a subroutine or branch command is completed

reference address, an address used to convert a relative address to an absolute address

reference axis, a base line used to assist in locating and identifying characters in an OCR system

reference listing, a list of program commands with their storage locations

reference table, program, a section of memory used to store operands, array references, subroutines, etc.

reflected code, in graphics, a numeric code in which each number inside a finite range differs from the previous number by one digit

reformat, the process of changing the representation of data from one form to another

refresh, a signal sent to volatile storage (RAM) to enable it to retain its information or to a CRT monitor screen to redraw (maintain) its image; to send such a signal

refresh buffer, temporary storage for screen display information as screen image is refreshed

refreshing, maintaining data in RAM or images on a CRT screen by repeatedly resending the data or image

regeneration, program logic which creates data from a formula; using part of the output of an amplifier as part of its input; same as **refreshing**

regenerative memory, memory which must be refreshed to retain its contents

regenerative reading, a read operation which writes data back to memory to prevent its deletion

register, a row of flip-flops which store a computer word while it is being processed

register, accumulator, a CPU register which stores the results of an arithmetic operation

register, address, the register in a CPU where an address is stored

register addressing, addressing by specifying the contents of a register, in contrast to directly stating the address

register, arithmetic, a register in the ALU on which arithmetic and logical operations can be performed

register, base, a computer register which modifies an instruction prior to its execution

register, block, a register which contains the address of storage blocks available for incoming data

register, cache, high-speed memory for storing frequently used data

register, circulating, a register which performs shift operations

register, control, a register which contains the address of the next program instruction; sometimes, the storage unit which contains the current instruction

register, double word, two computer registers which can be used together to accommodate a double length word

register, external, a register which is addressable by the program

register, general-purpose, a CPU register which is able to perform several functions

register, index, a hardware register which holds the index value of an element in a table or array; a hardware register which counts down the number of times a loop should be performed; a register in a loop which accesses consecutive locations in memory; a register containing a value used to modify an address

register length, the number of positions in a register; in effect, the number of bits, digits, etc. which a register can store

register pair, two registers, containing a single word, which can be addressed separately or as a double-length pair

register, program, the register which holds the instruction being executed

register, shift, a register in which the string of bits can be moved to the right or left to perform multiplication or division

register, standby, a register which holds the information being processed and which will be reused if there is an error in processing

register, temporary, a register which holds the output from an ALU while it is being sent to the destination register in case of transmission error

register, working, a register which holds work in process for quick access

registration, in optical character recognition, the positioning of data relative to a reference point or line

regression analysis, a statistical system for determining rate of change

regular branch, an unconditional instruction to move control to a new section of the program

relation, the association or connection between two or more elements

relational breakpoint, a breakpoint which takes place between two consecutive memory read or write operations

relational data base, a data base organized associatively by rows of related records, such as an employee list, and columns of fields containing like data elements, such as employee name or number

relational expression, a phrase which contains relational operators, or terms which express a relationship between items

relational operator, a term or symbol which indicates the relationship between two elements, such as *equal,* =, *greater than,* >, *less than,* <, etc.

relative address, an address which is to be altered to a direct address when a program is run

relative addressing, a method of providing absolute addresses by modifying a given address when a program is run

relative address label, naming the address where data is located in relation to yet another address

relative coding, machine instructions which contain relative addresses

relative time clock, a device which an executive program uses to audit for interrupts

relay, an electromagnetic switch

relay center, a location where incoming data is redirected to outgoing circuits

relay, electromagnetic, a relay which completes a circuit through the use of a magnetically activated switch

reliability, the probability that a system or peripheral will function without error or failure

reliability test, a stress test designed to evaluate the probability that a device will operate for a reasonable length of time without error or failure

relocatable, pertaining to an object program whose location in memory is not limited to one place

relocatable assembler, an assembler which generates an object program in which the addresses are relative to a base address

relocatable code, programs, routines, etc. whose location in memory is not limited to one place

relocatable program, a program which will run from any location in memory

relocate, to remove a program from one area of memory to another and correspondingly adjust address references

relocation dictionary, the part of a program which includes the data essential to adjusting the program's addresses when it is relocated

relocation, dynamic, changing the location in memory of a partly executed program without affecting the execution of the program

REM, remark; a key word in BASIC and MS-DOS® which indicates the beginning of a comment

remainder, the discrete value which is left after a division has been performed

remark, a comment included in a program by the programmer, to describe or explain an instruction or routine for future reference

remote, referring to a workstation, terminal or other peripheral which is located away from the immediate area of the main computer

remote access, referring to communication with a computer which is not in the immediate area

remote batch entry, the facility for assigning a task from a remote location for processing by a main computer which is linked to the remote location by communication channels

remote batch processing, batch processing from a remote location

remote console, a terminal which is located away from the computer and which is connected to it enabling normal communication

remote control, controlling a device or process from a distance as a main computer's control of a remote printer

remote control signal, a computer control signal which is initiated from outside the immediate area of the computer itself

remote inquiry, remote stations which are able to call up data from the computer, often used for a screen read of data regarding manufacturing processes monitored by the computer

remote job entry, the facility for entering a job from a remote location for processing by a main computer which is linked to the remote location by communication channels

remote job entry system, a system which provides for job entry from a remote terminal

remote processing, computer processing of messages, queries, etc. initiated from stations at a distance from the computer, often communicating over telephone lines

remote station, same as **remote terminal**

remote terminal, a terminal which is located away from the computer and which is connected to it enabling normal communication

REM statement, a comment by the programmer, preceded by the a key word or symbol, it is ignored by the computer when executing a program

repeatability, the ability to perform an operation in precisely the same way more than once, often used to describe a peripheral such as a plotter and its ability to return to precisely the same point as a determinant of its precision in producing clean lines and circles

repeat counter, a software routine which records the number of iterations of an event or other routine; also **cycle index counter**

repeating decimal number, a decimal number in which one or more digits repeats continuously in a pattern

repeat key, a terminal key which can be pressed in conjunction with any other key to cause it to repeat; in some application programs, a function key or key combination which repeats the last action

repetition instruction, a command which directs that an instruction be repeated and the number of times it is to be repeated

replacement, the exchange of one piece of equipment for another which performs the same or similar tasks; the exchange of a piece of equipment which has failed to function properly

replacement theory, a study of the failure of equipment over time, including, but not limited to, the prudence and economics of replacement in anticipation of failure compared to replacement at the time of failure

report, a document which furnishes the results of data processing and, often, an analysis of those results

report file, a computer file which contains a report generated by processing; in some application programs, a file which contains the user-defined parameters for a specific report to run from a specific database

report generation, producing a report on the computer, based on formatting and data input supplied

by the user

report generator, a program which creates reports; in some application programs, a program which writes the report program, designed for use by non-programmers

Report Program Generator, (RPG) a business-oriented programming language; an application program which automates or simplifies the task of creating customized reports from a database or spreadsheet file

report writer, a program which allows the user to generate a report by selecting fields and operators from a laundry list

representation, a combination of bits, codes, symbols, characters, etc. which depict something else

reproduce, to duplicate

reprogram, to replace one program with another in a computer; to reload a program after a shut down; to replace or revise a specific program; to correct or update a program; to reset manual controls, such as DIP switches, in a computer or peripheral

request for repeat, automatic, an error detection system which requests that transmission be repeated when an error in transmission is detected

rerun point, an element built into programs when stops are anticipated or when rerunning the entire program after a stop would entail a significant loss of data or time; the location in a computer program from which processing can be resumed after a stop

rerun routine, a routine which reconfigures data and variables after a stop, to prepare the program for a rerun

rescue dump, the programmed periodic recording of the entire contents of the computer so that the program can be rerun from the last dump in the event of failure

reserved word, a word which is part of a programming language's vocabulary and which may not be used for any other purpose, such as naming a variable

reset, to return an element to its original state, such as making a register or flip-flop equal to 0; to restart the computer

reset button, the button on a microcomputer which reboots after a crash without the necessity of shutting off the system

reset key, error, a button on the computer which is pushed to acknowledge recognition that an error occurred and to reset the error detector

resident, referring to anything which permanently resides in the computer's memory

resident compiler, a compiler program which resides within the computer for which it is compiling programs

resident macro assembler, a macro assembler program which resides in the memory of the computer for which it is used

resident program, a program which occupies memory set aside specifically for its use

resident software, software loaded into, or readily available to, stand-alone terminals, stations, or computers

residual error, the difference between a result and the anticipated result, often caused by rounding in computations

residual value, the assigned value of equipment at the end of a lease or after it has been depreciated

resistance, a measure in ohms of the difficulty encountered by a current flowing through a conductor

resistor, an electronic component of specified resistance, used to reduce the flow of current

resolution, the number of addressable picture elements on a view screen, a determinant of the quality of the image; **definition**

resolution, graphics, the relative quality of the reproduction of graphics on the printer, expressed as **dpi,** or dots per inch

resource, the hardware or software capacity available to the system; the system facilities required by a job or task

resource sharing, calls on a processor by several peripherals; accessing of the computer facilities by a number of users

response time, the time taken for a computer to respond to input

restart, to initialize the computer after a shut down; to resume execution of a program after a stop

restart point, the juncture at which a temporarily halted program can be restarted

restore, to return an element to its original state, such as making a register or flip-flop equal to 0

retrieval, the locating of stored data

retrofit, an adjustment to an existing system in order to expand or improve operation

return, a keyboard function key, also called *Enter,* which is used to move the cursor to the beginning of the next line or, in some programs, to direct execution of a selected command; in some word processing application programs, inserts an end-of-line or paragraph marker

return address, the address at the conclusion of a subroutine which returns control to the main program

return from interrupt, an instruction which restores the CPU to its condition prior to the interrupt

return key, a keyboard function key, also called *Enter,* which is used to move the cursor to the beginning of the next line or, in some programs, to direct execution of a selected command; in some word processing application programs, inserts an end-of-line or paragraph marker

reusable, referring to a routine which can be used in more than one place in a program

reverse Polish notation, a method of algebraic expression without parentheses to indicate the order of operations, in which the operands precede the operators; opposite of **Polish notation;** also called postfix notation

reverse video, a CRT monitor display showing dark characters on a light background

rewrite, to write data back to storage after a destructive read

RGB monitor, red/green/blue monitor; a color video monitor in which all of the colors are made up of combination of red, green, and blue signals

ribbon cable, a wide, thin transmission line in which the wires are aligned side by side

ribbon cartridge, a printer ribbon housed in a plastic container for ease of replacement in the printer

right-hand justified, in typesetting, the alignment of characters along the right margin; also described as *flush right*

right justify, the formatting of printed text with the copy aligned to the right margin

right shift, in a shift register, the process of moving the bits of a binary word one position to the right to effect a division

ring network, a network in which terminals and computers are connected in series with the last member connected back to the first to form a loop

RJE, remote job entry; the facility for entering a job from a remote location for processing by a main computer which is linked to the remote location by communication channels

robot, a machine designed to perform often complex repetitive tasks regulated by a computer

robot control language, a programming language created especially to control robots

robotics, the study of the design, fabrication, and programming of robots

roll over, a technique for the prevention of error when more than one character is entered from the keyboard at the same time

ROM, read only memory; special memory which can be read, but not altered

ROM bootstrap, a bootstrap loader in read only memory

ROM, keyboard, read only memory which stores the character codes associated with specific keys

root, same as **root directory**

root directory, the highest level directory on a magnetic disk; the primary directory, which is host to the command, configuration and system files which the computer system requires to begin operation as well as the first level of directories which hold all of the files and sub directories loaded onto the disk

rotate, shifting the bits in a register so that a bit which overflows one end is reinserted at the other end

rotation, a feature of a graphics program which allows an image to be turned or inverted around a reference axis

round, the process of adjusting the least-significant bit after truncation according to whether the truncated portion is greater or less then half the value of the base

rounding error, error in a final number induced by rounding during computation

round off, same as **round**

round off error, the error introduced by rounding off numbers in the course of several calculations

round up, a program instruction which directs that the least-significant bit after truncation be increased by one if the value of the truncated portion is greater than zero

route, the path of a communication signal; the process of assigning a path for data communications

routine, a set of instructions which perform a specific operation

routine, closed, a remote routine which is called up by the main program

routine, correction, a routine used after a malfunction to reconstruct

the program that was being run

routine, direct-insert, a subroutine which is written into the main program in contrast to being called up as a subroutine

routine, heuristic, a system in which the computer examines and tests a number of possible solutions, evaluates them at each step and selects the best

routine, input, a hardware or software routine which controls the reading of data into the computer

routine, interrupt control, a routine which stores the status of an interrupted program so it can be reentered when the interrupt is completed; a routine which stores the status of the computer at an interrupt to determine the cause

routine, loader, a program element which calls up other programs or routines

routine, open, a routine which can be inserted into a program other than that for which it was originally designed

routing, message, management of the transmission of a message through the system or from one system to another

RPG, Report Program Generator; a business-oriented programming language; an application program which automates or simplifies the task of creating customized reports from a database or spreadsheet file

RPN, reverse Polish notation; a method of algebraic expression without parentheses to indicate the order of operations, in which the operands precede the operators; opposite of **Polish notation**; also called postfix notation

RS-232, a standard 25-pin connector for interfacing computers and peripheral devices

RTC, real-time clock; time maintained in conventional manner in order to execute program instructions which contain real-time commands

RTE, real-time executive; a multitasking operating system manager

rules, syntax, the discipline which outlines the sentence structure, or the order of the elements of a sentence, in a programming language

run, the loading and execution of a program; a select word or command in BASIC which causes execution of the loaded program

run chart, a flow chart of a computer run which shows input and output

run indicator, a light which shows when the processor is in the run mode

run manual, a book of instruction and information about a computer, including specifications of the system, program logic, operating instructions, etc.

run phase, the part of a machine cycle during which a compiled program is run

run time, the time during which a program is being processed by the computer

run-time routine, a routine which is used by a program while it is running

run-time support package, a special routine which assists in running a program

S

SAM, sequential access method; a method of retrieving data by reading through all records sequentially until the search object is located

sample data, data used in a test run to determine whether a program works properly

sampling, a technique for monitoring a program by obtaining the value of a variable or input at regular intervals

satellite computer, a secondary computer which supports a larger system; a **satellite processor**

satellite processor, a computer which supports the main computer, and which is at least partially under its control, in order to increase productivity

saturation testing, trying out a program by inputting a large quantity of data to see if errors occur

save, to transfer a program or data to non-volatile memory

SBC, single-board computer; a computer which is designed with all of the vital components wired to a single printed circuit board

scalable font, a software program which contains a definition of the characteristics of a type face from which it can produce a font of any size within a given range

scan, to examine sequentially; to optically read and convert data for entry into a computer

scanner, a device which samples, or tests, various processes, conditions, etc.; a device which reads printed matter to convert it to signals which can be understood by the computer

scanner, analog input, a programmable device that connects any of several sensors to measuring equipment

scanner, bar code, any device used to read bar codes and translate them for the computer; same as **bar code reader**

scanning machine, a machine which reads printed matter or magnetic ink and inputs the data to the computer

scan rate, the frequency with which a computer verifies the process or condition it is governing

scheduled down time, the time during which a computer is undergoing regular maintenance

schema, the definition of the logical structure of a data base

schematic, a graphic representation of components and their connections in a circuit

schematic symbols, graphic representation of the elements of a circuit

scientific applications, mathematical fabrication of real world systems for objective study

scientific computer, a computer designed specifically to manipulate large, complex mathematical models

scientific notation, a system of expressing very large or very small numbers as powers of ten

scramble, a security technique which makes data or a transmission unreadable until reconfigured by authorized personnel

scrambled, referring to a message or signal which has been encrypted

scratch pad memory, a memory area used for temporary storage of the intermediate results of calculations

screen, a cathode ray tube or other device which provides a dynamic display of computer data

screen blanker, a software program which blanks the monitor screen or creates a random, moving pattern on screen if there is no keyboard activity for a user-specified length of time: the process prevents burning an image into the screen and is reversible by the movement of any key or a mouse

screen dump, a transfer of the data appearing on the screen to the printer or to storage; use of the **Print Screen** function key

screen forms, forms designed for use on a monitor screen either for data entry or display of information

screen refresh, scanning of a monitor screen to retain the image, normally about 60 Hz or 60 times per second to fool the eye into seeing an image which does not flicker; see also **VGA, super-VGA**

screen saver, same as **screen blanker**

screen size, the length of an imaginary diagonal line between opposite corners of a monitor screen

screen, touch-sensitive, a special monitor screen which transmits a signal when touched

screen type, the technology utilized to create a screen image, such as CRT, LCD, LED, etc.

scrolling, the horizontal or vertical movement of the image on a monitor screen to display the image which is outside the borders of the screen

SE, systems engineer ,a systems analyst who designs applications for the user

search, a systematic examination for the purpose of finding a particular item

search and replace, a word processing text editing function which locates a word or string in a file and replaces it with another

search and replace, global, a routine which seeks out a character string in a file and replaces it with another specified string, usually offering the user a choice of automatic replace or a prompt before replacing

search, global, a routine which finds every occurrence of a character string within a file or group of files; a file name search which includes all drives and directories in the system

search key, a field or data element on which a search is based

search time, the time required to locate a particular item in storage

secondary memory, same as **secondary storage**

secondary storage, an external storage device, such as disk or tape

second-level addressing, an instruction which contains the address of the memory which contains the address of the data

sector, a portion of a disk track; the amount of data which a computer can read into memory in one step

sector formatting, disk, part of the initialization of a disk; marking a disk to indicate the sectors and tracks

security, the techniques used to prevent unauthorized access to a computer or to certain files on the computer

seek, to search; the process of recovering data from a random access file; the positioning of the read/write head over the desired data track

seek time, the time required for a disk read/write head to move to a specific track

segment, a portion of a data file; a section of a program which may be processed in memory while the rest of the program is in mass storage

segmentation, a technique for dividing a program into parts so that they will fit into available memory

segmentation overlay, bringing a portion of a program into memory which overwrites the previous contents of the memory

segmented program, a program constructed in sections which can be brought into memory as needed, making the best use of main memory

segment mark, used in magnetic storage to delineate each section of a file

select, to choose from among a set of alternatives; to switch input/output channels in preparation for a transmission

selection check, a verification that the correct input/output device was selected for a routine

selection, priority, choosing the next job to run based on its priority and the availability of system resources

selective calling, a technique which allows a calling device to choose the receiver for its transmission

selective dump, a printout of certain sections of memory

selective trace, tracing specific elements of a program to test their function

selector channel, an input/output channel which provides a communications link between the computer and a peripheral device

self-adapting, a system which has the ability to change its attributes depending on the environment

self-checking code, a system for detection of errors by adding an extra bit to computer words

self-checking number, a number which includes an extra digit, used to detect errors in transmission

self-complementing code, a machine language in which the code of the complement of a digit is the complement of the code of the digit

self-correcting code, a system of coding numbers in which detection and correction of transmission errors is automatic

self-defining term, an expression whose value or function is identified by the expression itself

self-diagnostic, the ability of a device to monitor its own performance and signal when errors or faults occur

self-instructed carry, a carry which propagates itself automatically

self-learning computer, a computer which has been programmed to modify future action based on experience

self-relocating program, a program which adjusts its address constants so it can be loaded and executed from anywhere in memory

self-resetting loop, a circuit which resets input devices to their initial condition

self-test, the routine by which a device checks its circuitry and function when it is powered up

semanteme, a language element which expresses a precise image

semantic error, a programming error caused by the incorrect use of a

term in a program

semantics, the study of the meaning of words and symbols

semiconductor, an electronic element which can be made to alternate between a conductive state and a non-conductive state

semiconductor device, a chip

semiconductor, discrete, a semiconductor which serves a single function

semiconductor memory, same as **semiconductor storage**

semiconductor storage, memory chips, such as RAM or ROM

semi-random access, storage in which memory blocks may be accessed at random and specific elements within the blocks are located sequentially

sender/receiver buffer, temporary storage which allows input to be collected before being transmitted

sense, to read the holes in punched media or to detect the state of an electronic element

sense switch, a switch, either physical or contained in program instructions, which can be set to alter coded machine instructions

sensor, a device which reads analog signals

sensor based, of a computer which uses a sensing device to monitor a physical process

sensor device, an analog device which measures flow, pressure, temperature, etc.

sentinel, a mark or code which indicates the end of a unit of information

separator, a mark or code which indicates the break between units of data

sequence, to order elements into a

specific arrangement; elements so ordered

sequence check, a test to determine that data is arranged in the proper order

sequence, control, determination of the order in which program instructions are to executed; the processing of program instructions in order sequentially unless a branch is encountered

sequence counter, a register which contains the location in memory of the next instruction to be executed; same as **sequence register**

sequence error, an error caused by an instruction or a data record which is out of order

sequence number, a number attached to an item to indicate its relative position in a set

sequence register, a register which contains the location in memory of the next instruction to be executed; same as **sequence counter**

sequencing key, the field in a record which is the basis for a sort; in instruction which directs the order of a sort

sequential, stored or operating in order, one after the other

sequential access, a system that retrieves data by reading through all records sequentially until the search object is located contrasted to **random access**

sequential access device, a storage device which uses the sequential access method to locate records, data, files, etc.

sequential access method, a method of retrieving data by reading through all records sequentially until the search object is located

sequential access storage, mass storage which uses the sequential access method to locate files

sequential circuit, an electronic circuit that incorporates a logic element with storage element that provide data on the previous state of the inputs

sequential computer, a computer in which instructions are followed one after the other, in sequence

sequential control, the execution of instructions successively in order unless a branch is specified

sequential file organization, a scheme for organizing file records in a series in conformity to a key element

sequential logic, an arrangement of circuits in which the output is decided by the previous input

sequential operation, the execution of instructions in the order they are written, beginning one only after the previous instruction is completed

sequential search, the examination of a file by reading through all records sequentially until the search object is located; also called linear search

serial, the sequential manipulation of data; referring to time related activities

serial access, a system that retrieves data by reading through all records sequentially until the search object is located contrasted to **random access**

serial adder, an adder which operates on one digit at a time

serial arithmetic, mathematical operation on one digit at a time, in contrast to **parallel arithmetic**

serial by bit, moving bits one at a time in a fixed sequence

serial communications, transmitting data one bit at a time over a single communications line

serial computer, a computer which processes each bit, word or command one at a time, in order

serial input/output, transmitting and receiving data one bit at a time over a single circuit

serial input/output interface, a device which converts serial communication to parallel for processing

serial interface, a single channel connector between a computer and a peripheral which handles data one bit at a time

serially reusable, a routine which may be used for a task or in a place other than the one for which it was written without alteration

serial memory, memory which must retrieve data by reading records in sequence until the search object is found, contrasted to **random access**

serial operation, an operation which requires the handling of bits one at a time in order rather as a computer word

serial/parallel converter module, a device which changes between serial and parallel signals, to permit full duplex communication between devices

serial printer, a printer which prints one character at a time in sequence

serial printer interface, a device which can direct output to a printer from a terminal or computer

serial processing, processing file records in stored sequence, one at a time

serial programming, program instructions which direct a computer to perform one arithmetic or logical operation at a time

serial storage, storage in which data must be retrieved by reading records in sequence until the search file is found

serial transmission, sending data one bit at a time instead of in full computer words

series, a group of items which follow each other in order

server, a computer which provides file storage, a printer or any other device which is available to the users of a network

service bureau, an · organization which provides data processing services, such as computer time and personnel, to its clients

servo, a mechanical system in which response is an adjustment to input to make it match a target output

servo link, a mechanical amplifier which adjusts low power signals so that they may control devices which require higher power

servomechanism, a device that monitors a particular operation as it proceeds and makes necessary adjustments; a feedback control system

set, to return a device to its original state; a collection or group of related elements

set breakpoint, a place in a program where execution is interrupted, often as an aid in debugging

set name, the identifier or alias of a collection of data, instructions, etc.

set up, to prepare a system or data to begin processing a job

setup diagram, a graphic representation of the elements in a computer system

setup time, the time required to prepare a computer for a job

shadow batch, data which has not been added to a master file but which is available to queries

shared file, data which may be accessed by two or more users at the same time

shared logic, one computer which is available to two or more users at the same time

shared resource, a computer component or peripheral available to two or more users as a disk drive or printer

shared storage, main memory which can be accessed by two or more computers

shareware, non-commercial computer programs available at little or no cost, with the author usually requesting a donation if the program proves useful

sharing, the use of data. a device or computer by two or more users at the same time

sheet feeder, a special attachment which allows single sheets to be fed through a printer or scanner

shielded line, a line or circuit which is insulated to prevent interference from another line

shift, to move a series of bits, digits, or characters to the right or left

shift, arithmetic, moving binary digits in a register one place to the left or right which is the means of multiplying or dividing the number by 2

shift, character, a program code or printer switch which toggles control between outputting standard characters and graphics symbols

shift instruction, a machine instruction which causes the bits in a computer word to move one space to the right or left, as for binary multiplication and division

shift, keyboard, to change between the normal keyboard which produces numbers and lower case letters to the shifted keyboard which produces special characters and upper case letters

shift left in a shift register, the process of moving the bits of a binary word one position to the left to effect a multiplication

shift, letter, to change between lower case and upper case letters

shift, phase, a change in the relative time between parts of a signal wave form without change in the form of the signal

shift register, a register in which the string of bits can be moved to the right or left to perform multiplication or division

shift right, in a shift register, the process of moving the bits of a binary word one position to the right to effect a division

shortcut key, a key combination which executes a command, such as bringing a memory-resident utility to the foreground or executing a macro

short-instruction format, instructions which are one computer word in length

short-line seeking, a printer routine which returns the printing head to the side of the page nearest the end of the last line printed

sifting, an internal sorting method which involves the selection of records based on a bit pattern

sign, a mathematical symbol used to indicate whether the value of a number is positive or negative

signal, an event, instruction, electrical charge, etc. which conveys information

signal, analog, an electric signal which varies in amplitude or frequency to transmit information

signal conversion, the process of changing a signal from one form to another, as analog to digital

signal, digital, a signal whose various states are separated by discrete intervals

signal element, the basic unit of data in a communication system

signal, interrupt, the control signal which calls an interrupt to the CPU

signal processing, converting analog input to digital data

signal shaping and filtering, procedures applied in modems to limit a signal to a specific range and to exclude noise

signal-to-noise ratio, a comparison of the number of bad signals to the number of total signals over a transmission line

sign bit, a bit set to represent plus or minus

sign check, a test for change in the sign of a data field

sign digit, same as **sign bit**

sign flag, a flag which is set to 1 if the sign is minus

sign flip-flop, a flip-flop which stores the plus or minus sign of a number

significance, the quality of conditions which are not entirely the result of chance; the relative rank or order of magnitude or a number

significant digits, the digits place in a number which may not be rounded without a loss of accuracy

significant figures, the digits in a number recognized to be accurate or consequential

significant interval, the period of time during which a significant item is, or should be, transmitted

sign off, same as **log off**

sign on, same as **log on**

sign position, the position in a record field where the sign is located

silicon, a natural element used to make semiconductor devices

silicon wafer, a slice of silicon crystal on which integrated circuits are printed or etched

simplex channel, a channel able to communicate in only one direction

simulate, to represent one thing by means of another

simulation, a computer representation of a physical action or arrangement

simultaneous input/output, the use of buffers to temporarily store input or output from one operation while executing another

simultaneous processing, the performance of two or more data processing tasks at the same time

single address, a computer instruction which is limited to one command and involves one address; same as **one address**

single-board computer, a computer which is designed with all of the vital components wired to a single printed circuit board

single-board microcomputer, same as **single-board computer**

single density disk, a relatively low capacity floppy disk

single-level address, a procedure of directly accessing memory locations

single pass program, a routine which completes its task in a single run

single precision, referring to the use of one computer word for the storage of a number

single precision integer, an integer which can be depicted by a single computer word

single purpose LAN, a local area network devoted to a single application

single shot circuit, a circuit which standardizes imprecise input to produce output which meets the criteria of the target device

single-sided disk, a floppy disk which can record data on only one side

single step, to run a program one instruction at a time under user control

single-step debugging, checking for errors in a program after each instruction is completed

single-step diagnosis, same as **single step mode diagnosis**

single-step mode, a mode of operation in which the computer runs a program one instruction at a time and displays the results of each execution

single step mode diagnosis, detailed examination of a program, one step at a time, by stopping after each instruction is executed; examining a program's effect on memory, registers and flags after each instruction has been executed

16-bit microcomputer, a small computer which utilizes a 16-bit data word

16-bit microprocessor, a microprocessor which utilizes a 16-bit data word

16/32-bit microcomputer, a small computer which uses a 32-bit data word on a 16-bit bus

skeletal coding, pseudo code; preliminary coding of a program in which some information is completed later

skew, a measure of misalignment or non-synchronization in elements that are supposed to be parallel

skip, to disregard one or more instructions in a sequence of instructions

skip code, a code which directs the computer to skip specified memory fields

skip flag, a 1 bit which causes bytes to be skipped until another 1 bit is encountered

skip instruction, an instruction which causes the processor ignore it and advance to the next instruction or jump to another location

skip test, an instruction which examines the state of a device or content of a register to determine a jump to an alternative operation

slack, file, the percentage of the space on a disk or other storage medium, occupied by a file, which does not contain data

slave, a terminal or other device controlled by a computer

slave computer, a computer which is under the control of another computer as a backup against failure of the main computer, as a repository and controller of file storage, as a device for background processing, etc.

slave station, a station or data sink which can only receive data

slice, chip architecture which permits increased word size by stacking circuits

slice, time, the time period during which a portion of resources are allocated to a programs running concurrently with another program

slot, a position in a microcomputer where special operating or control boards may be added

slot, peripheral, a card slot in the computer case which holds the controller of a peripheral device

slow storage, an external storage device which provides relatively slow access compared to that of a resident hard drive or disk

small business computer, a microcomputer system configured to the needs of business applications rather than for games or simple home applications

smart card, a card, similar to a credit card, with a magnetic surface onto which data can be recorded

smart interactive terminal, a terminal connected to a main computer, but which has its own processor and the capability to perform certain functions independent of the main computer

smart peripheral, a peripheral which contains its own processor and memory, permitting it to functions, at least partially, under its own control

SME, Society of Manufacturing Engineers

SMIS, Society for Management Information Systems

snapshot, a printout of intermediate results of a program's execution; a technique which allows capturing an image on the monitor screen to a disk file for importing to another program

snapshot debugging, tracking the

state of a computer in a specific part of a program

snapshot dump, a printout of a computer program at a particular point in its operation

soft carriage return, an end of line code which signals the computer that the text which follows is a continuation of the previous text and is to be kept together with it; a line break after text which does not fill the line sufficiently to cause it to wrap to the next line, inserted by the user, pressing the CR or Enter key in combination with a shift key

soft copy, data displayed on a monitor screen, in contrast to **hard copy**

soft error, a programming error

soft font, a font which is stored in the computer and sent to the printer as needed; also called a downloadable font

soft hyphen, a special hyphen, imbedded between the syllables of a word by a hyphenation program or the user, and which is visible only if the word breaks at the end of a line

soft key, a keyboard key which can be programmed by the user or defined by software

soft return, same as **soft carriage return**

soft-sectored, a floppy disk in which the data storage format is not built into the disk and is set up by the computer

software, the programs which direct the operations of a computer, in contrast to the **hardware**, or equipment, on which the programs are run

software, canned, software designed for a specific application, but not a specific user, often available on the open market

software, compatible, software which can be run on a particular computer without modification; software programs which be used in conjunction with each other

software, custom, any program designed and written to meet the special requirements of a customer

software documentation, a printed text or manual which provides information needed to load and run packaged software

software emulator, a program which modifies another program to enable it to run on a computer other than the one for which the program was written

software house, a company which designs, develops and markets software

software interrupt, an interrupt called for in a program

software library, a collection of software which can be run on a particular type of machine

software maintenance, reworking and improving a program to keep it current and working properly; reviewing data files to archive or purge outdated information

software, multilevel, application programs in which the user interacts with the computer on one level other functions required to run the program are being handled on another level in the background

software, packaged, commercial application programs designed for specific purposes, such as word processing, data base, etc., offered for lease in retail establishments or by mail order; see also **proprietary program**

software protection, techniques designed to prevent or discourage the unauthorized copying and distribution of programs leased to a user

software, public domain, software to which no person or company lays claim of ownership and which can be freely used, copied, or modified

software publishing, the advertising and distribution of software packages, updates, peripheral programs, etc.

software, resident, software loaded into, or readily available to, standalone terminals, stations, or computers

software resources, the programs and data designed for, and available to, a computer system

software sealed-in, software built into ROM as a method of protection against unauthorized copying and distribution

software, system, a collection of programs which control a computer or peripheral's functions

software utility package, a set of utilities available for a microcomputer to assist the user in such tasks as disk management, formatting disks, recovering damaged disks, finding files, recovering deleted files, writing batch files, speeding computer and hard disk operation, etc.

solids modeling, generation of shapes on a monitor screen through the use of geometric construction techniques; see **Cartesian coordinate system**

solid state, referring to electronic devices composed of solid materials, in contrast to vacuum tubes

solid state circuitry, the solid state components in a computer

solid state device, a device made up of solid state circuits

S-100 bus, an assemblage of 100 parallel lines used as an interface throughout several parts of a computer

sort, to organize the elements of a group into a specific order

sorter, a machine which sorts punched cards

sort field, the field, specified in a program, on which records are to be sorted

sorting pass, one access of each record in the process of reordering a series of records

sorting phase, the operations of a sort program: initialization, internal, and merge phases

sort, internal, to sequence records within main memory as the initial phase of a multiple-pass sort program

sort keys, the fields in a record which identify it for the purposes of sorting

sort/merge program, a program that can sort a file or merge two sorted files

sort, multi-pass, a sort program in which only part of the records are sequenced in a single pass through the data so that additional passes are required to complete the sort

sound driver, a program which controls the reproduction of sound recorded on computer **sound files**

sound file, a file which contains the digital data to reproduce sound on the computer or through the computer, often used in conjunction with a visual presentation

sound generator, a device for converting digital signals to analog signals which drive a speaker

source code, the high-level language in which a program is written before conversion to machine code

source computer, a computer which prepares or stores input for another computer

source data, information which has been verified and is ready to enter into the computer; documents, hard copy, computer files, etc. which comprise the data to be processed by a computer program

source data capture, automatic recording of transactions as they are entered from a remote terminal, such as shop floor collection or at a cash register, etc.

source data entry, OCR, data entry by means of optical character recognition, through a device which reads and directly translates special characters from a source document

source deck, a source program on a deck of punched cards

source document, the origin or hard copy from which data or information is obtained for entering into the computer; when transferring data between computer files, the file from which transfer data is obtained

source editor, a type of word processing program used in the editing of a source program

source language, a high-level language in which a program is written, such as COBOL, Pascal, BASIC, etc.

source-language debugging, a debugging program which furnishes information in the syntax of the source language

source-language translation, the restatement of a high-level language program into another high-level language

source library program, an assortment of programs and routines in high-level or assembly language

source program, a program written in a high-level language before it is converted to machine language

source statement, a program statement written in a high-level programming language

SPA, Systems and Procedures Association

space, an area not occupied by a character, zero or blank; a special character which produces a space on a printed page or monitor terminal

special character, a character other than a letter or number

special interest group, users with a common interest, organized to facilitate the trading and sharing of information

special purpose, designed for a specific use

special-purpose computer, a computer designed to perform a specific function

special purpose language, a language created to work a specific type of problem or perform a special function

specific address, in absolute code, an exact storage location

specification, a precise description of software or hardware

specifications, functional, the design requirements of a computer system based on its intended use

specification sheet, a form designed for coding program statements

speech recognition, the ability of special computers to understand certain commands and instructions as spoken by a person; the technology which allows partial or total control of a computer by speech rather than keyboard

speech recognition terminal, an input terminal with speech recognition capabilities

speech synthesis, emulating human speech from digital data

speech synthesizer, a device that produces human sounding speech

speed, printer, the optimum rate at which a printer can produce hard copy under ideal conditions, usually expressed as characters per second, characters per minute or pages per minute

spell checker, a program, stand alone or part of a word processing application, which proofreads for errors in spelling

spike, an abrupt voltage increase

split screen, the capability of partitioning a monitor screen into two or more sections, each of which displays data independently

spooler, a hardware or software buffering device which allows printing or other output processing without disrupting foreground activity

spooling, the computer processing of input or output operations simultaneous with foreground activity

spreadsheet, electronic, a computer data manager comprised of rows and columns of cells into which may be entered an absolute value or a formula to calculate a value based on other cells in the current spreadsheet or cells in another spreadsheet to which it is linked

sprocket feed, the paper feed mechanism on a printer which aligns and drives the paper with pins which fit in holes on the sides of the paper; also called **pin feed**

squeezed files, computer files which have been compressed to save storage space

stable, not subject to sudden change

stack, an area of memory in which data is held for quick access when called by a program

stacked job control, the execution of programs in the sequence in which they are received

stacked job processing, same as **stacked job control**

stack pointer, a register which contains the address of the current top of a stack

stack pointer register, same as **stack pointer**

stack, program, a routine used by a program for the temporary storage of data and instructions

stack, push-down, a stack whose data is loaded and unloaded from the top

stack, virtual memory, a stack which exists in virtual memory instead of in RAM

stair step, the ragged aspect of a diagonal line displayed on a raster scan device

stand-alone, a device which can function without connection or control by another device

stand-alone capability, the ability of a device to function independently

stand-alone network system, a limited number of workstations connected to each other or to a common host or file server

standard, uniform practices and procedures; a generally accepted criteria for measuring the performance of a computer or peripheral device

standard interface, an interface which complies with one of the industry standards for linking a computer and peripherals

standby, equipment which is ready to be used if primary equipment fails; a ready state, in which resources may be utilized at any time

standby register, a register which holds the information being processed and which will be reused if there is an error in processing

star network, a network in which terminals and computers are each connected directly to a main computer

start bit, in asynchronous transmission, the bit which signals the start of transmission

state, the condition of a computer, device, circuit, etc. at a specific time

statement, the instructions which make up a unit of a computer program

statement, non-executable, a program statement which sets up a program or procedure as contrasted to a command which directs the performance of a task

statement number, the number of a line of code in a program used to locate it for debugging, etc.; synonymous with **line number**

static, undesirable interference in a signal; referring to non-volatile memory which retains its contents without power

static dump, a dump of the computer's state at a specific time

static memory, memory which does not need a refresh to maintain its contents

static storage, same as **static memory**

station, a communications terminal; any input or output device which requires a human attendant

station, remote, a terminal which is located away from the computer and which is connected to it enabling normal communication

statistical analysis, the examination and evaluation of data using mathematical techniques

statistical error, inaccuracies caused by random variations in the data being analyzed

statistical sample, a set of representative data, selected at random from the universe of data being assessed, used for statistical analysis

statistical universe, the sum of all the records in the data to be assessed

statistics, the science of predicting the characteristics of a universe of data based on a systematic sampling and analysis of the data

status, the condition or state of a device at a specific moment in time

status bit, a bit stored in a register which indicates the status of a computer or the information it is processing

status register, a register which records the status of a device or its operation

status word, a computer word containing status bits

status word register, a register

which contains a status word

step, a unit of processing relational to its reference, as, an instruction, a part of an instruction, a part of a program, a part of an action, one of a series of actions, etc.

step counter, a counter which records the steps in a multiplication, division, or shift operation

step-down transformer, a device which reduces input voltage for a lower voltage output

stepping switch, a switching unit which advances from one state to another with each input pulse

stochastic, conjectural; referring to the process of selecting from among a group of theoretically possible alternatives, those elements which will most closely approximate a desired result; procedures characterized by trial and error

stochastic variable, a statistical variable which reflects the probability that it may assume a particular value in a set

stop bit, in asynchronous transmission, the bit which signals the end of transmission of a group of data bits

stop, dynamic, a stop in a program caused by an instruction which branches to itself

stop element, same as **stop bit**

stop key, a button which stops the processing of a program after completion of the instruction being processed

stop, program, a processing halt called from the program

storage, non-volatile mass memory to which data is transferred for retrieval at a later date

storage allocation, the assigning of

certain data to specific locations in memory

storage access, cyclic, cyclic memory; memory which allows access at multiples of a fixed time interval

storage allocation, dynamic, the system of assigning storage to the first space available in order to make the best use of disk space

storage, auxiliary, any external storage available to the computer in addition to, but not including, its internal storage, such as magnetic tape, floppy disk, external hard drive, compact disk, etc.

storage block, a section of storage handled as a unit

storage, buffer, a device which temporarily stores information during transfer; a secondary storage for data to be transferred between internal and external storage; a synchronizing element between internal and external storage, devices of differing speeds, etc.

storage, bulk, large capacity external storage which supplements internal storage

storage capacity, the maximum number of bytes, character, etc. which can be stored in a device such as a disk, tape, etc.

storage cell, a basic unit of storage

storage circuit, a circuit which stores the value of the last signal received until changed by a subsequent signal

storage, common, a part of memory accessible to all programs

storage, common block, a section of main memory used by both the main program and a subprogram

storage, computer, the memory in a computer system, managed by the computer, where data, instruc-

tions, programs, etc. are stored

storage, coordinate, coordinate indexing

storage cycle, the sequence of events involving the transfer of data to or from a storage device

storage, dedicated, a portion of memory set aside for a specific purpose

storage density, the compactness of data on a storage medium; the characters per unit length of tape or unit area of disk

storage device, any memory unit, such as RAM, disk, tape, etc.

storage devices, direct-access, devices which allow fast access to storage locations such as disks or drums

storage, direct-access, storage in which access is independent of the last location accessed

storage, disk, computer memory using hard or floppy disks; the area in which are saved copies of data and program files

storage, drum, data storage on a magnetic drum

storage dump, a printout of the contents of memory; a memory dump or dump printout

storage, dynamic, dynamic memory; memory which can be altered

storage element, same as **storage cell**

storage, erasable, a storage medium which can be erased and used again, such as disks or magnetic tape

storage, external, external memory; a storage device which is not an integral part of the computer

storage, fixed, ROM

storage, flip-flop, binary data stored on a device which uses bistable elements to record its state

storage fragmentation, disk fragmentation; file fragmentation; a condition which occurs when files are updated frequently and various parts of the file are scattered in pieces throughout the disk

storage, high-speed, memory with faster access time than disk or tape storage

storage, input, temporary storage of input which is waiting to be processed

storage, intermediate memory, a section of memory used to temporarily hold data

storage, internal, the memory which is directly accessible to the CPU

storage key, a code or label attached to each word in a storage block

storage light, an indicator light on the control panel which indicates a parity error has been detected while reading a character into storage

storage location, the place in memory where a character, byte, or word is stored

storage location, temporary, a block of memory allocated for the temporary storage of data which is in a intermediate state of processing

storage, magnetic, mass storage on magnetic media, such as drum, tape or disk

storage, magnetic tape, mass storage on magnetic tape, often a backup system

storage, main, the RAM memory or working storage of a computer; **main memory**

storage map, same as **memory map**

storage, mass, devices, such as disk or tape, used for somewhat permanent storage of programs and data

storage medium, the devices on which programs and data are stored, such as punched cards, magnetic tape, magnetic disks, etc.

storage, non-erasable, storage elements or media which cannot be erased or changed, such as punched cards or paper tape; stored data which is coded as read-only such as ROM or protected files

storage, nonvolatile, computer memory which retains its content when power is off

storage, off-line, storage which is not under the control of the computer

storage, on-line, non-volatile memory which is connected to and controlled by the computer

storage, parallel, storage in which all bits of a word are processed simultaneously

storage, peripheral, mass storage which is outside the computer case, such as a disk or tape unit

storage, permanent dynamic, storage of data which can be altered but which is not lost when power is turned off, such as tape, fixed disk or floppy disk storage

storage, primary, the computer's main RAM memory

storage, program, the portion of memory where the program and its active routines are stored

storage, protected, sections of computer memory reserved for specific functions, not subject to overwriting by any other programs or data; sections of storage set aside for specific users and which may be accessed only by a special code or password

storage protection, the prevention of the reading or writing of data in storage such as disk or tape

storage, push-up, storage in which the first item entered is the first item retrieved; same as **FIFO**

storage, random access, refers to storage in which each site has a unique address so that the medium or the accessing device is able to move directly to any site specified; the ability to read and write data to any location in memory in a constant amount of time; a system which allows data to be addressed independent of the last access of data contrasted to **sequential access;** storage whose contents can be accessed directly and thus very quickly

storage, read-only, storage from which data can be read but which cannot be altered; **ROM**

storage, secondary, an external storage device, such as disk or tape

storage, semiconductor, memory chips, such as RAM or ROM

storage, sequential access, mass storage which uses the sequential access method to locate files

storage, serial, storage in which data must be retrieved by reading records in sequence until the search file is found

storage, shared, main memory which can be accessed by two or more computers

storage, slow, an external storage device which provides relatively slow access compared to that of a

resident hard drive or disk

storage, static, memory which does not need a refresh to maintain its contents; fixed storage of information which is available at any time, such as flip-flop or electrostatic storage

storage, volatile, RAM memory which loses its contents when the power is off

storage, volatile dynamic, dynamic storage which loses its contents when the power is off

store, to transmit information to a memory device for retrieval at a later time

store-and-forward, message switching in which a message is temporarily stored for transmission at a later time

stored program, a program in memory which is ready to use

straight line coding, program coding in which all instructions are written as needed, in contrast to the use of called routines and programmed loops

stream, a flow of data, transmitted without regard to meaning or function; to transmit data without dividing it into fields, records, files, etc.

stream, bit, the sequence of bits in a binary signal with no regard to stop bits, parity bits, etc.; a reference to a string of bits transmitted with no separation between groups of characters

stream-oriented file, a file containing unstructured data such as a text document which is recorded in the sequence it is entered

string, a group of characters manipulated as a unit

string, alphabetic, a series, or

string, of letters

string, bit, an array of binary digits in which the position of each is set as a separate unit

string, character, a series of characters processed as a unit

string, flip-flop, a series of flip-flops in a row

string length, the number of positions or characters in a string

string manipulation, the technique for processing or manipulating data or character strings

string processing, operations on strings, such as concatenation, comparison, replacing, etc.

string, quoted, a string of characters, enclosed by quotation marks, treated as a unit

stroke, in optical character recognition, a segment of a line used in the forming of a character

structured language, a computer language which is suited to structured programming

structured program, program instructions contained in modules or routines which are selected as needed from a main or control routine

Structured Query Language, a language designed to retrieve from a large data base, only those records which match a specific criteria

stylus, an input device which looks like a pen

stylus, light, a device which is used to select elements or modify the display on a monitor screen

subcommand, a command to which an instruction branches; a procedure within an instruction

subprogram, a program which functions under the control of another program

subroutine, a set of instructions which perform a particular task, called by the main program

subroutine, closed, an external routine which can be called from a specific location

subroutine library, a collection of basic routines available for use as needed by a program

subroutine, open, a subroutine which can be inserted where it is needed in a program

subroutine reentry, the repeated use of a subroutine before it has been exited from a previous call, as in a loop

subroutine status table, a special process which maintains a list of subroutines and administers their calling and storage by a program

subscript, a code or number which identifies an element in an array; in typesetting, a character which is usually smaller than, and set below the base line of, the rest of the type on the line, as the numbers in H_2SO_4

subscripted variable, an element in an array of variables, identified by its subscript, or position in the array

subsequence counter, a counter which records the incidence of parts of operations

subset, a set which is a part of another set

subset, language, parts of a computer language which can be used independent from the rest of the language

sub-string, a part of a string; a series of contiguous elements within a larger series

subsystem, a set of components which is part of a larger system

subtracter, an analog device which measures the difference between two input signals

subtrahend, a quantity which is to be subtracted from another quantity

successive approximation, a system of solving equations which involves estimating the solution, testing the estimate, then modifying the estimate and testing as many times as necessary until a solution of the required accuracy is found

suffix, a label which describes one item in a collection of similar items; in some operating systems, an addendum to a file name which serves to identify similar files, as .BAT for a batch file, .DOC for a document file, .SYS for a system file, etc.

sum, the result of an addition

sum, check, a number used to verify the accuracy of a transmission; the sum of a group of digits, such as the total of the ASCII codes for a block of data, used to verify accuracy by comparison with a previously calculated sum of the same digits

summarize, to abridge data for reporting, such as totaling fields, counting incidence, etc. in contrast to the detailed output of processing

summation check, verifying data by comparing the sum of a group of digits with a similar sum calculated earlier; comparing the **check sum** derived from different processing of the same data

summer, an analog device which calculates the sum of input signals

superconductor, a material which conducts electricity with little or no loss to resistance

superimpose, to move data to a memory location, overwriting the data previously written to that location

superscript, a letter or symbol written above the base line of, and often in a smaller size than, the rest of the text on the line, such as a power, 2^{10}, or an incidental mark, IBM®

super-VGA, a technology which allows the monitor screen to display at higher resolution than VGA, 800 pixels across by 600 pixels down or 1024 by 768 with a faster refresh rate than that displayed by EGA or VGA; also called extended VGA or VGA plus

supervising system, the operating system; the program which handles the routine functions of computer operation such as reading the keyboard, accessing memory, managing input and output, etc.

supervisor, same as **supervising system**

supervisor, overlay, a routine which controls and manages the overlaying of program segments

supervisory communications, the routines which control access to other terminals and computers

supervisory console, a console which includes a control panel in addition to the keyboard, printer, and control unit

supervisory control, a technique which permits an operator to monitor processing and operations

supervisory instruction, an instruction which controls the execution of routines or programs

supervisory operating system, same as **operating system**

supervisory program, same as **operating system** or **supervising system**

support, ongoing assistance by vendors to the users of their devices or software; any action by a software or hardware device which improves operation of the system

support chips, chips which are required to assist a CPU in the operation of a system

support package, run-time, a special routine which assists in running a program

support program, a program which assists the user in the operation of the computer, file management, etc.

support systems, any hardware, software or vendor service which is of assistance in the improved operation of a computer system

suppression, the elimination or prevention of an element or event; the faculty of a printer to disregard certain characters; programming which directs the ignoring of certain commands or functions; a programming technique which eliminates certain elements in data when it is recorded or printed

suppression, zero, programming which removes zeros to the left of a data field when it is printed

suppresser, line surge, a device which protects equipment from line surges

surge, an unexpected momentary increase in the voltage of a power line; also, **line surge**

surge protector, same as **surge suppresser**

surge suppresser, a device which protects equipment from line surges; also, **line surge suppresser**

swapping, temporarily holding a low-priority program to allow the processing of a program which has a higher priority

switch, a device which establishes a temporary connection between elements in a communication path; a **conditional branch,** which temporarily directs control to a different section of a program when certain conditions are met

switch, alteration, a switch, either physical or contained in program instructions, which can be set to alter coded machine instructions

switching circuit, a circuit which executes a switching function

switch, sense, a switch, either physical or contained in program instructions, which can be set to alter coded machine instructions

switch, toggle, a manual or electronic switch which maintains one of two stable states

symbol, a programmer-defined or language-defined representation of a program element

symbolic, referring to a character, image or label which represents something else

symbolic address, a location in memory identified by a name or other symbol instead of by its absolute address

symbolic addressing, identifying a location in memory by assigning a name representative of the data contained therein

symbolic code, same as **source code**

symbolic coding, coding using symbols instead of machine language

symbolic coding format, the rules

which govern the way in which various elements of a program are written according to the syntax of the language used

symbolic concordance program, a coding or language system which furnishes a cross-referenced list of the labels used in a program

symbolic language, any computer language which must be translated to machine language before running, hence, any language of a higher order than machine language; the use of symbols to represent logic instructions

symbolic logic, formal logic as represented by precise symbols

symbolic macro assembler, a macro assembler which permits the use of mnemonics and labels for the definition of machine instructions

symbolic math system, a computer program which solves algebraic equations and other mathematical operations which use unknowns, as in trigonometry and calculus

symbolic name, a label which identifies a program, a routine, a data set, a data file, etc.

symbolic programming, writing a computer program in a language which must be translated to machine language before running; the use of symbols to represent logic instructions

symbolic table, a list of the meanings of a set of symbols, either as another set of symbols or by definition

symbol, logic, a symbol which represents a logical operator

symbol, logical, a symbol which represents a logical operator

symbol library, the set of symbols which may be used for a particular application

symbol manipulation, the actions of a list processing language

symbol string, a string which contains or is made up of symbols; a symbol which is represented by a string of characters or code

symbol, variable, a representation of a program element which changes during the execution of a program; a symbol which can assume a range of values

synch, a signal which designates the beginning of a block

synchronization, the alignment of the relationship between elements

synchronization character, a character which keeps other elements in a synchronous transmission timed so as to be interpreted properly

synchronization, modem, the system of matching the speed and mode of two modems to function either asynchronous or synchronous

synchronization pulse, a pulse which keeps other elements in a synchronous transmission timed so as to be interpreted properly

synchronizer, a buffer which counteracts any variance in time between transmission and receiving

synchronizing clock, the device that produces clock signals and synchronizes messages sent to peripherals

synchronous, occurring at the same time; occurring in time with a timing device

synchronous computer, a computer in which operation is controlled by the pulses of a timing signal

synchronous data communication, the transmission of data between devices which are synchronized with a common timer signal

synchronous data transmission, same as **synchronous data communication**

synchronous gate, a gate which produces output in time with input

synchronous transmission, data transfer which is controlled by a timing signal

syntactic error, same as **syntax error**

syntax, the rules governing the structure and use of a language

syntax bug, same as **syntax error**

syntax checker, a program which monitors source statements for violations of the syntax of a language

syntax error, a computer program error caused by failure to follow the rules for structure and use of the programming language

syntax recognizer, a program subroutine which interprets the syntax of a programming language

syntax rules, the discipline which outlines the sentence structure, or the order of the elements of a sentence, in a programming language

synthesis, the combination of compatible elements to form a working unit which fills a specific requirement

synthesis, speech, emulating human speech from digital data

synthesis, systems, the analysis of a problem and the detailed planning for its solution

synthesizer, a device which produces sound from digital instructions

synthetic language, an artificial or non-spoken language designed to serve a particular purpose, as a pseudo code or symbolic language

system, a computer with its peripheral devices and software which interact with each other as a cohesive unit

system, accuracy control, a system which detects errors and signals their presence

system, adaptive, a computer or program which learns from past activity; for example, a scanner or hyphenation system which, when corrected, retains a record for future use.

system, application development, a series of programs used for the development of custom designed applications

system, assembly an assembly language with its assembler

system, audio, computer equipment which can process and store data from voice input

system, backup, a standby system available for use when the primary system is down and which takes control either automatically or at the user's command; a system combining several sophisticated techniques for the detection and correction of errors

system, basic input/output, (BIOS) the part of the CP/M or MS-DOS operating system which controls the screen, the keyboard, printers and other peripheral devices

system, basic operating, a program which controls the essential functions of computer operation, such as reading the keyboard, accessing disk drives, monitor display, communicating with the printer, etc.

system, binary, the number system in base 2

system, block parity, a system which uses parity bits to detect errors in block data transfers

system, broad band, in data transmission, the ability to handle a greater frequency range than voice grade

system, Cartesian coordinate, a system for indicating the shape of a solid by means of three planes intersecting at right angles to each other at a point called the origin from which any point in space with coordinates x, y, and z can be located; the means used in a CAD system to represent a three dimensional object on screen

system, cassette-user tape a system which includes hardware and software necessary to store data and programs on a cassette tape

system chart, a schematic of a system which shows the information flow

system check, a test of system performance

system, closed loop, a technique in which a program controls an external program or process without human involvement

system commands, instructions which direct the computer to perform tasks relegated to the operating system, such as setting system parameters, displaying list of files in a directory, copying a file or directory, backing up, etc.

system, communications, a computer which manages real-time, on-line applications

system, computer, a computer or computers and all of the associated peripherals and software

system, computer communications, a microcomputer system which handles real-time applications; the hardware which makes up a communication system which is controlled by computer such as telephone and fax modems, etc.

system, contention, a system of transmitting data in which the sender tests for conflict, i.e., a busy line, and does not attempt to transmit until the channel is free

system control panel, a panel which allows the computer operator to control the internal functions of a computer, to intercede in the processing of a program, and to debug software

system, conversational, a system in which the user or a device employed by the user can communicate directly with the computer

system, data collection a system which collects, sorts and stores data from remote collection stations

system, data communications, data processing which involves the use of terminal devices, communications software, and the transmission and receiving of data over common and private lines

system design, complete specifications for the components of a computer system and the working relationship between them

system, disk operating, (DOS) an operating system for microcomputers; the program which controls all of the computer functions and from which other programs are run

system, disk, the components required for disk management including drives, heads, support chips, and software

system, dual, a system which runs the same program on two computers and compares the results to confirm accuracy

system, dual processor, a computer system which incorporates a second processor as an emergency backup

system, electronic data processing, the assortment of hardware, software and people which together perform electronic data processing

system, electronic switching, a telephone switching system which is controlled by a digital computer

system, executive, a set of routines which manages the sequencing and executing of programs; an operating system which provides for the running of several programs at one time or multi-tasking

system, fail-safe, a computer system designed to record and periodically move changes to a special backup file which can be retrieved after a power or system failure

system, file management, the part of a disk operating system which controls the use of disk files; a set of operational procedures for the creation and maintenance of an organization's files; a software program which assists in the organization and maintenance of files

system, financial planning, a software package which permit the user to explore and rate options before making an investment decision

system flowchart, a graphic illustration of the flow of information through a system

system, hard disk, the components required for disk management including drives, heads, support chips, and software

system, hierarchical file, a file system which allows cataloguing files in directories and sub-directories depending on their relationship

system, home security, a system for the home, controlled by a computer, which can control and monitor the operation of burglar alarms, smoke detectors and lights as well as locks for windows and doors

system, information, the procedures for storing and retrieving data in a particular situation or organization and making it available to those who need it

system, input/output control, a set of routines for managing I/O operations

system, integrated, a method of combined processing which provides that data need not be reentered to be used in succeeding operations

system, interactive, a system which allows the user or a peripheral device to communicate with the computer and alter its actions during processing

system, interactive debugging, a program which allows examination of a program line by line by simulating a run of the program and providing an accompanying hexadecimal display of memory states

system interface, a device which connects components in a microcomputer

system language, a language in which instructions relate directly to machine language statements

system life cycle, the useful life predicted for a computer system, considering workload, future needs and changes in technology

system loader, a program which places assembler or compiler output into computer memory

system, management the organizational structure of the personnel who direct the operations of an organization

system, management information, the procedures for storing and retrieving data in a particular situation or organization and making it available to those who need it

system, management support, the computer analysis of information to assist management in decision making

system, master/slave, an arrangement of computers in which all are controlled by one

system, microcomputer, a complete computer system operated by a microprocessor including the CPU, memory, keyboard, CRT monitor, and any peripherals

system monitor, a set of routines which supervise the order and execution of programs in a multitasking environment

system, multiple process operating, an operating system which is capable of accessing more than one application and executing more than one function at a time

system, multi-computer, a computer system which operates with two or more CPU's

system, multi-user, a computer system with multiple terminals, all of which may be used at the same time

system, natural language, a computer system that accepts a spoken language as contrasted to a machine language

system, on-line, a procedure whereby data is fed into the computer directly from its point of origin, as in some cash register, banking and airline systems

system, open-ended, a computer or computer system which may be modified or to which additional input/output devices may be added without disrupting the original system or the purpose for which it was intended

system, open loop control a routine for checking transmission without feedback, in which the check data is contained in the transmission data, such as a parity check

system, operating, the program which handles the routine functions of computer operation such as reading the keyboard, accessing memory, managing input and output, etc.; **main program**

system, output module control, a device which stores program commands and converts them into control signals

system, peripheral disk, file storage on a disk system outside the computer

system, phonetic, a system of machine generated or voice sourced speech synthesis which constructs words from phonemes

system, point of sale, a scheme which computerizes the functions related to retail transactions including, but not limited to, recording and reporting transactions, summarizing activity, tracking and adjusting inventory, etc.

system, program development, the hardware and software used to design, write, test and debug software applications

system prompt, a symbol, character or series of characters which indicate the command line, or insertion point for instructions to be typed to a computer system

system, real-time, a system which processes information so that the output can be used by the process supplying the information

system, remote job entry, a system which provides for job entry from a remote terminal

systems analysis and design, the process of analyzing and designing solutions to a data processing problems

systems analyst, a person who specializes in the analysis and design of computer applications

systems architect, a person who specializes in the internal design of microprocessors or computer systems

systems compatibility, the compatibility of components in a computer system

systems engineer, a systems analyst who designs applications for the user

systems engineering, the technique of analyzing needs and designing, or specifying, a computer system to fill those needs; establishing a strategy for implementing an existing computer system to fill the needs of an organization

systems manual, a handbook of detailed specifications, and instructions for operating, a computer system

system software, a collection of programs which control a computer or peripheral's functions

systems program, a program which controls the operation of the computer; same as **operating system**

systems programmer, a person who designs and writes programs necessary for the system to function

systems study, an examination of the practicality of modifying a computer system or installing a new one

systems, support, any hardware, software or vendor service which is of assistance in the improved operation of a computer system

systems synthesis, the analysis of a problem and the detailed planning for its solution

systems testing, verifying the operation of a computer system by running a set of programs of known operation and results

system support programs, programs which aid in the operation of the system

T

tab, a preset location on a line of copy; to send the screen cursor to a preset location on a line

table, a two-dimensional array with columns and rows of related data

table, decision, a graphic aid which displays possible courses of action for a given situation

table, look-up, data stored in referenced columns and rows which allows easy access when the value of a variable is required

table look-up, the use of a known value to locate a variable in a referenced data array

table, program reference, a section of memory used to store operands, array references, subroutines, etc.

tablet, graphics, a drawing surface which converts the position of an electronic stylus into digital data which can be displayed on a monitor screen

tabulate, to arrange in a table or list; to calculate the totals for groups of data

tactile keyboard, a flexible membrane printed to look like the standard keyboard which it replaces and which sends the appropriate signals to the computer when touched; same as **touch-sensitive-membrane keyboard**

tag, a marker or label; a **flag**; part of an instruction which references an index register whose contents modify the address in the instruction; information attached to data which identifies the field or record to which it belongs

take-up reel, the spool onto which tape is wound as it is being read for processing

talking terminal, a terminal with speech synthesis capability, designed to communicate with the blind

tape, a plastic or paper strip for recording digital data; **magnetic tape** or **paper tape**

tape backup, a copy of the data and programs from a computer saved to magnetic tape to protect against loss as a result of disk failure; a system designed to create such a backup, usually at regular intervals

tape cable, a cable comprised of flat metallic ribbon conductors

tape cartridge, magnetic tape which is enclosed in a protective container

tape cassette, a self-contained package of reel-to-reel magnetic tape, such as that used in stereo systems and video recorders can be used to store computer data

tape deck, a magnetic tape drive including read/write heads and controllers

tape drive, a device which operates with tape reels or cartridges, in contrast to cassettes

tape head, the read/write head in a magnetic tape system

tape label, the first record on a magnetic tape which contains a description of its contents

tape, magnetic, recording tape used for the storage of computer programs and data

tape mark, a machine-readable mark on a magnetic tape indicating the end of the tape is imminent

tape, master, a tape which contains the operating system program, the main program or control program of an integrated set of programs or a master data file

tape, paper, tape which stores data in rows of holes and spaces; also called **perforated tape** or **punched tape**

tape, punched paper, same as **paper tape**

tape speed, the rate at which tape moves past the read/write head during normal operation

target computer, a computer specifically designated to run a program which is being written or translated; a computer designated as the receiver of data or instructions from another computer

target program, a program which

has been translated into a particular machine language

task, a job for the computer; an instruction or set of instructions

task management, instructions in a control program which allocates the use of system resources

task queue, all the task control blocks in the system at any one time

technique, a method or procedure for accomplishing a specific task

telecommunications, transmission of data between remote locations

template, programmer's, a card which contains traceable cutouts of symbols, used in preparing a flowchart

temporary register, a register which holds the output from an ALU while it is being sent to the destination register in case of transmission error

temporary storage, same as **temporary storage area**

temporary storage area, the memory area set aside for temporary files and work in process

temporary storage location, same as **temporary storage area**

term, an element in a mathematical equation; a word or phrase used by a programming language

terminal, a remote terminal with a monitor screen and keyboard input used for communications or offline jobs; a data station; a workstation

terminal, ASCII, a keyboard terminal capable of sending and receiving the full set of ASCII codes

terminal, graphics, a terminal with graphics input capabilities

terminal, intelligent, a terminal with built in input/output and

other processing operations which to some extent free it from dependence on the host

terminal, interactive, a terminal equipped with a keyboard for data entry

terminal interface, the connector which interfaces a terminal with a computer

terminal, job-oriented, a terminal which is designed for a specific application

terminal keyboard, an alphanumeric or numeric keyboard which is part of, or connected to, a terminal

terminal, master, the terminal in a network which is controlling the computer, its peripherals and communications with other terminals in the system

terminal, multi-drop, one of several workstations connected to a single line

terminal, speech recognition, an input terminal with speech recognition capabilities

terminal symbol, a flowchart symbol which denotes the starting and ending points of a procedure

terminal, talking, a terminal with speech synthesis capability, designed to communicate with the blind

terminating symbol, a symbol on tape which marks the end of a block of information

term, self-defining, an expression whose value or function is identified by the expression itself

test, to check for certain conditions; to determine the accuracy of an operation, or the state of devices; running data whose output is known to verify a program

test data, data which will deliver known output, used to verify the operation of a program

test, diagnostic, a special routine, sometimes inserted in an existing program, to locate and identify a malfunction in a device or a program

testing, marginal, the testing of hardware to ascertain which components are most likely to fail under stress; **bias checking**

testing, on-line, test equipment connected directly to the CPU for monitoring tasks as they are performed

testing, parameter, using a parameter in a test routine to ensure that input produces the desired output

testing, saturation, trying out a program by inputting a large quantity of data to see if errors occur

test, leapfrog, a program used to detect computer malfunctions

test pattern generator, a device which generates special messages for verifying that communications equipment is operating correctly

test problem, a routine designed to determine whether a computer or a program is functioning properly

test, reliability, a stress test designed to evaluate the probability that a device will operate for a reasonable length of time without error or failure

text, words displayed on a printer or monitor screen; information; the body of a letter or memo

text editing, altering a text file, whether a programming or word processing function

text editor, a program with minimal word processing functions and without the ability to format printout usually in ASCII

text mode, the configuration of a monitor screen or printer in which only characters can be displayed or printed, in contrast to **graphics capability** or **graphics mode**

thermal printer, a dot-matrix printer which uses hot wires to form characters on heat-sensitive paper

thesaurus, a list of words; commonly, a dictionary of synonyms and antonyms

thrashing, switching parts of a program between mass storage and the computer in a slow, inefficient manner

three-dimensional array, a layered array made up of sequential sets of two-dimensional arrays with columns, rows, and layers

three dimensional digitizer, a device which inputs three dimensional coordinates by moving a stylus over a three dimensional object

three-dimensional graphics, line drawings which use perspective to create the impression of a third dimension

three dimensional line drawing, a line drawing in perspective to simulate a three dimensional, or solid, object; a graphic representation used in computer aided design; **three dimensional graphics**

threshold, a logic operator which returns true only if a stated number of statements are true; the level at which a change of state occurs

throughput, productivity; the quantity of data processed by a computer in a measured time period

tie-breaker, circuitry which prevents two CPUs from attempting to communicate simultaneously with a single device

tightly coupled, descriptive of devices in a computer system which are dependent on each other

time, access, the lapsed time between the moment when the computer asks for data from a storage unit and the moment when the data becomes available

time, cycle, the time required for the completion of a particular function

time, decay, the time it takes for voltage to drop to 10% of its maximum value

time division multiplexer, a device which interleaves signals from several sources at timed intervals

time, down, the time during which a computer is not operating regardless of the reason

time gate, a gate which produces output at specified intervals

time-out, the time which the computer waits for a task to be performed before reporting on error condition

time, real, referring to processing which is not delayed, generally in an interactive program, accepting data as it is input and producing output as required

time, response, the time taken for a computer to respond to input

timer, interval, an internal clock which keeps track of the time of day and has the ability to interrupt if specified to do so

timer, programmable, same as **programmable clock**

time, search, the time required to locate a particular item in storage

time-sharing, several users connected to a computer at the same time; a system whereby an organization which cannot justify a computer installation buys time from another organization which has open time on their computer

time-sharing monitor, a program which coordinates and controls time-sharing

time slice, the time period during which a portion of resources are allocated to a programs running concurrently with another program

time-slicing, allocating computer time sequentially in turn between programs or users to provide simultaneous access to all

timing circuits, circuits which control the timing of events within a computer

timing error, an error caused by an operation which takes more or less time than anticipated

timing signals, signals sent at timed intervals which synchronize the internal operation of a computer

toggle, a flip-flop; any device which has two stable states; to set a control to one of two states

toggle switch, a manual or electronic switch which maintains one of two stable states

tolerance, the allowable variation from a specified value or condition

tone generator, a sound generator that produces musical tones

top down design, same as **top down programming**

top-down programming, a problem solving technique which involves, in order: analysis of the problem, design of the program or solution in terms of broad objectives, designing the modules and subroutines needed in the program and, finally, writing the detailed code

topology, the study of the relationships of points in space; the physical or logical placement of stations in a computer network

total, batch, the sum of selected data in a batch of data records often to validate the run

touch-sensitive membrane keyboard, a flexible membrane printed to look like the standard keyboard which it replaces and which sends the appropriate signals to the computer when touched

touch-sensitive screen, a special monitor screen which transmits a signal when touched

touch terminal, a terminal which allows the user to select input by touching an area of the screen

trace, to monitor the execution of a program, one instruction at a time, observing the results for debugging

trace program, a program which has the capability to track the actions of another program for debugging

trace, selective, tracing a program for only specified elements

tracing, interpretive, a debugging system which simulates the operation of a program by interpreting each step

tracing routine, a routine which provides a record of the contents of registers and the value of variables during a program run

track, a single concentric circle on a disk, on which data is recorded

trackball, a moveable ball mounted on a base, which operates in a fashion similar to that of a mouse,

used for moving the cursor on a monitor screen

tractor feed, a part of the paper feed mechanism on a printer which helps move continuous form paper through a printer

trailer, a record indicating the end of a file or group of records, and which contains information about that file or record group

trailer label, same as **trailer**

transaction, any single activity or documentation of an activity, such as an order, a record, an instruction, etc.

transaction code, one or more elements in a field which distinguish the type of transaction represented by the record

transaction file, a register of transactions used to update a master file; a **detail file**

transaction listing, an itemized list of data entered, operations performed and result of the processing

transaction processing, processing of data by the computer as it is entered

transaction terminal, a station on a shop floor or in a store which allows entry of data to the computer as transactions take place

transceiver, a device which transmits and receives signals

transcribe, to copy; to enter data into the computer; to move data from one storage medium to another

transfer, to move; to shift control from one location or peripheral to another; to copy from one location or storage device to another; the act of transferring

transfer check, verification of the accuracy of a transfer of data

transfer, conditional, an instruction to move control to a new section of the program if a certain condition is met; a **conditional branch**

transfer rate, the speed with which data can be transferred between one location or device and another

transform, to change the format or structure of data without altering its meaning

transformation, graphics, the alteration of a graphics display by changing size, position, or perspective

transformer, a device which changes the voltage and frequency of an electrical power supply

transient, temporary

transient area, a memory area available for user programs, temporary storage of data, etc.

transistor, an electronic device which controls the flow of electrical current in the computer

transistor-transistor logic, (TTL) a type of integrated circuit used for input/output and control functions in microcomputers

transition, a change from one condition to another

translate, to convert signals, data, programs, etc. from one form to another

translation, the conversion of communication signals to binary data; restating a computer program in a different language; revision of a file format for acceptance by an applications program other than the one for which it was originally intended

translation, machine, the conversion of programs or data from one form to another, such as from OCR to a data file, one program language to another, etc.

translator, a program which translates other programs from one computer language into another

translator, input, the portion of a program which converts entries from the keyboard into machine operators

transmission, sending an electronic signal from one location to another

transmission error, the loss or distortion of data during transfer from one location to another

transmission error correction, the accurate repeat transfer of data which initially contained transmission errors

transmission loss, a decrease in signal power during transmission

transmission, parallel, a system communication in which all bits in a block or string are sent simultaneously

transmission, serial, sending data one bit at a time instead of in full computer words

transmission speed, the rate at which data is transmitted, often expressed in bits per second; **baud rate**

transmission, synchronous, data transfer which is controlled by a timing signal

transparency, communications, the ability of a computer to communicate in the background with no apparent interrupt or delay in foreground operations

transparent, referring to computer processing which takes place in the background without user intervention

transport, to transfer in bulk, as a unit, or as a whole from one storage device to another

transportable microcomputer, a microcomputer small enough to be easily carried from place to place; **laptop computer; notebook computer**

trap, a device which causes a transfer of control; a programming device which suspends running and displays an error message when an error is detected

tray, a storage drawer for punched cards

tree, a branched structure in which each item is linked to the one above it and all items below it

tree structure, the organization of data which involves linking each item to two or more related items; a **hierarchical file system** of directories which contain files and directories of a lower order, and which are in turn linked to their parent or higher level directory, all of which branch from the root or base directory

trial run, running a program with sample or test data of known output to verify the accuracy of program procedures

trigger, an electronic device which uses stored information to test conditions and initiate actions based on those conditions

triple precision, the use of three times the normal number of bits or words to delineate a number

troubleshoot, to identify and correct a problem in hardware or software

truncate, to shorten by cutting off the less significant parts, as the rounding of a decimal number to a limited number of places

truncation, cutting off one or more of the least significant digits from a number

truncation error, a mathematical error caused by rounding, usually in intermediate calculations

trunk, same as **bus**

truth table, a two-dimensional array which represents the output values for all possible combinations of input

TSR, terminate and stay resident; referring to a memory-resident utility such as a scratch pad, alarm clock, or spell checker, which remains in the background while other programs are processing and can be called up by the user whenever needed from anywhere in the computer; **memory resident**

TTL, transistor-transistor logic; a type of integrated circuit used for input/output and control functions in microcomputers

TTL compatible, memory which can interface with TTL devices without additional buffering or circuitry; memory which has been rendered able to interface with TTL devices

tube, cathode-ray, a display device attached to a computer or used as a remote terminal; a vacuum tube which sprays a stream of electrons onto a fluorescent screen such as a television set or computer display

Turing machine, a theoretical machine with four functions, used to identify the kind of problems which can be solved by machine

Turing test, a test for artificial intelligence

turn around document, a document which, in the normal course of business would be returned, or a copy returned, to the sender, as an invoice

turn around time, time required for feedback: the time the computer takes to produce data from the processing of a program; the time required to fill a third party request for data which involves scheduling the computer time based on work load; the time to allow for delivery of parts, hardware, software and supplies; etc.

turnkey, a computer system designed for a specific application which can be operated immediately, without any modification; a system designed and installed by an outside vendor so that it is ready to run without modification after installation

turtle, a cursor which operates under program control, used to create geometric figures on a monitor screen

turtle geometry, the mathematics of programming a turtle to create graphics

tutorial, programmed lessons in the use of a system, program, or device

two-address, an instruction which identifies the address of the operand and the address for the result of the operation

two-dimensional array, data which is arranged in rows and columns of similar content

two-dimensional line drawing, a graphic representation of a single plane or side of an object

two-level subroutine, a nested subroutine; a subroutine which contains another subroutine

type-ahead buffer, a keyboard buffer which allows typing faster than characters can be echoed to the monitor screen; a technique for holding a user-defined number of entries from the keyboard while awaiting processing, often providing for a warning beep when the quantity is exceeded; also called *n* **key rollover**

typeball, a printing element which contains raised characters on the surface of a metal or plastic sphere

type font, a specific size and style of a type face, such as Time Roman, 12 point, italics

U

UART, universal asynchronous receiver/transmitter; a circuit which exchanges data between parallel and serial formats

UCSD P-system, an operating system developed by the University of California at San Diego for microcomputers which compiles its programs in P-code, so that use on a computer entails creating a P-code interpreter for that machine's language

UCSD Pascal, an extended version of Pascal used for P-code

ultrasonic, sound frequencies above the range of human hearing

unallowable instruction digit, a set of bits, or character, not recognized as a valid operation code

unary operator, a logic operator with one state only

unblanked scope, a scope in which the Z-axis, or depth, is simulated by differences in intensity

unblind, to allow the display of transmitted data which is normally not printed

unblock, to separate one or more records from a block in memory

unbundled, selling separately, hardware, software, and services which are usually sold as a package

uncommitted storage list, blocks of memory which have not been allocated for a particular use

unconditional, without exception

unconditional branch, an absolute or unqualified instruction to move control to a new section of the program

unconditional jump, an unconditional branch; an absolute or unqualified instruction to move control to a new section of the program

unconditional transfer, same as **unconditional branch**

uncorrectable error, a mistake in a program which cannot be understood by the compiler

underflow, a quantity which is too small for the computer to display

undo command, in some applications, an instruction which reverts a document, spreadsheet, etc. back its condition before the last command was executed

unidirectional, one-way communication between devices

uniform spacing, referring to a type font in which the space occupied by each character is the same width, as contrasted to **proportional spacing**

uninterruptible power supply, a special battery backup which provides short-term power when external power is lost, allowing an orderly shutdown or continued operation

unipolar, having only one pole

unit, a device having a particular function; a basic element, as of hardware or a program

unit position, the rightmost position in a field; the numeral to the immediate left of the radix point

universal asynchronous receiver/transmitter, a circuit which exchanges data between parallel and serial formats

universal language, a language which can run on several different computers

Universal Product Code, a code assigned to a distinct product which identifies the product, the manufacturer or source, etc. represented by a pattern of lines which can be read by an optical device

unpack, to restore **packed data** in order to allow the computer to access it

unrecoverable abend, an abend with no provision in the program to restart or to determine the cause

unused-command check, a test for illegally coded instructions

unwind, to code explicitly all the operations of a cycle

up and running, referring to a computer or peripheral which is in operation and functioning properly

UPC (Universal Product Code)

update, to post changes and additions to a master file

UPS, uninterruptible power supply

up time, the time during which equipment is functioning properly

upward compatible, the ease with which a computer or system may be upgraded at a future time instead of being replaced; the provision in a system to take advantage of improvements anticipated to be available in the future

user, a person who utilizes the computer facility to perform specific tasks although not necessarily the operator of the system

user area, the storage area available

for user programs and data in contrast with areas reserved for system functions

user definable keys, function keys which may be programmed by the user to perform specific functions

user friendly, easy to use; generally referring to computers and applications which require little or no experience to use, usually menu driven with on-line context sensitive help

user group, an association of individuals or representatives of organizations which use computers, formed to share information and ideas, usually relating to a particular type of computer or application

user hotline, a phone number provided by the supplier of hardware or software to provide the user assistance in the use of the supplier's products

user interaction, exchange of communication between a user and a computer system

user library, general purpose routines or subroutines available to the user

user memory, RAM which has not been set aside for computer system functions and is available for use by the user

user memory map, an area of memory available to an individual user, distinct from areas available to other users

user-oriented, a system designed for ease of use by those who have only minimal knowledge of the computer; **user friendly**

user-oriented language, a programming language which somewhat resembles English and does not require the programmer to have a

working knowledge of machine language

user program, an interactive application program which is run by the user, in contrast to a program in which the user's primary interest is the output from the run; a program or routine written or modified by the user, as contrasted to a packaged program designed for a specific task and which cannot be altered

user terminal, a remote terminal with a monitor screen and keyboard input used for communications or off-line jobs; a data station; a workstation

utilities, system maintenance or general purpose software which aid in managing file systems, backing up files, recovering lost files, enhancing computer performance, etc. as well as making the user more efficient with such things as note pads, appointment calendars and alarm clocks

utility, a program which enhances the operation of a computer; the running of a program or the efficiency of the user

utility debug, a debugging program included as part of a compiler or assembler package

utility functions, ordinary system operations such as printing, reading keyboard input, etc.

utility program, a program which assists in the operation of a computer, such as a backup program, a disk compactor, etc.; a program which enhances the operation of another program such as a grammar or spell checker in a word processing program, etc.; a **peripheral program** or **support pro-**

gram

utility routines, software which makes frequently used computer functions easier

V

vaccine, an **anti-virus program**

validation, insuring, insofar as possible, that data to be input is correct

validity checking, the set of procedures for detecting invalid results of computation or invalid data for input

value, absolute, the magnitude of a number without regard to its sign

value-added reseller, a company which customizes and bundles hardware components into completed devices or systems for resale under their own or someone else's name

value, residual, the assigned value of equipment at the end of a lease or after it has been depreciated

variable, alterable or changing; a symbol, code or name representing a value which changes during the execution of a program

variable, Boolean, a logic variable with one of two values: 1 (true) or 0 (false)

variable connector, a flowchart symbol representing a conditional connection; a routine that may introduce other routines depending on the operation of the program; a multiple branch point

variable, global, a variable which is available to the entire program; in an applications program, a variable which is available through all files created with the program

variable length field, a field which

is not limited to predetermined number of positions

variable length record, a record which is not limited to a predetermined number of fields

variable length record file, a file consisting of records which are not restricted to a specific length

variable, local, a variable used by a subroutine and not available to the rest of the program

variable, manipulated, a variable which is altered in order to regulate a condition

variable name, the identifier of a program element which can assume a range of values

variable, stochastic, a statistical variable which reflects the probability that it may assume a particular value in a set

variable, subscripted, an element in an array of variables, identified by its subscript, or position in the array

variable symbol, a representation of a program element which changes during the execution of a program; a symbol which can assume a range of values

variable symbol, global, in assembly programming, a variable symbol which transfers values between macros or between a macro and the main program

VCR, video cassette recorder

VDT, video display terminal; a monitor screen; an interactive unit which displays data from the computer and data being prepared to enter into the computer

vector, a quantity which has both magnitude and direction; a one-dimensional array

vectored interrupt, an interrupt

which identifies its source and directs a jump to a special routine based on the cause of the interrupt

vector quantity, a quantity which has both magnitude and direction

Venn diagram, a graphic illustration of the relationships between sets of data

verification, comparison of two sets of data to ensure accuracy; also **key verification**

verify, checking a copy of data against the original to avoid errors in transcribing; insuring, insofar as possible, that data which is to be entered is correct

vertical parity check, a test for data error which entails a count of redundant bits in a computer word.

vertical redundancy, an error condition occurring when a computer word fails a parity check

vertical redundancy check, (VRC) a system for checking data transmission errors in which a parity bit is assigned to each character transmitted

vertical scrolling, shifting the image on a monitor screen up or down to display information which is beyond the borders of the screen

VGA, video graphics array; a computer monitor screen technology which offers a 256 color mode and 640 pixels across by 480 pixels down resolution

VGA plus, same as **super VGA**

video, compressed, a system of transmitting video signals over telephone lines

videodisk, a medium for storing visual information on a disk and which can also be used to store digital data from a computer

video display generator, a device which controls the image displayed on a CRT

video display terminal, (VDT) same as **video terminal**

video graphic display, a system which displays graphic images on a CRT controlled by a computer

video image generation, the use of vector or raster technology to translate digital data into a video image

video monitor, a cathode ray tube

video, reverse, a CRT monitor display showing dark characters on a light background

video terminal, a computer terminal which includes a CRT

video terminal code, one of a set of control codes which governs the display of an image on a CRT

virtual, simulated, as if real

virtual address, an immediate or real-time address

virtual array, an array in linear form which simulates a two or more dimensional array

virtual machine, a computer which can imitate the operation of other computers or computer environments

virtual memory, disk storage used as an extension of the computer's main memory

virtual memory stack, a stack which exists in virtual memory instead of in RAM

virtual storage, same as **virtual memory**

virus, computer, any undesirable instruction which adversely affects the performance of a computer or program; a program or instruction maliciously hidden in another program which replicates itself and destroys files, changes files, clogs the system or performs any other action which is detrimental to the computer and its programs

visual display console, an operator's console which allows a visual display of computer contents

visual display unit, a **video terminal**

visual scanner, a device which reads print or graphic images into the computer; a device which reads optical data designed for scanner recognition and converts it into digital data

vocabulary, a list of operating codes or reserved words which are acceptable for writing a program in a particular language

voice acceptance terminal, a terminal which accepts and is able to act on voice commands

voice frequency, the frequency of sounds within the range of human hearing

voice-grade channel, a channel which is capable of handling the transmission of speech

voice output, computer output in the form of a synthetic or recorded voice

voice recognition, computer recognition of the human voice

voice synthesis, reproduction of the human voice by a succession of recorded vocal sounds or by synthesizing from digital data

void, unoccupied or empty; the absence of a portion of a printed character which is to be read by a scanner, making recognition difficult, or even impossible

volatile, not stable

volatile dynamic storage, dynamic storage which blanks when the power is off

volatile memory, random access memory which blanks when the power is off

volatile storage, same as **volatile memory**

volatility, the inclination to change or lose electric charge

voltage multiplier, a circuit that converts low-voltage alternating current to high voltage direct current

volume, a unit of peripheral storage, such as a disk pack or a reel of tape

volume label, the name which identifies a disk, displayed when a directory listing is requested

voting processors, a technique in which three or more microprocessors handle the same instruction and, if results differ, those which agree continue to operate while the others are taken out of service for repairs

VRC, vertical redundancy check; a system for checking data transmission errors in which a parity bit is assigned to each character transmitted

W

wafer, the silicon ingot from which slices are cut for the manufacture of computer chips; the slice of silicon crystal itself, on which integrated circuits constructed

wait, any delay time in computer processing: the time between calling a file from storage and when it is loaded into memory, the time between reading a command and beginning to execute the command, etc.

waiting list, a queue; a list of programs or data awaiting processing as for printing, transmission, etc.

waiting state, the lapsed time between the receipt of an interrupt and when it becomes active

wait state, the time during which the CPU is idle

walk-through, an interactive tutorial which demonstrates by example, the workings of a system or application program; any interactive training device used on the computer, not necessarily related to computer training

wand, a hand-held optical reader

warm boot, a boot, or restart, performed while the system is running, in contrast to a **cold boot**

warning marker, destination, a reflective spot on magnetic tape which is sensed photoelectrically to indicate proximity to the end of the tape

wave, the configuration of electromagnetic radiation

wave form, the graphic representation of an electromagnetic wave

wave form analyzer, a device which measures the amplitude and frequency of a wave form

weighted average, a statistical device for calculating an average which places added emphasis on values that are considered more important than others

weighted value, the relative value assigned to an element

"what if" model, a problem solving technique which involves projecting the consequence of various actions, or the way in which results would be altered by introducing or changing the value of elements affecting the problem

wheel printer, a line printer which has a wheel in each character position, with formed characters around the face of the wheel

white noise, random signals which convey no messages

whole number, a number which has no fractional part

wild card, a variable which replaces one or more of the characters in a file name, used select a group of files which have part of their name or extension in common or to find a file, the name of which is partly known

window, a viewing area on a computer monitor screen

windowing, dividing a computer monitor screen display into several sections, each of which is able to display different data

wire, a strand of conducting material; the strike element in a wire printer

wire board, an electrical panel which is wired by the user to change its function

wired program computer, a computer in which the program instructions are characterized by wired connections on a board

wired in, referring to components which are permanently wired, in contrast to being plugged in

wire frame representation, a graphic illustration of a three-dimensional object as transparent so that all outlines are visible

wire printer, a printer which forms characters by using an array of wires to strike the paper or ribbon; a **dot-matrix printer**

word, a set of contiguous characters which form part of a message or instruction; a fixed-length sequence of bits manipulated as a unit in processing and memory storage; a **computer word**

word, banner, the first word in a data file

word, call, the word used to identify a computer program subroutine

word, computer, a fixed-length sequence of bits manipulated as a unit in processing and memory storage; a unit of data in a computer

word, control, a computer word which is the first or last word of a record or a block which contains information pertinent to that record or block; a word which transmits processing information

word, device status, a computer word in which the bits indicate the status of a device

word, double length, a computer word depicting a number represented by a binary number of double the binary digits that the computer's word length allows and which uses two registers or storage locations

word, half, a series of bits which is half the length of a computer word and addressable as a unit

word, identifier, a computer word which is compared to stored information in a search

word, information, a computer word which expresses data as contrasted to controls or instructions

word, instruction, a computer word which contains, or is, an instruction

word, I/O command, a computer word which controls an I/O device

word, I/O status, a computer word which reports the status of an I/O

device

word length, the number of bits in a computer word

word, machine, a fixed-length sequence of bits manipulated as a unit in processing and memory storage; a unit of data in a computer; a **computer word**

word mark, a signal which indicates the beginning or ending of a word

word, microprocessor, a series of bits which are processed as a unit; a computer word

word, numeric, a computer word comprised of numerals

word, parameter, a word which contains the parameters, or the address of parameters, which define or limit the action of a subroutine

word pattern, the smallest unit of language; one of the unique syllables which make up the words which comprise a language

word processing, the recording, editing, formatting, and printing of documents

word processing machine, a machine designed to perform the functions of word processing

word processing terminal, a terminal designed primarily to handle word processing applications

word processor, a **word processing machine;** a program which performs word processing functions on the computer

word processors, communicating, desktop computers which are connected to other devices such as phone and fax modems; word processors programmed for direct communication with other units in the system

word, reserved, a word which is

part of a programming language's vocabulary and which may not be used for any other purpose, such as naming a variable

word size, the number of bits in a computer word

word time, the time required for a computer word to pass a given point

word wrap, a word processing function in which text too long to fit on a single line is automatically continued on succeeding lines; a desktop publishing feature which prevents text from overwriting a graphics element by fitting the copy around it

work area, a place in memory where the intermediate results of an operation are stored

working environment, same as **environment**

working register, a register which holds work in process for quick access

working storage, same as **work area**

work load, the amount of work or number of jobs awaiting processing

worksheet, an **electronic spreadsheet**

workspace, the amount of memory required by a program for processing, intermediate results, etc.; the memory available for processing

work station, a remote terminal with a viewing monitor and keyboard input used for communications or off-line jobs; a terminal; a data station

WORM drive, write once, read many drive; an optical disk drive for storing large quantities of data which, once written, cannot be erased

worst case, an assessment of the most difficult set of circumstances to overcome in solving a problem; a forecast of the maximum stress which will be placed on a system

worst case design, design of an element which will allow it to function in the worst possible circumstances

wpm, words per minute; one of the measures of the speed of a typist or printer

wraparound, the process of returning to the first of a series or set of positions after the last position in the series is encountered; in desktop publishing, to continue text around a graphics element

write, to enter or transfer data to an output device or a location in memory

write enable, a routine which permits the computer to write data to a storage device, such as a disk

write error, a condition in which information is incorrectly written or can not be written onto disk or tape

write head, the device used to write data to a magnetic medium; a **read/write head**

write inhibit ring, a device which prevents writing data to magnetic tape

write key, a code which specifies whether or not data may be written to a specific location in memory

write protect, a software code or physical device which prevents writing data to a memory device or a file

WYSIWYG, what you see is what you get; an acronym for a combination of monitor and software which displays type and graphics on the screen as it appears when printed

X

X-axis, in a Cartesian coordinate system, the horizontal axis

xerographic printer, a photoelectric printer

xerography, photoelectric copying in which the elements which are to appear in color are statically charged, causing dry ink to adhere to them

X-Y loading, formatting a monitor screen by first indicating the starting position of copy as X-Y coordinates, or row and column, for each copy string

X-Y plotter, a plotter which draws lines based on X and Y coordinates

Y-axis, in a Cartesian coordinate system, the vertical axis

yoke, a set of read/write heads which move together to access tracks on multiple disks or tapes, or multiple tracks on a single disk

Z

zap, to intentionally clear the screen, a block of data on the screen or a working copy of a file; to accidentally overwrite a file

Z-axis, an axis at right angles to the Cartesian X and Y axes; the third dimension

zero, a numeral representing the absence of magnitude; a place holder for numbers; of no value, or too small to be considered of any value

zero address instruction, an instruction which includes the address of the data to which it applies or on which it will operate

zero bit, the first high-order bit of a program counter, which is set to 1 if the accumulator content is 0

zero elimination, a program device to eliminate printing of zeros to the left of a stored number

zero fill, using zeros to pad the leading spaces in a computer word

zeroize, to fill a section of computer storage with zeros in order to assure that the area is clear of extraneous data

zero level address, immediate address; an address of data included in the instruction which operates on that data

zero page addressing, loading or accessing instructions in the first 1024 bytes of memory

zero state, the condition of an electromagnetic device which indicates zero

zero suppression, programming which removes zeros to the left of a data field when it is printed

Appendix

ASCII Control Characters

Name	Decimal	Hex	Typed	
NUL	0	00	CTRL @	
SOH	1	01	CTRL A	
STX	2	02	CTRL B	
ETX	3	03	CTRL C	Interrupt Program
EOT	4	04	CTRL D	
ENQ	5	05	CTRL E	
ACK	6	06	CTRL F	
BEL	7	07	CTRL G	Beeper
BS	8	08	CTRL H	Backspace
HT	9	09	CTRL I	Horizontal Tab
LF	10	0A	CTRL J	Line Feed
VT	11	0B	CTRL K	Vertical Tab
FF	12	0C	CTRL L	Form Feed
CR	13	0D	CTRL M	Carriage Return
SO	14	0E	CTRL N	Optional Type Mode*
SI	15	0F	CTRL O	Optional Type Mode*
DLE	16	10	CTRL P	
DC1	17	11	CTRL Q	Select Printer
DC2	18	12	CTRL R	Optional Type Mode*
DC3	19	13	CTRL S	Deselect Printer
DC4	20	14	CTRL T	Optional Type Mode*
NAK	21	15	CTRL U	
SYN	22	16	CTRL V	
ETB	23	17	CTRL W	
CAN	24	18	CTRL X	Cancel Line Print
EM	25	19	CTRL Y	
SUB	26	1A	CTRL Z	End of File Mark
ESC	27	1B	CTRL [	Escape
FS	28	1C	CTRL \	
GS	29	1D	CTRL]	
RS	30	1E	CTRL ^	
US	31	1F	CTRL _	
DEL	127	7F	DEL	Delete Character

* Optional Type Mode commands are instructions to select or deselect a printer style such as Double-wide Characters or Condensed Characters.

Note: The effect of control characters varies from one computer or printer to another; the above list merely reflects the more common assignments.

ASCII Print Characters

Decimal	Hex	Character		Decimal	Hex	Character
32	20	space		71	47	G
33	21	!		72	48	H
34	22	"		73	49	I
35	23	#		74	4A	J
36	24	$		75	4B	K
37	25	%		76	4C	L
38	26	&		77	4D	M
39	27	'		78	4E	N
40	28	(		79	4F	O
41	29	)		80	50	P
42	2A	*		81	51	Q
43	2B	+		82	52	R
44	2C	,		83	53	S
45	2D	_		84	54	T
46	2E	.		85	55	U
47	2F	/		86	56	V
48	30	0		87	57	W
49	31	1		88	58	X
50	32	2		89	59	Y
51	33	3		90	5A	Z
52	34	4		91	5B	[
53	35	5		92	5C	\
54	36	6		93	5D	]
55	37	7		94	5E	^
56	38	8		95	5F	-
57	39	9		96	60	`
58	3A	:		97	61	a
59	3B	;		98	62	b
60	3C	<		99	63	c
61	3D	=		100	64	d
62	3E	>		101	65	e
63	3F	?		102	66	f
64	40	@		103	67	g
65	41	A		104	68	h
66	42	B		105	69	i
67	43	C		106	6A	j
68	44	D		107	6B	k
69	45	E		108	6C	l
70	46	F		109	6D	m

continued next page . . .

ASCII Print Characters (continued)

Decimal	Hex	Character	Decimal	Hex	Character
110	6E	n	119	77	w
111	6F	o	120	78	x
112	70	p	121	79	y
113	71	q	122	7A	z
114	72	r	123	7B	{
115	73	s	124	7C		
116	74	t	125	7D	}
117	75	u	126	7E	~
118	76	v			

EBCDIC Print Characters

Decimal	Hex	Character	Decimal	Hex	Character
64	40	blank	122	7A	:
			123	7B	#
76	4C		124	7C	@
77	4D	<	125	7D	`
78	4E	+	126	7E	=
79	4F			127	7F	"
80	50	&			
			129	81	a
90	5A	!	130	82	b
91	5B	$	131	83	c
92	5C	*	132	84	d
93	5D	)	133	85	e
94	5E	;	134	86	f
			135	87	g
96	60	-	136	88	h
97	61	/	137	89	i
107	6B	,			
108	6C	%			
109	6D	_			
110	6E	>			
111	6F	?			

continued next page . . .

EBCDIC Print Characters (continued)

Decimal	Hex	Character		Decimal	Hex	Character
145	91	j		209	D1	J
146	92	k		210	D2	K
147	93	l		211	D3	L
148	94	m		212	D4	M
149	95	n		213	D5	N
150	96	o		214	D6	O
151	97	p		215	D7	P
152	98	q		216	D8	Q
153	99	r		217	D9	R
162	A2	s		226	E2	S
163	A3	t		227	E3	T
164	A4	u		228	E4	U
165	A5	v		229	E5	V
166	A6	w		230	E6	W
167	A7	x		231	E7	X
168	A8	y		232	E8	Y
169	A9	z		233	E9	Z
193	C1	A		240	F0	0
194	C2	B		241	F1	1
195	C3	C		242	F2	2
196	C4	D		243	F3	3
197	C5	E		244	F4	4
198	C6	F		245	F5	5
199	C7	G		246	F6	6
200	C8	H		247	F7	7
201	C9	I		248	F8	8
				249	F9	9

Binary–Hexidecimal Equivalents

Decimal	Binary	Hex		Decimal	Binary	Hex
0	0000	0		8	1000	8
1	0001	1		9	1001	9
2	0010	2		10	1010	A
3	0011	3		11	1011	B
4	0100	4		12	1100	C
5	0101	5		13	1101	D
6	0110	6		14	1110	E
7	0111	7		15	1111	F

Decimal – Hexidecimal Equivalents

Decimal	Hex		Decimal	Hex		Decimal	Hex
0	00		27	1B		54	36
1	01		28	1C		55	37
2	02		29	1D		56	38
3	03		30	1E		57	39
4	04		31	1F		58	3A
5	05		32	20		59	3B
6	06		33	21		60	3C
7	07		34	22		61	3D
8	08		35	23		62	3E
9	09		36	24		63	3F
10	0A		37	25		64	40
11	0B		38	26		65	41
12	0C		39	27		66	42
13	0D		40	28		67	43
14	0E		41	29		68	44
15	0F		42	2A		69	45
16	10		43	2B		70	46
17	11		44	2C		71	47
18	12		45	2D		72	48
19	13		46	2E		73	49
20	14		47	2F		74	4A
21	15		48	30		75	4B
22	16		49	31		76	4C
23	17		50	32		77	4D
24	18		51	33		78	4E
25	19		52	34		79	4F
26	1A		53	35		80	50

continued next page . . .

Decimal – Hexidecimal Equivalents (continued)

Decimal	Hex	Decimal	Hex	Decimal	Hex
81	51	120	78	159	9F
82	52	121	79	160	A0
83	53	122	7A	161	A1
84	54	123	7B	162	A2
85	55	124	7C	163	A3
86	56	125	7D	164	A4
87	57	126	7E	165	A5
88	58	127	7F	166	A6
89	59	128	80	167	A7
90	5A	129	81	168	A8
91	5B	130	82	169	A9
92	5C	131	83	170	AA
93	5D	132	84	171	AB
94	5E	133	85	172	AC
95	5F	134	86	173	AD
96	60	135	87	174	AE
97	61	136	88	175	AF
98	62	137	89	176	B0
99	63	138	8A	177	B1
100	64	139	8B	178	B2
101	65	140	8C	179	B3
102	66	141	8D	180	B4
103	67	142	8E	181	B5
104	68	143	8F	182	B6
105	69	144	90	183	B7
106	6A	145	91	184	B8
107	6B	146	92	185	B9
108	6C	147	93	186	BA
109	6D	148	94	187	BB
110	6E	149	95	188	BC
111	6F	150	96	189	BD
112	70	151	97	190	BE
113	71	152	98	191	BF
114	72	153	99	192	C0
115	73	154	9A	193	C1
116	74	155	9B	194	C2
117	75	156	9C	195	C3
118	76	157	9D	196	C4
119	77	158	9E	197	C5

continued next page . . .

Decimal – Hexidecimal Equivalents (continued)

Decimal	Hex	Decimal	Hex	Decimal	Hex
198	C6	218	DA	238	EE
199	C7	219	DB	239	EF
200	C8	220	DC	240	F0
201	C9	221	DD	241	F1
202	CA	222	DE	242	F2
203	CB	223	DF	243	F3
204	CC	224	E0	244	F4
205	CD	225	E1	245	F5
206	CE	226	E2	246	F6
207	CF	227	E3	247	F7
208	D0	228	E4	248	F8
209	D1	229	E5	249	F9
210	D2	230	E6	250	FA
211	D3	231	E7	251	FB
212	D4	232	E8	252	FC
213	D5	233	E9	253	FD
214	D6	234	EA	254	FE
215	D7	235	EB	255	FF
216	D8	236	EC		
217	D9	237	ED		